GRAPHIC DESIGN USA: 20

The Annual of the American Institute of Graphic Arts

The Annual of the American Institute of Graphic Arts

Written by Steven Heller, Paula Scher, Véronique Vienne, and Lorraine Wild
Designed by Beth Crowell, Cheung/Crowell Design
Jacket/cover designed by Fred Woodward
Editorial production by Marie Finamore

Copyright © 2000 by the American Institute of Graphic Arts.
First published in 2000 in New York by the American Institute of Graphic Arts, 164 Fifth Avenue, New York, NY 10010, and Watson-Guptill Publications, a division of BPI Communications, Inc., 1515 Broadway, New York, NY 10036.

Distributed to the trade by Watson-Guptill Publications, 1515 Broadway, New York, NY 10036.

ISBN: 0-8230-7234-7

First printing, 2000.

Distributed outside of the United States and Canada by HarperCollins International,
10 East 53rd Street, New York, NY 10022-5299.

Printing: Syl, Barcelona, Spain
Color Separation: Syl, Barcelona, Spain
Paper: Creator Silk 135 gsm
Page layouts were composed in
Adobe QuarkXpress 4.0 on a Macintosh G4.
Typefaces: Sabon, Univers, Bubbledot ICG

Contents

he medal of the AIGA, the most distinguished in the field, is awarded to individuals in recognition of their exceptional achievements, services, or other contributions to the field of graphic design and visual communications. The contribution may be in the practice of graphic design, teaching, writing, or leadership of the profession. The awards may honor designers posthumously.

Medals are awarded to those individuals who have set standards of excellence over a lifetime of work or have made individual contributions to innovation within the practice of graphic design.

Individuals who are honored may work in any country, but the contributions for which they are honored should have had a significant impact on the practice of graphic design in the United States.

The Design Leadership Award recognizes the role of perceptive and forward-thinking organizations that have been instrumental in the advancement of design by applying the highest standards, as a matter of policy.

The AIGA's 1999 awards committee was chaired by Michael Vanderbyl and included Dana Arnett, Philip Meggs, Jennifer Morla, Christopher Pullman, and Paula Scher. Commenting on the three medalists, Jennifer Morla said, "Individually, they have inspired us by illuminating history, challenging the dogma of design education, and encouraging us to question the status quo. But their impact on design is even more evident when reviewed in concert: three original voices that, when heard in unison, make us reconsider design in a more meaningful way."

Steven Heller is the art director of the *New York Times*, chair of the graduate program in graphic design at the School of Visual Arts, editor of the *AIGA Journal of Graphic Design*, chair of the annual "Modernism and Eclecticism" seminar at SVA, and the editor or co-author of more than sixty books on graphic design. "Steve early on gave voice to a profession that was almost mute," Christopher Pullman said. "With ever more prodigious output, Steve has taken us on a forced march through our history, practitioners, and values. Though a person with his own strong opinions about the profession, his great contribution has been in helping many other voices to be heard."

Tibor Kalman, who passed away in May 1999, was the founder/principal of the influential studio M&Co, the creative director of Benetton's innovative publication Colors, and a provocateur/anti-corporate conscience of the graphic design profession. Christopher Pullman remarked, "Every now and then, somebody comes along with such an original and quirky sensibility that it offers up to the profession a new model of what it means to be a graphic designer. By reminding us at every turn that graphic design is all about language and the magic interplay of words and images, and by putting his money where his mouth is on the tricky issue of where you are going to put your energy and influence as a communicator, Tibor managed to charm or piss off just about everybody who has a brain and a conscience."

1971 to 1995, Katherine McCoy co-chaired (with her husband, industrial
er Michael McCoy) the design department at the Cranbrook Academy of Art.
their leadership, as Philip Meggs has written, the department "became a
t for people interested in pushing the boundaries of design, as well as a light-
rod for criticism about the new design discourse." Christopher Pullman
ented, "Through it all, her career has been marked by incredible energy, a high
of social purpose, a keen and articulate intellect, and an abiding generosity in
g what she has learned. She strikes me as the perfect role model for a young
er."

towing the 1999 Design Leadership award on Alfred A. Knopf Inc., the
ittee explained, "Although recently opened up from its deep roots in print, the
profession still traces its lineage from that mother of all design assignments:
ok. The most recent crop of Knopf book designers, who have so refreshingly
gned what a book can look like, are only the latest expression of a corporate
itment to quality and innovation in publishing that goes back farther than most
can remember." The committee is also acknowledging Knopf's embodiment
founder's commitment to excellence, and reaffirming the AIGA's own long-held
ation of Alfred A. Knopf himself, who was awarded the AIGA Gold Medal in
As reported in the *AIGA Journal* (vol. III, no. 1, 1950), Knopf was "cited as
inguished publisher, informed collector, consistent exponent of fine bookmaking;
pioneering and sustained efforts to raise the standards of design in American
book publishing; for this interest which has led the general reader to a greater
t in good design."

Graphic Design Chronicler

Steven He

By Paula Scher

If you notice anything peculiar about this particular medalist essay, it is probably one of the very few that is not written by Steven Heller.

Steven Heller, the ubiquitous, tireless chronicler of our design times, is the author, co-author, or editor of more than sixty books on design-related topics (with fourteen more due to be published as we speak). A journalist, critic, and commentator, he has written for a wide array of publications, including *Print, U&lc, I.D. Magazine, Affiche, Graphis, Creation, Eye, Design, How, Oxymoron, Design Issues, Mother Jones, Speak* magazine and the *New York Times Book Review*. Steven Heller has also been editor of the *AIGA Journal of Graphic Design* since its inception as a serious forum for design writing and criticism, in the early '80s.

Apparently, all of this has been nothing but a sideline because the same Steven Heller is also a full-time, salaried employee (senior art director) of the *New York Times Book Review*, a *weekly* publication that closes on Wednesdays. In this capacity, Heller has launched and nourished the careers of innumerable successful and influential illustrators. But that alone would be worthy of a whole other medal from a whole other graphic arts organization.

If we keep our discussion here restricted to this particular AIGA medal, then we are talking about lifetime achievement that comes from a workday existing roughly between 4:30 and 8:45 A.M. — FOUR-THIRTY TO EIGHT FORTY-FIVE A.M. — before a full workday at the *Times,* to produce sixty some books; edit a bunch of magazines; write innumerable articles, reviews, forewords, and obits; plan the annual *Modernism and Eclecticism* symposium; and chair a graduate program at the School of Visual Arts. I've known Steve for about twenty years and have never been able to figure out this math.

In this process of impossible Herculean output Heller has managed to completely chronicle the past hundred years of graphic design to such an extent and depth that his influence cannot help but be felt by every design student and practitioner everywhere in the world. He is the Samuel Boswell of our graphic design age.

Heller came to his Boswellian role by a strange and circuitous route. A product of both a military school and a progressive prep school on the Upper West Side of Manhattan, Heller never received a formal art education. In 1968, his leftist leanings led him to the *New York Free Press.* He was seventeen years old and became art director. He had no qualifications whatsoever for that job. He used his press pass to attend some New York University lectures on a variety of subjects during the student sit-in strikes. That seems to have been the extent of college education for this author of over sixty books.

At the *Free Press* he met a brilliant young illustrator named Brad Holland, who persuaded Heller that page layouts and type

Early work art directed by Steven Heller. Above: *The New York Free Press* (1968). Below, clockwise: *Mobster Times* (1972), illustrated by Brad Holland. *Rock* magazine (1970). *The New York Ace* (1972), illustrated by Bill Griffith. *Screw* (1973), illustrated by Doug Taylor.

Facing page: Covers of the *New York Times Book Review*, art directed by Steven Heller. Illustrators, left to right, from top row downward: C.F. Payne (1998), Robert Grossman (1998), Juliette Borda (1996), Ed Lam (1999), Brad Holland (1997), Milton Glaser (1997), Etienne Delessert (1997), Julian Allen (1996), Mirko Ilic (1996), Mirko Ilic (1996), Art Spiegelman (1996), and John Hovell (1997).

choices actually mattered. Heller had been more or less oblivious to design. He had read a copy of *Simplicissimus* for its political content and thought the design "looked nice." But Heller's personal tastes ran more toward political cartooning and conceptual illustration. In 1974, after brief stints at *Interview, Rock, Screw, Rat,* and the *Evergreen Review,* he wound up as art director for the *New York Times* Op-Ed page, home of political illustration, surrealism, and social comment. His respect and passion for illustration led him to produce a variety of collections on the subject. The first, *Artists' Christmas Cards,* was followed by *Man Bites Man: Two Decades of Satiric Art, Jules Feiffer's America,* and a number of others.

By the early '80s Heller had become interested in design, an interest that was ignited by two important relationships. The first was his friendship with Seymour Chwast. Both had a passion for publishing. Heller was interested in politics and history, while Chwast was interested in type and imagery. Heller knew what was important; Chwast knew what was good. Together they produced a slew of books, including *Art Against War, The Art of New York,* and *Graphic Style,* a compendium that has become a bible for graphic designers.

At the same time, Heller had begun dating graphic designer Louise Fili, whom he would marry in 1983. Fili was then art director of Pantheon Books. Heller had sent her a fan letter because he

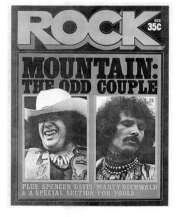

The New York Times **Book Review**

Wolfe Burns Atlanta

Sherman first, then Margaret Mitchell. In their wake, Tom Wolfe's novel 'A Man in Full' is a comedy of fear, race, angst and fallen values. *Reviewed by Michael Lewis* 17

Jim Shepard on the stories of T. C. Boyle 7

Emily Eakin on Francine du Plessix Gray and her biography of the Marquis de Sade 8

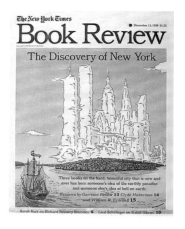

The New York Times **Book Review**

The Discovery of New York

Three books on the hard, beautiful city that is now and ever has been someone's idea of the earthly paradise and someone else's idea of hell on earth.
Reviews by Garrison Keillor 13 *Clyde Haberman* 14 *and William R. Everdell* 15

Sarah Kerr on Richard Brinsley Sheridan 6 · Liesl Schillinger on Kahlil Gibran 10

The New York Times **Book Review**

It Wasn't Always Like This

A battered wife tries to recall herself as she used to be in Roddy Doyle's new novel, 'The Woman Who Walked Into Doors.' *Reviewed by Mary Gordon* 7

Reviews of books by Christopher Darden and Robert Shapiro 14-15

The New York Times **Book Review**

The News This Year Oh Boy!

A lucky President made the grade, with a little help from his enemies and even his friends. Which was George Stephanopoulos? Gary Wills looks into that 4 Tom Goldstein reviews Michael Isikoff's 'Uncovering Clinton' 5 And Michael Oreskes examines 'Monica's Story,' by Andrew Morton 6

The New York Times **Book Review**

Things Children Know

Deborah Eisenberg's short stories speak the language of the almost intuitions. *Reviewed by Jim Shepard* 9

Gary Krist on Will Self's 'Great Apes' 7 Maxine Kumin on horses 12

The New York Times **Book Review**

Yo Picasso!

The second volume of John Richardson's life of the gigantic artist, with about 1,000 illustrations. *Reviewed by Richard Howard*

Katha Pollitt on a biography of Pearl S. Buck 13 Daphne Merkin on Diana Trilling 43

The New York Times **Book Review**

'The Island Of the Colorblind'

Oliver Sacks searches the Pacific for neurological mysteries and peculiar adaptations. *Reviewed by D. M. Thomas* 7

Joan Acocella on Allegra Kent 6 Gary Giddins on Ralph Ellison's stories 13

The New York Times **Book Review**

A Spoiled Child, but So Smart!

Orson Welles at 23 terrified America with 'The War of the Worlds.' At 26, he enraged Hearst with 'Citizen Kane.' Simon Callow's 'Orson Welles: The Road to Xanadu' is the first volume of a biography of this oversize prodigy. *Reviewed by Stanley Kauffmann* 7

Richard Wollheim on Diderot 9

Claire Messud on Carol Shields 12

The New York Times **Book Review**

Will Time Run Out For Nigeria?

In 'The Open Sore of a Continent,' the Nobel laureate Wole Soyinka tells the sorry story of the rise and fall of nationhood in Africa's most populous country; now, he fears, 100 million Nigerians may be engulfed by complete social collapse. *Reviewed by Robert D. Kaplan* 9

Anne Rice's novel 'Servant of the Bones.' *Reviewed by Daniel Mendelsohn* 5

Margaret Drabble's biography of Angus Wilson. *Reviewed by Peter Parker* 7

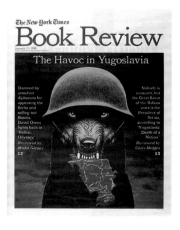

The New York Times **Book Review**

The Havoc in Yugoslavia

Damned by armchair diplomats for appeasing the Serbs and selling out Bosnia, David Owen fights back in 'Balkan Odyssey.' *Reviewed by Misha Glenny* 12

Nobody is innocent, but the Great Satan of the Balkan wars is the President of Serbia, according to 'Yugoslavia: Death of a Nation.' *Reviewed by Chris Hedges* 13

CRIME AND MYSTERY

Robert B. Parker on a new Raymond Chandler/22

Edward I. Koch's murder mystery reviewed by Wendy Wasserstein/23

Robert Lacey on Nicholas Pileggi's 'Casino'/28

R.W.B. Lewis reviews the latest from Ruth Rendell/29

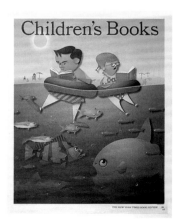

Children's Books

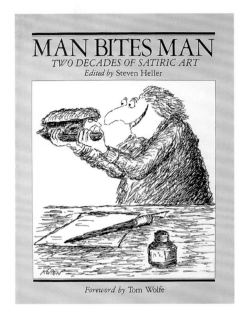

noticed that all the book jackets he liked in the bookstores were always her designs. He became serious about learning about typography, largely because it was a good way to impress his date. Heller and Fili later became husband-and-wife collaborators on a series of books for Chronicle on Italian Deco, French Deco, British Deco and other beautifully designed compendiums, which have become highly popular with designers everywhere.

In the early '80s Heller also became editor of the *AIGA Journal of Graphic Design*. He turned a chatty, amateurish newsletter into a serious journal of critical writing, inviting academics, practitioners, sociologists, lawyers, and so on to contribute articles on a broad variety of topics in themed issues. *Looking Closer*, volumes one and two, are compilations of articles culled from the *AIGA Journal* as well as other publications. The *Journal* became a forum of lively debate and ushered in a mature age of critical design writing.

Through the *Journal*, Heller launched and nourished the careers of many fledgling design writers now prevalent in current

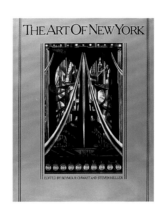

1982	1983	1984
Jules Feiffer's America: From Eisenhower to Reagan, by SH (Alfred A. Knopf)	*The Art of New York,* edited by SH and Seymour Chwast (Harry N. Abrams)	*Art Against War: Four Hundred Years of Protest in Art,* by D.J.R. Bruckner, Seymour Chwast, and SH (Abbeville Press)
War Heads: Cartoonists Draw the Line, edited by SH (Penguin)		*The Art of Satire: Painters as Cartoonists and Caricaturists from Delacroix to Picasso,* by Ralph Shikes and SH (Horizon Press)
Malik Verlag (exhibition catalogue), by James Fraser and SH (Goethe House)		

design publications. Most of these publications, in authorship or editorial mix, cannot help but, in one way or another, be influenced by Steven Heller.

There is no quintessential Heller book. He operates in an ad hoc manner, seemingly a jack of all trades. Some of his books are eclectic mixes, illustrating specific genres or approaches, like *That's Entertainment, Jackets Required,* or *Graphic Wit.* Others are "how-to" books that relate to design careers and business. Others still are portraits of individual designers, notably the recently published tome on Paul Rand. *Design Literacy* was a collection of Heller essays, revisited and assembled as a view of specific designs he deemed important and influential for a variety of reasons.

The one common denominator of Heller's work is that the design and/or the designer is always the star. Heller maintains a journalistic narrative that allows the design and the designer to stand out. His compendiums are always inclusive, usually illustrating a broad and varied range of work. This stands in sharp contrast with other recent design compendiums where work of a specific contemporary style is collected and a thesis is written about the work. While the compendium will contain the work of many designers, the work appears so similar that the individual designer disappears and only the author of the thesis is visible.

Steven Heller has been graphic design's biggest fan. There is not a symposium, conference, show, book, publication or graphic organization that does not continually rely on his counsel and recommendations. For any question asked of him, he responds with twenty ideas, and if those aren't the right ones, he finds another twenty.

We easily take for granted our design history books, our magazines, and our conferences. We are accustomed now to seeing design work from all over the world and from any time in history without working terribly hard to find it. But before 1980, design books, magazines and design conferences were few and far between. Steven Heller has immortalized our graphic past and made coherence of our present. The debt that future graphic designers owe him simply cannot be calculated.

1985	1986	1987

Seymour Chwast: The Left-Handed Designer, edited by SH (Harry N. Abrams)

The Fifties Revisited, by SH and Seymour Chwast (Universe)

The Little Theatre Presents A Christmas Carol, edited and produced by SH, text adapted by Dan Weaver (Viking)

Innovators of American Illustration, edited by SH (Van Nostrand Reinhold)

New York Observed: Artists and Writers Look at the City, 1650 to the Present, by Barbara Cohen, Seymour Chwast, and SH (Harry N. Abrams)

Design Career: Practical Knowledge for Beginning Illustrators and Graphic Designers, by SH and Lita Talarico (Van Nostrand Reinhold)

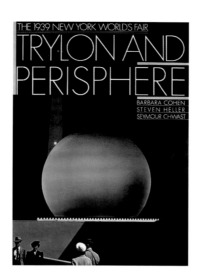

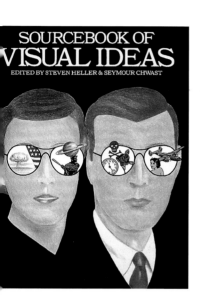

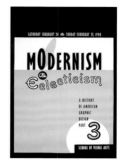

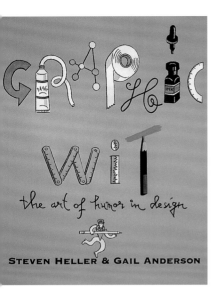

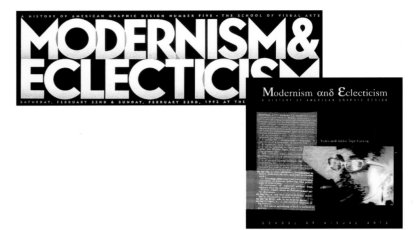

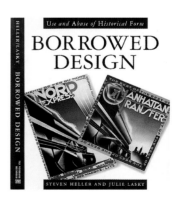

1991	**1992**	**1993**

Graphic Wit: The Art of Humor in Design, by SH and Gail Anderson (Watson-Guptill Publications)

Angry Graphics: Protest Posters of the Reagan/Bush Era, by Karrie Jacobs and SH (Peregrine Smith Books)

You Must Have Been a Beautiful Baby: Baby Pictures of the Stars, by Vicki Gold Levi, SH, and Seymour Chwast (Hyperion)

School Days, by SH and Steven Guarnaccia (Abbeville Press)

Borrowed Design: Use and Abuse of Historical Form, by SH and Julie Lasky (Van Nostrand Reinhold)

The Savage Mirror: The Art of Contemporary Caricature, by SH and Gail Anderson (Watson-Guptill Publications)

Italian Art Deco: Graphic Design Between the Wars, by SH and Louise Fili (Chronicle Books, 1993)

Covers and Jackets! What the Best-Dressed Books and Magazines Are Wearing, by SH and Anne Fink (PBC International, 1993)

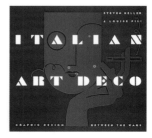

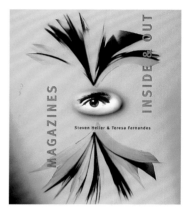

1994	**1995**	**1996**

Dutch Moderne: Graphic Design from De Stijl to Deco, by SH and Louise Fili (Chronicle Books)

Designing For Children: The Art of Graphic Design in Children's Books, Posters, Magazines, Etc., by SH and Steven Guarnaccia (Watson-Guptill Publications)

Looking Closer: Critical Writings on Graphic Design, edited by Michael Bierut, William Drenttel, Steven Heller, and D.K. Holland (Allworth Press)

American Typeplay, by SH and Gail Anderson (PBC International)

Streamline: American Art Deco Design, by SH and Louise Fili (Chronicle Books)

Jackets Required: An Illustrated History of American Book Jackets, 1920–1950, by SH and Seymour Chwast (Chronicle Books)

The Business of Illustration, by SH and Teresa Fernandes (Watson-Guptill Publications)

100 Best Posters of Europe and America, edited by SH and Alain Weill, executive editor Milton Glaser (Toppan)

Japanese Modern: Graphic Design Between the Wars, by James Fraser, SH, and Seymour Chwast (Chronicle Books)

Newsletters Now: From Classic to New Wave, by SH and Eleanor Pettit (PBC International)

That's Entertainment, by SH and Anne Fink (PBC International,)

Cover Story: American Magazine Covers 1900–1950, by SH and Louise Fili (Chronicle Books)

Magazines: Inside and Out, by SH and Teresa Fernandes (PBC International)

Food Wrap: Packages That Sell, by SH and Anne Fink (PBC International)

Deco Type: Stylish Alphabets of the '20s and '30s, by SH and Louise Fili (Chronicle)

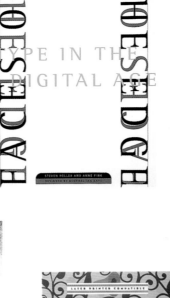

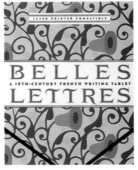

1997	1998	1999

French Modern: Art Deco Graphic Design, by SH and Louise Fili (Chronicle Books)

Faces on the Edge: Type in the Digital Age, by SH and Anne Fink (Van Nostrand Rhinehold)

Looking Closer II: Critical Writings on Graphic Design, edited by Michael Bierut, William Drenttel, SH, and D.K. Holland (Allworth Press)

Deco España: Graphic Design of the Twenties and Thirties, by SH and Louise Fili (Chronicle Books)

The Digital Designer: The Graphic Artist's Guide to the New Media, by SH and Daniel Drennan (Watson-Guptill Publications,)

Design Literacy: Understanding Graphic Design, by SH and Karen Pomeroy (Allworth Press)

Design Culture: An Anthology of Writing from the AIGA Journal of Graphic Design, by SH and Marie Finamore (Allworth Press and AIGA)

Teenage Confidential: An Illustrated History of the American Teen, by SH and Michael Barson (Chronicle Books)

British Modern: Graphic Design Between the Wars, by SH and Louise Fili (Chronicle Books)

Design Dialogues, by SH and Eleanor Pettit (Allworth Press)

German Modern: Graphic Design from Wilhelm to Weimar, by SH and Louise Fili (Chronicle Books)

The Education of a Graphic Designer, edited by SH (Allworth Press)

Less Is More: The New Simplicity in Graphic Design, by SH and Anne Fink (Northlight)

Typology: Type Design from the Victorian Era to the Digital Age, by SH and Louise Fili (Chronicle Books)

Paul Rand, by SH (Phaidon)

Becoming a Graphic Designer, by SH and Teresa Fernandes (John Wiley & Sons)

Looking Closer 3: Classic Writings on Graphic Design (Allworth Press)

Design Literacy: Continued, by SH (Allworth Press)

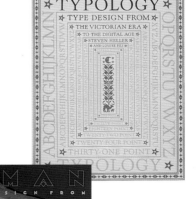

Covers of the *AIGA Journal of Graphic Design,* edited by Steven Heller. Clockwise from top left: "Love Money Power" (1991), designed by Julie Riefler, illustrated by Barbara Kruger. Censorship issue (1991), designed by Julie Riefler, illustrated by Brad Holland. "Can You Read the Writing on the Wall?" (1992), designed by Julie Riefler, illustrated by Yolanda Cuomo and Fran Bull. The Literacy issue (1997), art directed by Michael Ian Kaye. "Design in the Real World" and "Designing in Tongues" (1995), art directed by Laurel Shoemaker. Bordertowns (1999), Motion (1998), and Music (1997) issues art directed by Michael Ian Kaye. "What's Next" (1994), designed by Lisa Naftolin. "In Spin We Trust" (1998), art directed by Michael Ian Kaye.

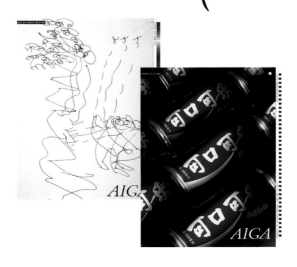

Provocateur

No. Tibor Kalman

By Steven Heller

In the mid-1980s two names changed graphic design: Macintosh and Tibor.

The former needs no introduction. Nor, with various books and articles by and about him, does the latter. Tibor Kalman, who died on May 2, 1999, after a long, courageous battle with non-Hodgkin's lymphoma, was one of the few graphic designers whose accomplishments were legend within the field and widely known outside as well. Tibor may not be as influential on the daily practice of graphic design as the Mac, but his sway over how designers think — indeed, how they define their roles in culture and society — is indisputable. For a decade he was the design profession's moral compass and its most fervent provocateur.

I first saw Tibor in the 1980s when, as master of ceremonies of the annual AIGA/New York "Fresh Dialogues" evening, he transformed the navel-gazing event into a cultural circus. He assembled a cast of a dozen relative unknowns and a few prematurely forgottens to enlighten and entertain, each through five-minute offerings about the overall visual culture, rather than their own design work. Though at times it was reminiscent of an elementary school show-and-tell, most of the presentations shed light on generally ignored issues of environmental waste, the virtues of unsophisticated design, and the divisions between Modernism and postmodernism. Some were funny, others serious — together they were truly fresh dialogues.

Tibor was a tough ringmaster. If any speaker went thirty seconds beyond his or her allotted time (or if Tibor felt that the talk was unbearably dull) the amplified sound of barking dogs would pierce the presenter's soliloquy, signaling the end of the segment. In addition, Tibor introduced quirky short films, an unexpected pizza delivery (by a nonplussed delivery boy), and souvenir handouts (designed by a job printer and reproduced at QuickCopy) that showed design at its most rudimentary, yet communicative. As a new twist on the old ventriloquist's dummy, Tibor's onstage straight man was a Mac Classic with a happy face that quipped at programmed intervals. This was the first of many public salvos against the status quo. It was also vintage Tibor.

Not since the height of American Modernism during the late 1940s and 1950s had one designer prodded other designers to take responsibility for their work as designer-citizens. With a keen instinct for public relations, a penchant for Barnum-like antics, and a radical consciousness from his days as an organizer for SDS (Students for a Democratic Society), Tibor had, by the late 1980s, become known as (or maybe he even dubbed himself) the "bad boy" of graphic design.

When the clothing company Esprit, which had prided itself as being socially liberal and environmentally friendly, was awarded the 1986 AIGA Design Leadership award, an irate Tibor anonymously distributed leaflets during the awards ceremony at the

Facing page: Tibor Kalman. Photograph copyright © Markku Nyytäjä, Helsinki.

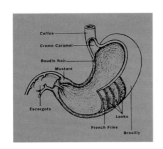

Above: Florent Morellet/
Restaurant Florent "Stomach"
postcard (1990), designed by
Dean Lubensky and Tibor Kalman.
Below: Detail from the David
Byrne CD "Uh-oh" (1991).
Designed by Tibor Kalman and
Scott Stowell, illustrated by Brian
Dewan. Sire Records.

Facing page: Projects designed
for Florent Morellet/Restaurant
Florent. Above and center:
"Symbols" postcard (1986) and
matches (1987), designed by
Alexander Isley and Tibor Kalman.
Below right: "Potato" advertise-
ment (1992), designed by Scott
Stowell and Tibor Kalman. Below
left: "Give/Help/Eat" advertise-
ment (1989), designed by Tibor
Kalman with Dean Lubensky.

AIGA National Design Conference in San Francisco protesting
the company's exploitation of Asian laborers. Tibor believed that
award-winning design was not separate from the entire corporate
ethic and argued that "many bad companies have great design." In
1989, as co-chair with Milton Glaser of the AIGA's "Dangerous
Ideas" conference in San Antonio, he urged designers to question
the effects of their work on the environment and refuse to accept
any client's product at face value. As an object lesson and act of
hubris, he challenged designer Joe Duffy to an impromptu debate
about a full-page advertisement that he and his then partner,
British corporate designer Michael Peters, had placed in the *Wall
Street Journal* promoting their services to Fortune 500 corporations. While most designers admired this self-promotional effort,
Tibor insisted that the ad perpetuated mediocrity and was an
example of selling out to corporate capitalism. This outburst was
the first, but not the last, in which Tibor criticized another designer in public for perceived misdeeds. By the early 1990s, Tibor
also had written (or collaborated with others in writing) numerous
finger-wagging manifestos that exposed the pitfalls of what he
sarcastically called "professional" design.

Tibor saw himself as a social activist for whom graphic
design was a means of achieving two ends: good design and social
responsibility. Good design, which he defined as "unexpected and
untried," added more interest, and was thus a benefit, to everyday
life. Second, since graphic design is mass communication, Tibor
believed it should be used to increase public awareness of a variety
of social issues. His own design firm, M&Co (named after his wife
and co-creator, Maira), which started in 1979 selling conventional
"design by the pound" to banks and department stores, was transformed in the mid-1980s into a soapbox for his social mission.

He urged clients like Restaurant Florent to use the advertising
M&Co created for them to promote political or social messages.
He devoted M&Co's seasonal self-promotional gifts to advocate
support for the homeless. One Christmas he sent over 300 clients
and colleagues a small cardboard box filled with the typical
Spartan contents of a homeless-shelter meal (a sandwich, crackers,

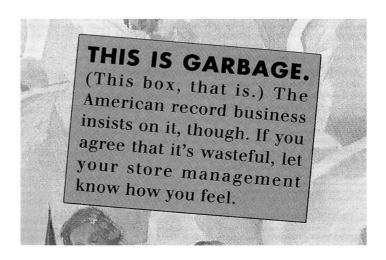

THIS IS GARBAGE.
(This box, that is.) The
American record business
insists on it, though. If you
agree that it's wasteful, let
your store management
know how you feel.

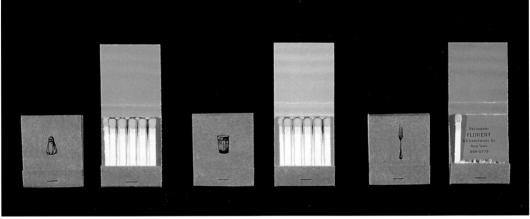

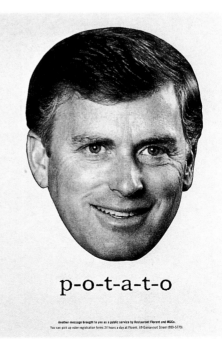

21

A BOOK?!??

Just a cruddy old book?

OK, we had a hard time
coming up with a gift for you
guys this year.

We thought about giving you a . . .

Maybe what M&Co can do is
provide you with the **means**.

Still isn't enough to get something good.

Let's face it, it's not that much.

You could give it away.

There are plenty of really
good causes these days.

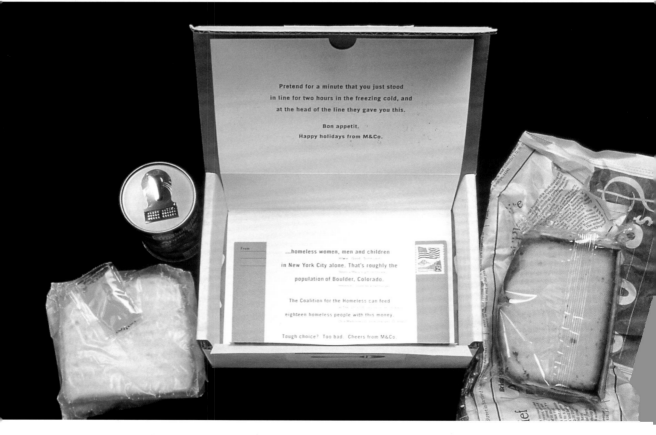

Pretend for a minute that you just stood
in line for two hours in the freezing cold, and
at the head of the line they gave you this.

Bon appetit.
Happy holidays from M&Co.

...homeless women, men and children
in New York City alone. That's roughly the
population of Boulder, Colorado.

The Coalition for the Homeless can feed
eighteen homeless people with this money.

Tough choice? Too bad. Cheers from M&Co.

Above left and right: Brochure and signage for Red Square, a housing development on New York's Lower East Side (1989). Designed by Tibor Kalman with Marlene McCarty. Text by Danny Abelson, photo by Ken Schless. Sundered Ground. Center: Optimism, the 1991 M&Co holiday gift to clients and friends, a foul-smelling perfume in honor of the war in the Persian Gulf. Designed by Tibor Kalman with Maira Kalman and Emily Oberman.

Facing page, top and center: The $26 book, M&Co's 1989 holiday gift, a cheap used book interspersed with cash and notes from the studio. Designed by Tibor Kalman with Dean Lubensky and Emily Oberman. Below: Lunch box for the homeless, the M&Co 1990 holiday gift. Designed by Tibor Kalman with Scott Stowell.

candy bar, etc.) and offered to match any donations that the recipients made to an agency for the homeless. The following year he sent a book peppered with facts about poverty along with twenty dollars and a stamped envelope addressed to another charity.

Tibor was criticized for using the issue of homelessness as a public relations ploy to garner attention for M&Co. And indeed he was a master at piquing public interest in just this way. But he was also sincere. Perhaps the impulse came from his childhood, when as a seven-year-old Hungarian immigrant fleeing the Communists in 1956, he and his family were displaced — virtually homeless — in a new land. Although he became more American than most natives, he never forgot the time when he was an "alien."

He savored the nuances of type and had a fetish for vernacular design — the untutored or quotidian signs, marquees, billboards, and packages that compose mass culture — but understood that being a master of good design meant nothing unless it supported a message that led to action. Even most stylistic work must be viewed in the context of Tibor's persistence. Everything had to have meaning and resonance. A real estate brochure, like one for Red Square, an apartment building on the Lower East Side of Manhattan, had to be positioned in terms of how it would benefit the surrounding low-income community. One message was never enough. When Tibor sold a "design" to a client, he did not hype a particular typeface or color, but rather how the end result would simultaneously advance both client and culture.

Tibor did not, however, rebel against being a professional — M&Co was in business to be successful and he enjoyed the rewards of prosperity. But he questioned the conventions of success. "Everyone can hire a good photographer, choose a tasteful typeface and produce a perfect mechanical," Tibor once railed. "So what? That means ninety-five percent of the work exists on the same professional level, which for me is the same as being mediocre." Tibor ardently avoided any solution, or any client, that would perpetuate this *bete noir*. About clients, Tibor said: "We're

This page, descending from top: "CK Chicken" cover design, *New York Times Magazine* (1998). Designed by Tibor Kalman with Diane Shaw. Cover of *Next Stop Grand Central* by Maira Kalman (1998). Designed by Tibor Kalman, illustrated by Maira Kalman. Spreads from *Tibor Kalman: Perverse Optimist,* Princeton Architectural Press (1998): South Korean National Assembly Vice President Hwang Nakjoo struggling to speak in the final moments of the 1994 budget debates. Photo by Yeohong Yoon. Alexander Calder's desk, Roxbury, Connecticut. Photo by Inge Morath/Magnum. Bill Gates getting a pie in the face, Brussels, 1998. Photo by Herwig Vergult/Belga/Agence France Press. Zaire. Photo by José Azel/Aurora. Poor white family, South Africa. Photo by Louise Gubb/The Image Works. New York City. Photo by Jeff Mermelstein. World leaders as women. Photo illustration by Kathy Grove. Opening of the Hypermarché Auchan Bel Est, France. Photo by Pascal Sittler/REA. Christmas in Managua, Nicaragua. Photo by Carl Purcell. Opening of Ponape airport, Micronesia. Photo by Michael Fride/Rex Features. The Vatican. Photo by Adriano Mordenti/AGF/Franca Speranza. All text by Tibor Kalman.

not here to give them what's safe and expedient. We're not here to help eradicate everything of visual interest from the face of the earth. We're here to make them think about design that's dangerous and unpredictable. We're here to inject art into commerce."

With little patience for mundane and insipid thinking, whether it came from clients, other designers, or M&Co, Tibor was intolerant of mindless consistency and was not reluctant to make people angry — including associates, friends, and allies. For example, in a speech before the Modernism and Eclecticism design history symposium, he accused two friends, Charles Spencer Anderson and Paula Scher, who revived historical styles at that time, of being grave-robbers who abrogated their responsibility as creators. Curiously, M&Co had developed a house style of its own based on vernacularism, the "undesign" that Tibor celebrated for its unfettered expression, which also fed into the postmodern penchant for referring to the past. While Tibor's ire sometimes

Descending from top: Cover of *Tibor Kalman: Perverse Optimist,* Princeton Architectural Press (1998). *Maam* magazine spread (1997). Designed by Jenny Holzer with Tibor Kalman. "The People of 42nd Street" installation (1998). Designed by Tibor Kalman and Kim Maley. Photographs by Neil Selkirk. Installation photo by Kim Maley. 42nd Street Development Project.

Above: *Artforum* cover
(September 1987). Designed by
Tibor Kalman. Photograph by
William Wegman. Edited by Ingrid
Sischy. John(ny Rotten) Lydon
cover of *Interview* (January 1991).
Designed by Tibor Kalman, pho-
tographed by Kurt Markus, edited
by Ingrid Sischy. Below left: Cover
of *Colors* 8 (September 1994)
and below right: Cover of *Colors* 1
(Fall 1991). Both photographed by
Oliviero Toscani.

seemed inconsistent with his own practice, he rationalized M&Co's
use of vernacular as a symbol of protest — a means of undermining
the cold conformity of the corporate International Style.

M&Co left scores of design artifacts behind, but Tibor
will be remembered more for his critiques on the nature of consumption and production than for his formal studio achievements,
which were contributed to by many talented design associates.
Despite numerous entries in design annuals, and the catalogue
of objects in his own book, *Tibor Kalman: Perverse Optimist*
(Princeton Architectural Press, 1998), the heart of Tibor's accom-
plishment was enlarging the parameters of design from service
to cultural force. And this was no more apparent than in his later
work. For when Tibor realized that stylish record albums, witty
advertisements, and humorous watches and clocks had a limited
cultural value, he turned to editing.

First, he signed on as creative director of the magazines
Artforum and *Interview*. But he mostly guided the look, not the
content, of these publications. In fact, without total control he
was frustrated by his inability to experiment with a new pictorial
narrative theory that he was developing. As a teenager he was an
avid fan of *Life* magazine, and believed that in the age of electronic
media, photojournalism was still a more effective way to convey
significant stories. While editing pictures for the photographer
Oliviero Toscani, who had created the pictorial advertising identity
for Benetton, the Italian clothing manufacturer, Tibor helped
produce a series of controversial advertisements focusing on AIDS,
racism, refugees, violence, and warfare that carried the Benetton
logo but eschewed the fashions it sold. For him, this was sublimely
subversive.

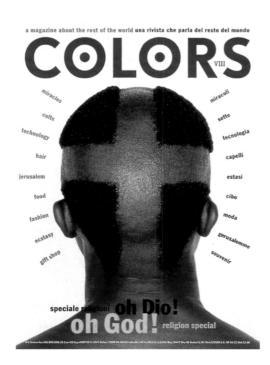

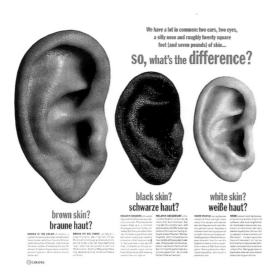

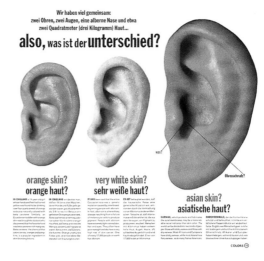

Above: Spread from *Colors* 4 (Spring 1993). Racial retouching by Site One, New York. Original photos by Ronald Woolf/Globe Photos. Center left: Spread from *Colors* 7 (June 1994). Reagan photo by Rota/Camera Press/Grazia Neri. Image computing by Site One, New York. Center right: Spread from *Colors* 7 (June 1994). Photo by Sergio Merti/Studio MDA.

Productless commercial advertisements were not altogether new. In the 1980s Kenneth Cole and Ben and Jerry's Ice Cream companies devoted advertising and packaging space to promote social and environmental causes. But in the 1990s Benetton went a step further with what began as The United Colors of Benetton, a product-based series of multicultural kids promoting ethnic and racial harmony, which evolved into captionless double truck journalistic photographs. Ultimately the ads led to the creation of Benetton's own magazine, *Colors*, for which Tibor became editor-in-chief and where he continued to reject fashion magazine clichés in favor of sociopolitical issues. *Colors* quickly became the primary outlet for Tibor's most progressive ideas. And shortly after launching the magazine, he closed M&Co's doors and moved to Rome.

Colors was "the first magazine for the global village," Tibor announced, "aimed at an audience of flexible minds, young people between fourteen and twenty, or curious people of any age." It was also the outlet for Tibor's political activism. In his most audacious issue devoted to racism, a feature titled "How to Change Your Race" examined cosmetic means of altering hair, lips, noses, eyes, and, of course, skin color to achieve some kind of platonic ideal. Another feature in the same issue, "What If..." was a collection of full-page manipulated photographs showing famous people racially transformed: Queen Elizabeth and Arnold Schwarzenegger as black; Pope John Paul II as Asian; Spike Lee as white; and Michael Jackson given a Nordic cast. "Race is not

Above: "Cigarette" OpArt, *New York Times* (January 15, 1997). Designed by Tibor Kalman, produced by Alan Hill. "Your Ad Here," OpArt, *New York Times* (May 22, 1998). Designed by Tibor Kalman. Below: Legal paperweight (1984). Designed by Tibor Kalman. M&Co Labs.

the real issue here," Kalman noted. "Power and sex are the dominant forces in the world."

Through its vivid coverage of such themes as deadly weapons, street violence, and hate groups, *Colors* was a vivid contrast to Benetton's fashion products. Even the way it was printed, on pulp paper, which soaked up ink and muted the color reproductions, went counter to the brightly lighted Benetton shops with happy clothes in vibrant colors. Yet *Colors* served to "contextualize," as Tibor defined it, Toscani's advertising imagery. Indeed, the basis for criticism leveled at Benetton's advertising campaign had been the absence of context. Without a caption or explanatory text the images appeared gratuitous — shocking, yes, but uninformative. The campaign signaled that Benetton had some kind of a social conscience, but the ads themselves failed to explain what it was. With *Colors* the advertisements appeared as teasers for a magazine that critically addressed war and peace, love and hate, power and sex.

In 1997, cancer forced Tibor to return to New York, where despite grueling chemo and radiation therapy, he re-established M&Co with a mission to take a pro-active approach to design and art direction. Foreseeing his last chance to do meaningful work, Tibor accepted only projects that would have lasting impact. He began writing OpArt critiques for the OpEd Page of the *New York Times*, attacking smoking and noise pollution, among other issues. He designed an outdoor installation of photographs of real people commenting on their relationship to Times Square, which hung on the scaffold around the Conde Nast tower in Times Square. He taught a weekly class in pictorial narrative in the MFA/Design program at the School of Visual Arts until a week before he died. And he continued to contribute articles on popular and vernacular culture to various magazines. As his last testament he designed "Tiborocity," a retrospective exhibition at SFMoMA, constructed as thematic "neighborhoods" that integrated Tibor's work with his graphic influences from the '60s and '70s.

Of the two names that changed design in the '80s and '90s — Mac and Tibor — one changed the way we work, the other the way we think. The former is a tool, the latter was our conscience.

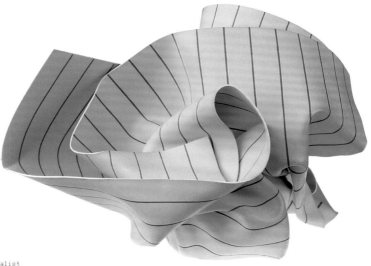

July 6, 1949
Born in Budapest, Hungary.

1956
Kalman family flees Communists in Hungary and moves to the United States.

1967–1970
Attends New York University; joins Students for a Democratic Society; covers the student occupation of Columbia University for the NYU newspaper.

1970
Drops out of NYU and briefly moves to Cuba as a member of the "Venceremos Brigade" to cut sugar cane and learn about Cuban culture.

1968–1979
Works for company that becomes Barnes & Noble.

1979–1990
Founds and is principal of M&Co.

1987–1988
Art directs *Artforum*.

1989–1991
Is creative director of *Interview*.

Spring 1991–Fall 1993
Is founding editor-in-chief of *Colors,* in New York City.

Fall 1993–Fall 1995
Moves to Rome, is editor-in-chief of *Colors* full-time.

Fall 1995
Moves back to New York.

Summer 1997
Reopens M&Co.

May 2, 1999
Dies in Puerto Rico.

Source: *Tibor Kalman: Perverse Optimist* (Princeton University Press, 1998).

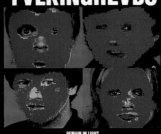

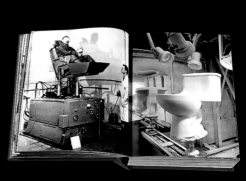

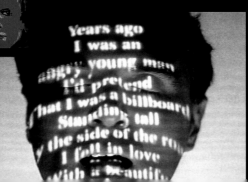

29

Expanding Boundaries

Katherine McCoy

By Lorraine Wild

I have to begin this essay with a confession: it is not easy to write about an old friend and teacher, someone to whom I owe so much. I have been in awe of Katherine McCoy's talents and accomplishments for the almost thirty years that I have known her, and that admiration is framed by my experience of being her student at Cranbrook back in the '70s. When I heard that Katherine McCoy was being awarded the AIGA Gold Medal, I interpreted it as a sign that the AIGA was honoring design education through this specific award to such a consummate educator. My reaction may be an automatic reflection of the stubborn split between those designers who perceive themselves primarily as educators, and those who see themselves primarily as professionals. And I am sure there are designers out there who think Katherine McCoy comes purely from the educator's side, and is somehow detached from the pragmatic concerns of day-to-day practice. But what I wish to describe is how the work of Katherine McCoy has been concentrated in education, and yet has had an enormous impact on design practice in the United States during the last two decades, and conversely, how the professional work and activities that she has engaged in have also functioned as educational, and have made a terrific contribution to the maturing of design in the broadest sense.

Katherine often has said that it was a visit to the Museum of Modern Art (on a family trip to the New York World's Fair in 1964) that made her realize she was most interested in the power of design. After majoring in industrial design at Michigan State University and graduating in 1967, she took a job in the Detroit offices of Unimark International, design consultants who produced some of the largest and most notable corporate identity projects of the period. The offices of Unimark, where she received her real typographic training, were famous for the strict, clean "Swiss" Modernism of their designs, which at that time was still unique, almost exotic to corporate communications. Not only did Unimark sell their work to their clients, they also promoted a hyper-rational problem-solving approach to corporate communications, detached from advertising or marketing. The house journal, *Dot Zero*, published some of the earliest arguments in the United States in support of the Modern style. Immersed in the ideology of problem solving through "objectivity" in form, she spent hours poring over the office copies of the "Swiss Bibles," typographic books by Müller-Brockmann, Ruder, Gerstner, and Hofmann.

Her experience at Unimark was followed by a year at Chrysler Corporation's corporate identity office, and then by a Boston office, Omnigraphics, that consulted with Muriel Cooper at the MIT Press, which provided further opportunity to hone the typographic approach she had developed at Unimark, and a design office in Detroit, Designers and Partners, which was quite a different place altogether. Designers and Partners was oriented toward working with advertising agen-

CRANBROOK

Facing page: Katherine McCoy.
Above: Cranbrook logotype,
Cranbrook Educational
Community (1994). Designed as
a principal of McCoy & McCoy.

Above: Supplier Communications
Manual (1968). Designed while
a staff designer at the Chrysler
Corporation Identity Office.

Facing page, above: Frontier
Airlines ticket counter posters,
designed as a junior designer
at Unimark International (1967).
Center left: Graphic Artists
Guild call for entries poster
(1971), designed while co-chair
of Cranbrook design department.
Center right and below: Cranbrook
Academy of Art graduate design
recruitment posters (1974),
designed while co-chair of the
Cranbrook design department.

cies, mostly on automotive accounts, and had a staff that consisted of all sorts of graphic arts "professionals," including illustrators, cartoonists, and "lettering men" as well as graphic designers. Although she did not particularly enjoy the work with advertising clients (finding the focus on selling to be contrary to her interests in communication), Katherine was exposed to a very lively group — including her colleague Edward Fella, who was later to become one of the more influential participants (as both a critic and a graduate) in the Cranbrook design department, and whose aesthetic was as eclectic as Unimark's was pure.

In 1971, Katherine and her husband, Michael, an industrial designer, were founding their partnership, McCoy & McCoy Associates, when they were asked by the Cranbrook Academy of Art to become co-chairs of the design department. Under the direction of Eliel Saarinen from the '30s to the '50s, Cranbrook's graduate-level design department had nurtured and produced several students who went on to become major forces in American architecture and design — Harry Bertoia, Eero Saarinen, Florence Schust (Knoll), and Ray and Charles Eames, among others. But all schools go through cycles and not much had happened in design at Cranbrook after that. After some hesitation, Michael and Katherine accepted the position, walking into a department that had a great past but no present — although it did have the incredible and subtly beautiful Saarinen-designed campus as a daily reminder of what could be accomplished in that place.

The McCoys were free to reinvent the programs in 2-D and 3-D design however they wanted. Katherine recalls that she combined the "objective" typographic approach that she knew through professional practice with an interest in the social and cultural activism that was in the air in the late '60s. One early recruitment poster for the program features text that describes the goals of the design program in almost completely Utopian terms, combined with a collage that reproduces fragments of provocative design from both the professional and avant-garde design traditions of the twentieth century. The beginning of the McCoys' program at Cranbrook can be seen as part of a wave of activity in U.S. design programs that was directed toward more high-level experimental work. California Institute of the Arts, the Kansas City Art Institute, and the Rhode Island School of Design, among other schools, started to offer alternatives to the graduate program at Yale, one of the advanced programs in graphic design studies that not only trained people for professional practice, but encouraged them to work speculatively, beyond the professional model.

The tensions and contradictions between the Modernist obsession with process and methodology versus the fascinations with both historical and speculative form were always in play at Cranbrook. Katherine McCoy describes her role as a "parade organizer" or a "coach," concerned with setting the scene for

Saint Louis

Frontier

Kansas City
Saint Louis
Tucson
Oklahoma City
El Paso
Dallas
Las Vegas
Salt Lake City
Billings

GAG 5

CRANBROOK

GRADUATE

DESIGN

Location

Sixteen miles north of the center of
Detroit on a 300-acre wooded campus
in the heart of Bloomfield Hills,
Cranbrook's location combines an
unique rural environment with the
advantages offered by the nation's
fifth largest city.

Facilities

Individual studio spaces, shops,
darkrooms, gallery spaces,
dormitories, recreational facilities
and an 18,000 volume art library set
to Saarinen architecture.

Information

Write for catalog and application to
Admissions Office, Cranbrook
Academy of Art, 500 Lone Pine Road,
Bloomfield Hills, Michigan 48013.

Cranbrook Academy of Art admits
students of any race, color, and
national or ethnic origin.

Program

Two-year graduate concentrations,
stressing self-directed, self-motivated
study. Limited undergraduate program
available to advanced candidates
entering the junior year of study.

Student body

150 graduate students working closely
with a 12-member resident faculty in
the major departments of
architecture, ceramics, design, fiber,
metalsmithing, painting, photography,
printmaking, and sculpture.

Financial aid

Financial assistance available to both
first and second year students in the
form of scholarships, assistantships
and tuition grants as well as the
College Work Study Program, the
Federally Insured Loan Program and
a special scholarship grant provided
by the Ford Foundation.

Cranbrook Academy of Art

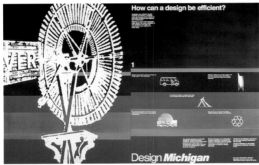

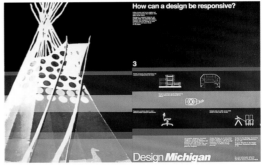

Top: Cranbrook Academy of Art academic catalogues (1972–1978); Thomas B. Wedell, photography. Center left and right: *Design Michigan* educational posters # 1 and #3 (1977), conceived, written, and designed by a faculty/student team including Katherine and Michael McCoy and Cranbrook design department graduate students.

a rich interchange between students. The remarkable thing about Cranbrook under the direction of the McCoys that is not well understood is how, on the surface, a department with so little structure actually worked. The art school was run without classes, grades, requirements, or deadlines other than a final thesis show, and yet the place was a beehive of activity. This has lots of anecdotal explanations — winter weather so bad that there was nothing to do but work, or haunted dorm rooms — but the truth as usual is more complex. The McCoys had a good eye for the right students, and really knew how to create an interesting mix of personalities in the studio. After a brief foray into interdisciplinary projects, the students were segregated into projects but not into separate studios, so graphic designers were exposed on a daily basis to the problems of industrial designers, and vice versa. Students sat in on one another's critiques without regard to specialty. It is true that Katherine leaned on her Modernist typographic background at the beginning (I remember Kathy handed me a copy of Ruari McLean's translation of Jan Tschichold's *Asymmetric Typography* and said, "Here, read this, it's all you really have to know about type.") but she soon evolved a short sequence of introductory projects for the graphic design majors that would accelerate their progress from standard typographic skills into the ability to play more fluidly and expressively with typography.

Over the years Katherine designed a lot of material for the

Camera & Eye poster announcing a Detroit Institute of Arts traveling photography exhibition (1975). Bicentennial jazz concert series, Cranbrook Academy of Art Museum (1976). Both designed as a principal of McCoy & McCoy.

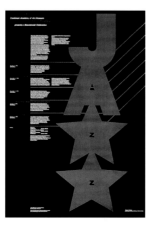

Cranbrook educational community, quarterly magazines, catalogues, and posters, along with other projects that she and Michael produced as McCoy & McCoy. Within the tradition of the atelier there were many opportunities for students to collaborate with Katherine on the design of works that were actually realized. This is the counterbalance to the experimental work of the Cranbrook students, which was so often reproduced yet not understood to be part of a wider range of projects undertaken in the department. However, that interest in process and progress that the McCoys had brought to the program transformed itself into an obsession with the possibilities of change and transformation of design practice itself. At the studios and the critiques at Cranbrook, discussions often centered on the possibility of breaking away from the norms of everyday practice. Katherine and Michael required the students to read about both historical and contemporary design and theory, to really understand the context in which each student was going to be entering. In retrospect, this might have seemed a bit presumptuous for a design department in a somewhat obscure art school in the northwestern suburbs of Detroit, but the internal expectation set up by Katherine and Michael was simply that they (the McCoys and the students) were in this not only to make interesting work, but to make their mark upon the development of the field. And Katherine's ongoing work outside of Cranbrook, with its orientation toward public education, such as the *Design Michigan* project of 1977, the *Colorado Native American Heritage* poster project of 1978, or the *Fluxus* book of 1981 constantly set the example of work that worked, both formally and conceptually, for its audience.

Something else that Katherine and Michael McCoy gave their students — although it was obviously never taught, it was offered purely by example — was the idea of living a life that could not be divided simplistically between life and work, but that integrated life and love and design and work absolutely seamlessly. The McCoys, like all the Cranbrook faculty, lived and worked on campus, although they were the only teachers who worked as a team, as a creative partnership, and as a married couple. Every day the students witnessed what prodigious things could be accomplished under such an arrangement! The power and positive energy implicit in the creative partnership of McCoy & McCoy (that simple equation, one plus one) proved to be exponential, and again only emphasized the importance of commitment both inside and outside of the design studio.

Katherine took two leaps in the design of the design program during the late '70s, which led to its second, very influential phase. First, she began to alter the introductory typography projects to allow a semiotic interpretation to begin to drive the solutions, and she allowed the students to depart from the stricter Modernist vocabulary of previous years, to include stylistic elements that had previously been underused by Modernist typographers, such as

This page, above: McCoy &
McCoy capabilities brochure
(1977), designed as a principal
of McCoy & McCoy; Thomas
B. Wedell, photography.

Facing page, top row and
center right: Covers and interior
spreads from Cranbrook
Academy of Art academic
catalogues, all designed while
co-chair of Cranbrook design
department. Top left: 1983
catalogue, Constance Birdsall,
design assistant; Thomas B.
Wedell, photography. Top right:
1978 catalogue, photography
by Thomas B. Wedell. Center
right: 1988 catalogue, Andrew
Blauvelt, design assistant;
Thomas B. Wedell, photography.
Center left: Cover and interior
spread of *Fluxus Etc.*, Cranbrook
Academy of Art Museum exhibition catalogue on international
neo-Dada art movement (1981),
designed as a principal of
McCoy & McCoy. Lori Barnett,
Lynnette Silarski, and Kenneth
Windsor, design assistants;
Thomas B. Wedell, photography.
Bottom: Packaging and signage
for Tivoli, an upscale gift shop
(1977). Designed as a principal
of McCoy & McCoy; Thomas B.
Wedell, photography.

historical or vernacular type forms or images. The second leap was
to let the students, who were more than ready and able, to take
the lead on the exploration of theory, but to insist that it always
be resolved as a visual problem rather than an academic one.
This again emanated from Katherine's honest assessment that the
strength of the Cranbrook tradition was one of making meaning
through making real work. Also, what cannot be underestimated
is Katherine McCoy's ability to put together classes of students who
would challenge without competitively destroying each other, and
her ability to articulate an ethic of community that somehow
encouraged this high level of productivity.

It is important to note that while Katherine was running
the 2-D program at Cranbrook and consulting on myriad design
projects, she also served as the first woman president of the
Industrial Design Society of America (1983–1985), sat on the
national advisory board of the AIGA, and chaired the Design Arts
Fellowship Grant Panel for the National Endowment for the Arts
for three years. The generous amount of time she spent on the
development of professional organizations during these years of
growth came out of her conviction that it constituted an extension
of her teaching time — that the organizations were critical to the
ongoing development of the design itself. She has a holistic view of
the interrelationship between the academies and the design offices,
and sees the professional organizations as the natural link, a force
for education that does not stop with school.

Another aspect of Katherine's influence has been her writing,
which has always been cogent, jargon free, and clear in its commitment to the continuing education of all designers, not just those in
school. After she and Mike took a sabbatical in Holland, she wrote
an essay in *I.D. Magazine* titled "Reconstructing Dutch Graphics"
(1985), which was one of the first explorations of the new Dutch
work to appear in an American design magazine. It did a lot to
draw the attention of young American designers to the high level
of contemporary design being produced there and helped to insti-
gate many exchanges between American and Dutch graphic designers during the next few years. But most of Katherine's writing has
been focused on issues specific to education or to attitudes that
affect design practice, inside and outside of the classroom. A con-
tinual theme running through her writing is that of authenticity and
ethics: in education (working through ideas about understanding
the criteria to judge effective programs to teach design) and in
professional practice (exploring the idea of commitment to social
and cultural and political activity and the tension between that and
the stubborn notion of the disengaged professional). Also, she has
used writing to spur her own research into the articulation of new
ideas in design, and in the process has often found the words to
explain what we are experiencing visually at that moment. That
writing, which would include her essays on typography and now on

new media, has entered the syllabi of studio and seminar courses in design schools across the country.

In 1991, the McCoys (with a large team of 2-D and 3-D students) produced the book *Cranbrook Design: The New Discourse* (Rizzoli International Publications). The book documented the high-octane visuals of the work that had been produced in the Cranbrook studios during the 1980s, and it probably sealed the reputation of the school as being a place where the visual quality of the work, sometimes generated by a highly creative (or even mistaken!) interpretation of theory took precedent without regard to the "needs" of the profession. Again, the critique that often met the work represented in that book was often voiced without knowledge of the actual discourse of the studio critique, driven by the McCoys, that challenged the experimentation to be as real as possible, out of a dedication to realizing the Utopian ideal of design that informed, delighted, and somehow liberated its users.

The McCoys gave up their chairmanship at Cranbrook in 1995 after sustaining twenty-four years of coherent and energetic work. They moved to Chicago, where they spend every fall semester as senior lecturers at the Illinois Institute of Technology's Institute of Design. Katherine in particular has somewhat moved away from studio teaching, and has instead been concentrating more on theoretical issues having to do with both the teaching and practice of graphic design in the context of new media. In fact, this has brought her back to issues of design methodology, information and communications theory and the audience, not far from where she started both under the influence of Unimark and the

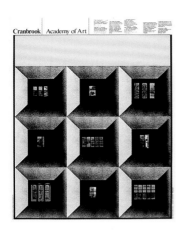

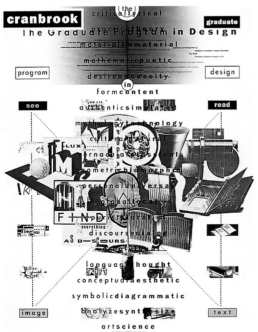

late '60s obsession with process over form. Like many other educators facing the shift in technologies brought on by design for electronic media and the Web, Katherine recognizes that we are facing a profound shift that cannot be answered with the same set of principles that framed the backbone of the last several decades of design for print. But she does bring a depth of experience and perspective to this new challenge (and, again, phenomenal energy for study and research). She initiated and chaired the American Center for Design's "Living Surfaces" conference in 1992, the first U.S. design conference on the subject of new media, and has written many articles and lectures devoted to this new phase of her ongoing work.

Katherine and Michael spend the rest of the year in the mountains of Colorado, in what, from afar, looks like semi-retirement. But up close the image shifts completely: in their totally wired encampment they continue their projects and their research. Even the teaching doesn't really stop — this year Katherine and Michael have launched "High Ground," a series of studio charette workshops open to professional designers in their studios. Katherine has often advised younger designers that they must regard the design of their own careers as a project itself, and that they must choose their paths carefully. Even in that remote location, the path that Katherine has taken, and continues to take, integrating life and art and design and work, resonates in the work of so many others from coast to coast. It is for work accomplished, but an exemplary process still in progress, that this AIGA Gold Medal seems most appropriate.

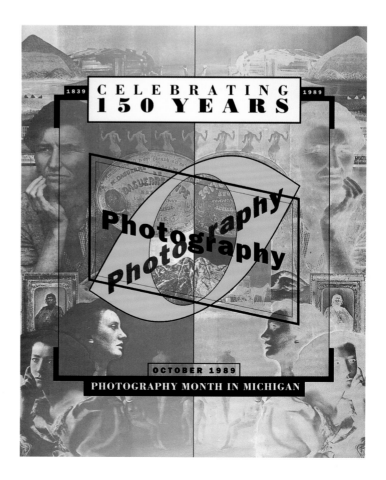

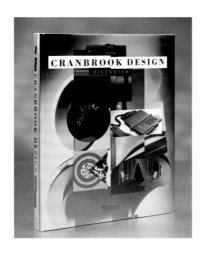

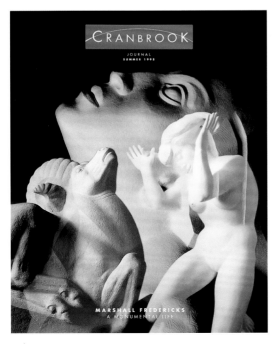

Alfred A.K

By Véronique Vienne

If you were to peruse your bookshelves at home in search of hardcover books published by Alfred Knopf, Inc., as I did when researching this writing, you might be surprised to discover that many of your favorite books sport on their spine a running Borzoi dog — the famous Knopf trademark.

Whether it is a faded copy of *The American Language,* by H. L. Mencken, with its original 1919 copyright, or a well-preserved 1955 edition of *Collected Poems* by Wallace Stevens, or a reprint of the Julia Child's 1961 classic *Mastering the Art of French Cooking,* or *Landscape and Memory,* the 1995 bestseller by art historian Simon Schama, they are the books you would not want to part with. Also by Knopf are slimmer volumes on your night table — three or four must-read novels by contemporary authors. Each time you pull one of these books from the shelf, you are compelled to leaf through it slowly, as each page beckons you to linger. What makes them so special? Is it the quality of their paper, the elegance of their typefaces, the careful layout of their pages — or simply their subject matter? Puzzled, you make a mental note to investigate Knopf titles the next time you go into a bookstore. Forget judging a book by its cover — maybe you should start judging it by its trademark.

"Look for the Borzoi label and then buy the book!" a 1920 Knopf advertisement used to advocate. It was wishful thinking, of course. Privately, Alfred A. Knopf, a larger-than-life mustachioed character who imposed his views with Olympian poise, admitted that, in fact, "few people ever remember the name of the publisher of any book." But, during his fifty-five-year career, he did his best to break down this ignorance by insisting that publications bearing his imprint be the best-looking books in America. "For me, book design is a personal thing," he was fond of saying. The company he founded in 1915 with his wife, Blanche, has not only endured till the end of the twentieth century and maintained its position as a leader in the field, it has come close to becoming what is now called a "brand."

When asked what makes the Knopf books stand out among the dizzying array of books published today, Carol Devine Carson, vice president and art director of the Knopf imprint, does not hesitate. "Respect for books," she says. "And our relationship with authors." She explains that Knopf authors are treated as full-fledged partners, with final say on the cover of their book — even if this privilege is not stipulated in their contract. Some authors come with preconceived ideas (such as their name in large type!), but most writers are open to her suggestions, simply because they know that at Knopf, design is never an afterthought.

Also part of the Knopf mystique, she adds, is "A Note on the Type," the brief paragraph at the back of each book describing the origin and characteristics of the typeface used to set the text. That's where you learn, for instance, that the celebrated goldsmith

Facing page: Alfred A. Knopf. Photograph by Tom Hollyman (1972). This page, below: Borzoi logo by Warren Chappell.

Above: *Transport* (1929). Designer unknown. Below: Various spines designed by W. A. Dwiggins in the 1930s.

Francesco Griffo designed Bembo in 1495. That the typeface called Janson was not in fact designed by Dutchman Anton Janson but by Nicholas Kis, a Hungarian protégé of Dirk Voskens. Or that what makes Trump Mediaeval unique is the subtlety of its italic letterforms. The printer, paper company, binder, illustrator, and designer involved in the creation of the book are also mentioned in this colophon as well. Introduced in 1926, "A Note on the Type" reflects the tradition of readability and graphic elegance makes Knopf books so distinctive.

Last but not least, the playful Knopf logo, a.k.a. the Borzoi, is probably one of the most beloved pets in the history of publishing. The borzoi, a wolfhound, is a crossbreed between an Arabian greyhound and a Russian sheepdog. On spines and on title pages, its long yet muscular silhouette is a pretext for an exercise in graphic wit. There is no official version of this trademark, whose variations are too many to be counted. Some look like Victorian engravings, others have an Art Deco signature, and still others capture the likeness of the running dog with only a couple of smart curlicues. Even Paul Rand designed a Borzoi, turning it into a cabalistic sign. Legend has it that Blanche Knopf came up with the idea. "Knopf" was deemed hard to pronounce, while the alliterative sound of "Borzoi Books," she figured, would provoke curiosity. "Borzoi are decorative, but not good as dogs," Alfred Knopf once remarked, with his usual abrupt candor.

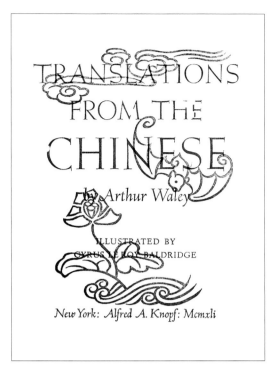

Above, from left: Title page of *The Snow Goose,* designed by George Salter. Title page of *Translations from the Chinese,* designed by Richard Ellis and Cyrus LeRoy Baldridge. Both from the AIGA *Fifty Books of the Year* exhibition. Below: Various spines designed by W. A. Dwiggins.

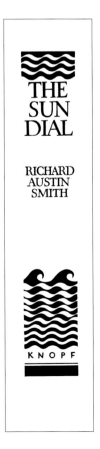

WALT WHITMAN'S

Leaves of Grass

THE COMPLETE AND DEFINITIVE TEXT
FROM WHITMAN'S "DEATHBED EDITION"

Preface by Bernard Smith

THREE OF A KIND
three short novels

JAMES M. CAIN
AUTHOR OF "SERENADE," ETC.

Willa Cather
On Writing

With a Foreword by Stephen Tennant

CRITICAL STUDIES
ON WRITING AS AN ART

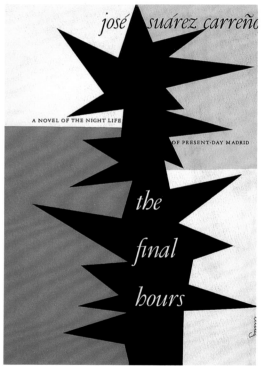

josé suárez carreño

A NOVEL OF THE NIGHT LIFE
OF PRESENT-DAY MADRID

the

final

hours

Leave me Alone
a novel by David Karp
author of One + All Honorable Men

The Doctor and the Soul

From Psychotherapy to Logotherapy

A new approach to
the neurotic personality
which emphasizes man's
spiritual values and the
quest for meaning in life

by Viktor E. Frankl, M.D.

Second, expanded edition

Peter Wahlöö

*The
Thirty-First
Floor*

*A terrifying novel
of a nation
demoralized by
a publishing empire*

*Translated from
the Swedish
by Joan Tate*

Though there is no design formula for achieving the Knopf look, one thing is sure: the key word is quality, or, as Knopf himself used to say, "Better-than-average design calls for better-than-average materials to do it justice." Carol Devine Carson explains that the tactile appeal of Knopf books is the result of a number of small but important details that include design and typography but also the quality of the paper, of the binding, and whether the edge of the pages are smooth or rough. Letterpress is still used for poetry books, and once in a while she can stain the top of the pages.

Alfred Knopf was a tyrant when it came to book production. He required editors, publicists, and sometimes even accountants to attend his long, tedious meetings with the head of manufacturing. Vastly experienced in bibliophilia, but also in music, history, sociology, gastronomy, and nature preservation, he asked the most involved questions. Often, he overruled editors and authors who tried to interfere with the work of William Addison Dwiggins, the artist who designed more than 320 books for Knopf over thirty years. Since 1923, when Dwiggins, whom everyone called "WAD" or "Dwig," joined the firm, Alfred Knopf had consistently relied on his taste and judgment. In front of the staff, he would tell WAD, "Go ahead and make a book."

In 1950, Knopf was awarded an AIGA Gold Medal as a "distinguished publisher, informed collector, consistent exponent of fine bookmaking; for his pioneering and sustaining efforts to raise the standards of design in American trade book publishing; for his interest which has led the general reader to a greater interest in good design." For Knopf, though, good design was not a new concept but an old-fashioned idea. He did not accept, as did other industry leaders, the then-fashionable idea that "good design is good business." Never under the illusion that attractive books necessarily sold better, he was nonetheless willing to add to the production cost of a book just because he wanted it to "look right."

Well-mannered, but short with fools, Knopf didn't waste time with other people's marketing schemes. Unapologetically aristocratic in his approach to business, he did only what pleased him, and, as an editor remembers, "was whatever he felt like being." His eccentricities added to the cachet of his Borzoi imprint. Between 1915 and 1984, when he died at age ninety-one, his firm had published more than 5,000 books, including the work of sixteen Nobel prize winners and twenty-six Pulitzer recipients.

Since Knopf's official retirement in the late 1960s, two men have assumed leadership of the Borzoi imprint: Robert Gottlieb, who stayed at the helm for two decades, and Sonny Mehta, who took over in 1986. Each man, in his own way, managed the remarkable feat of easing the publishing house into the bottom-line economy without betraying the "Knopfitude" of the man who, all his life, bemoaned the growing commercialism of the publishing industry.

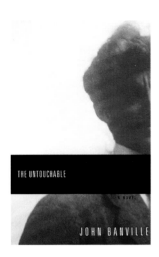

The Untouchable (1997), designed by Carol Devine Carson.

Today, in 1999, the AIGA is bestowing a second medal to Alfred A. Knopf — but this time the Design Leadership Award goes to the vibrant corporate culture he created, which has been sustained for close to a century. "The design profession still traces its lineage from that mother of all design assignments — the book," wrote the AIGA committee that selected Alfred A. Knopf Inc. for this award. "The most recent crop of book designers, who have so refreshingly redefined what a book can look like, are only the latest expression of a corporate commitment to quality and innovation in publishing that goes back farther than most of us can remember."

Indeed, most of the people who remember working with Alfred Knopf are long gone. Luckily, many of them were writers who committed to paper their recollections of the man who knew how to make them feel so important. Alfred himself loved to pen his reminiscences and tell how he discovered and developed his passion for beautiful books.

Born in New York City on September 12, 1892, Alfred Knopf wrote his first book reviews in 1911 for the campus news-paper of Columbia University, where he was studying. His acquaintance with many writers whose works he would later publish dates from this time. In 1912, during his postgraduate summer tour of Europe, he was introduced to a number of Bristish novelists, among them John Galsworthy, Frank Harris, Katherine Mansfield, and John Middleton Murry. Though impressed by these famous authors, he was even more impressed by the design and physical quality of their books, most of them far superior to anything he had seen in the States.

Back in New York, he worked first for Doubleday, where he quickly got involved with the manufacturing of books, and later for Mitchell Kennerly, where he met type designer Frederic Goudy. By 1915, at age twenty-two, young Alfred was ready to start his own firm. Borrowing $5,000 and a desk from Samuel Knopf, his father, he set to work with one assistant, Blanche Wolfe, whom he had met in his Columbia days. Their first book, Four Plays, by Emile Augier, was set in Cheltenham monotype — "a face," Knopf said, "I have never since had the courage to use." The binding was orange and blue, establishing bright colors as part of the Knopf trademark. Just as revealingly, the book was advertised by emphasizing its imprint rather than its author or its subject. Knopf's ambition, and his desire to be hailed as a famous publisher, would serve him well throughout his life.

Within the year, Blanche and Alfred were married. They had published twenty-nine books, including a first bestseller, Green Mansions, by W. H. Hudson. By 1918, a son, Pat, was born and the firm was incorporated: Alfred was president, Blanche vice-president, and Samuel Knopf treasurer, a position the ex-advertising executive would keep until his death in 1932. Over the next fifty years,

Clockwise from top left:
The Tiny One (1999), designed
by Carol Devine Carson. *About
Schmidt* (1996), designed by
Carol Devine Carson. *The House
on R Street* (1994), designed by
Archie Ferguson. *Winchell:
Gossip, Power, and the Culture
of Celebrity* (1995), designed by
Barbara de Wilde. *The Blue
Afternoon* (1995), designed by
Chip Kidd and Carol Devine
Carson.

ABOUT SCHMIDT

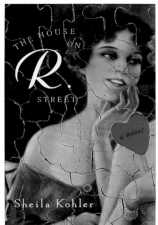

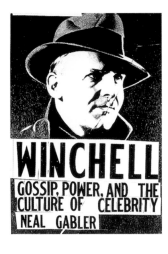

A

H A N D B O O K

F O R

D R O W N I N G

Clockwise from top left:
A Handbook for Drowning (1993),
designed by Chip Kidd. *This Side
of Paradise, Everyman's Library
edition* (1996), designed by
Barbara de Wilde. *Skinned Alive*
(1995), designed by Archie
Ferguson. *Dreaming in Cuban*
(1992), designed by Chip Kidd.
Gut Symmetries (1997), designed
by Archie Ferguson.

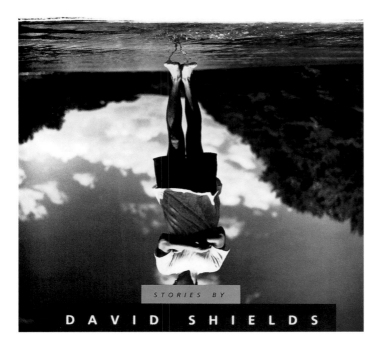

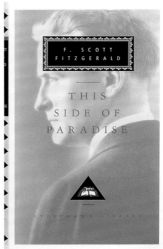

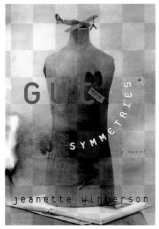

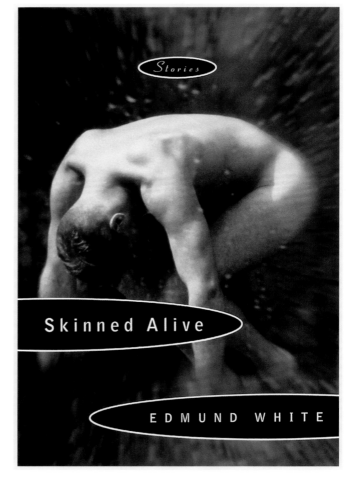

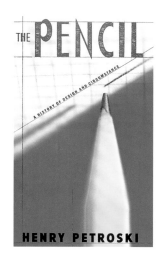

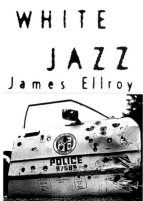

the Knopf husband-wife team was a success. "Alfred and Blanche are like Jupiter and Juno," noted writer Robert Nathan. Everyone knew who the boss was, though. William Koshland, who joined the company in 1934 and eventually became its president and CEO in 1972, when Knopf retired, couldn't resist this remark: "Alfred and Blanche were equal, but Alfred was always more equal."

Blanche brought to the party her suave manner and a formidable ability to spot literary talent here and abroad. She signed many French *écrivains*, such as André Gide, Simone de Beauvoir, Jean-Paul Sartre, and Albert Camus, as well as South American and Japanese writers, Jorge Amado and Yasunari Kawabata among them. Soon, the Borzoi imprint was known for introducing American readers to a bevy of authors with an international reputation: Franz Kafka, Sigmund Freud, Thomas Mann, T. S. Eliot, John Cheever, John Updike, Dashiell Hammett, James Baldwin, and many more.

Though less celebrated than the authors, the designers who contributed to the Knopf legend were — and still are — some of the most illustrious in the field. The first book designer to join

The Pencil: A History of Design and Circumstance (1990), *White Jazz* (1992), and *Darling* (1992). All designed by Chip Kidd.

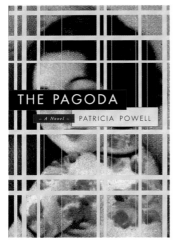

The Loser (1991), designed by Chip Kidd. *The Pagoda* (1998), designed by Susan Carroll. *Push* (1996), designed by Archie Ferguson.

Knopf in 1915 was Claude Bragdon, an architect and scenic designer. In the 1920s, graphic artist Rudolph Ruzicka left his mark with numerous versions of the Borzoi logo. At about the same time, Dwiggins burst onto the scene. A prolific lettering artist, stencil cutter, woodcut illustrator, puppeteer, cartographer, pamphleteer, humorist, writer — not to mention book designer — he also crafted the Caledonia and Electra fonts. In 1940, Warren Chappell, a calligrapher, illustrator, and historian of printing, got involved, and went on to design more than 150 Knopf titles. In the 1950s, Bruce Rogers, known as "the dean of American book design" and the creator of the Centaur font, also became a contributor. And the list goes on, with Elmer Adler, Herbert Bayer, Lovat Fraser, Carl Hertzog, Paul Rand, and Vincent Torre.

Today, Carol Devine Carson has assembled a staff of designers that includes Chip Kidd, Barbara de Wilde, Archie Ferguson, Susan Caroll, and Abby Weintraub. "Though there are more books published today than ever before, the number of good book designers is surprisingly small," she notes. "We are able to deliver a consistent level of excellence because we have worked together for a long time. I haven't lost anyone on my staff in twelve years." Together, they are responsible for close to 200 books a year. Although art photography, which brings an emotional edge to the title of a book, has replaced on jackets the more decorative illustrations that were in favor in the past decades, the design of the books themselves still celebrates the timeless qualities of typography at its best.

"To me, a book is first meant to be read," Knopf wrote in 1946. "Therefore it is of the greatest importance that the page be readable. This means a typeface that doesn't trouble the eye — and sometimes an otherwise pretty face does just that. It means type of a proper size, sufficient leading, and, above all, not too wide a line."

Today, the way we "consume" information has changed drastically, but, fortunately, the way we curl up with a book has not. The pleasure we get from a page is still directly proportionate to its level of comfort and elegance. That's why, for almost a century, the greatest honor for a writer is to be published by Knopf.

EVER AFTER

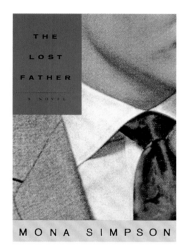

GRAHAM SWIFT

THE
LOST
FATHER

A NOVEL

MONA SIMPSON

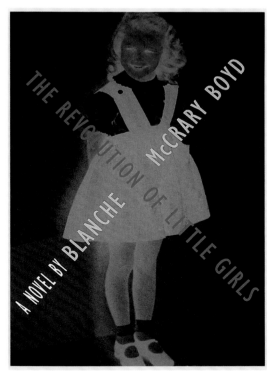

Clockwise from top left: *Ever After* (1992), designed by Carol Devine Carson. *Peppers: A Story of Hot Pursuits* (1992), designed by Chip Kidd. *The Revolution of Little Girls* (1991), designed by Barbara de Wilde. *American Owned Love* (1997), designed by Archie Ferguson. *The Lost Father* (1992), designed by Barbara de Wilde.

Communication Graphics 20

What did you make of 1998?

Fast companies, big budgets, and branding obsession contributed to a banner year for business, but does economic prosperity beget great design?

Communication Graphics 20 **explores this issue by examining the creative products of the past year. In retrospect, 1998 appeared to be the obvious time to quantify the value of design and creative problem solving with bottom-line contributions. In a seemingly golden age of professional opportunity, what did designers carve out for themselves? Did we further our mission to advance excellence in graphic design as a discipline, profession, and cultural force? What do we have to show for this block of time?** *Communication Graphics 20* **recognizes solid design and strategic applications that provided clarity of thought in an age of excess.**

Bill Grant *Chair*

Dan Boyarski

Dan Boyarski is a communication designer with twenty-six years' experience in education and the profession. He is a professor of design at Carnegie Mellon University's School of Design, where he has taught for sixteen years. As director of graduate studies, he coordinates two masters programs: one in interaction design, the other in communication planning and design, a joint program with the English department. He teaches courses at both the graduate and undergraduate levels in typography, information design, and human-computer interaction design. Boyarski is interested in how words, images, sound, and motion may be combined to produce effective communication.

Cover of *Design Issues*, Summer 1999
Design Firm *Boyarski/Boyarski, Pittsburgh, PA*
Designer/Photographer *Dan Boyarski*
Typeface *Meta*
Publisher *The MIT Press*

Quilt #2 and Quilt #4
Design Firm *Boyarski/Boyarski, Pittsburgh, PA*
Designer/Illustrator *Dan Boyarski*

Bill Grant

Bill Grant, chairman, is president of i.e., design, a multidiscipline design firm located in Atlanta. Prior to i.e., design, he was a principal of Design! from 1984 until 1996. He is the current president of AIGA/Atlanta and has served on the chapter's board of directors since 1994. The work of i.e., design has been featured in *Communication Arts, Print, Step-By-Step Graphics, IIDA Perspective, Interior Design, Interiors,* the New York Type Director's Club annual, the AIGA's own annual, *Graphic Design USA,* and *Graphic Design in America 2,* among other publications.

Blue Ridge Break Room and Training Center
Design Firm *i.e., design, Atlanta, GA*
Art Director/Designer *i.e., design*
Architectural Photography *Steve Hall/Hedrich Blessing Chicago*

leave it at the office

Get carried away with Weavepoint, a new commercial carpet from Lotus. Dial 800.222.1437.

LOTUS CARPETS

Lotus Carpets Trade Advertisement
Design Firm *i.e., design, Atlanta, GA*
Art Director/Designer *i.e., design*
Photographer *Geof Kern*
Client *Lotus Carpets*

57

Diti Katona, along with her partner, John Pylypczak, is a principal designer and creative director of the Toronto-based firm Concrete Design Communications. Her work has been exhibited and published widely throughout North America and Europe. The projects range in diversity from corporate annual reports and consumer magazines to ad campaigns and websites. Katona has also been on the teaching faculty at both York University and the Ontario College of Art. In addition to her design practice, she is kept busy by her two daughters, Camille and Greta.

Tom Brochure
Design Firm *Concrete Design Communications, Inc., Toronto, Ontario*
Art Directors *Diti Katona and John Pylypczak*
Designer *John Pylypczak*
Photographer *Karen Levy*
Typeface *Centennial*
Printer *Arthurs Jones Clarke*
Paper *Lustro Gloss*
Client *Keilhauer Industries*

Azure **Magazine**
"Think Skin" Cover (May/June 1999)
Design Firm *Concrete Design Communications, Inc., Toronto, Ontario*
Art Directors *Diti Katona and John Pylypczak*
Designer *Theresa Kwan*
Photographer *Mike Webb*
Typeface *Trade Gothic*
Printer *Annan & Sons Lithographing Ltd.*
Paper *Garda Silk*

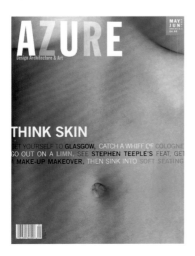

Steven Liska

Steven Liska is the president of Liska + Associates, Inc., a communication design firm with offices in Chicago and New York. Currrently, Steve is chairman of the 27 Chicago Designers, chairman of the To Make the World a Better Place Foundation, a director of F3, a Chicago-based investment firm, and a partner in Drymartini.com, a new e-commerce company. He is a former national board member of the AIGA and past president of AIGA/Chicago. A frequent design judge and lecturer, he has taught graduate-level design at the School of the Art Institute of Chicago, Kent State University, and Syracuse University.

www.kleinbikes.com

Design Firm *Liska + Associates, Chicago, IL*
Art Director *Steve Liska*
Designers *John DeVylder,*
Tim Messman, and Matt Raettig
Photographers *Steve Grubman and Various*
Typefaces *Scala Sans, Verdana*
Interface Designers *John DeVylder,*
Tim Messman, and Matt Raettig
Client *Klein Bicycles*

Modern Organic Products Packaging

Design Firm *Liska + Associates, Chicago, IL*
Art Director *Marcos Chavez*
Designer *Susanna Barrett*
Typefaces *Arial, Swiss*
Client *Modern Organic Products*

Allison Muench Williams is principal, with J. Phillips Williams, of design: m/w, in New York. They have done extensive work for Takashimaya New York, Banana Republic, Buttenpapierfabrik Gmund, Champion International, Isabella Rosselini's Manifesto cosmetics, Mohawk Paper, Neiman Marcus, Sotheby's, and Vera Wang. Since its inception in 1993, the firm has received numerous awards from a variety of organizations, including *Communication Arts, Graphis, I.D. Magazine,* American Center for Design 100, Clio, the Art Directors Club, Society of Publication Designers, the Type Directors Club, and the AIGA. Muench Williams is a visiting critic at Yale University.

Isabella Rossellini's Manifesto Brochure
Design Firm *design: m/w, New York, NY*
Art Director *Allison Muench Williams*
Designers *Mats Hakansson and Yael Eisele*
Photographer *Miles Aldridge*
Printer *Hennegan*
Paper *Parilux*
Client *Lancaster*

Takashimaya Volume 5
Design Firm *design: m/w, New York, NY*
Art Director *Allison Muench Williams*
Photographer *Maria Robledo*
Printer *Hennegan*
Paper *French Parchtone*
Client *Takashimaya New York*

Ann Willoughby

Ann Willoughby is principal of Willoughby Design Group, the company she founded in 1978. Her firm of fifteen specializes in retail corporate and brand identity, packaging and visual merchandising. Over the past twenty years, Ann has evolved a unique studio environment that fosters the creation of outstanding design. She has taught at the University of Kansas and the Kansas City Art Institute and is a frequent speaker and judge for various design organizations.

Orbiting the Giant Hairball

This little book reflects a seventeen-month collaboration between Gordon Mackenzie and our design firm. The challenge was to deliver a serious message in a provocative manner to both corporate management and creative audiences about how to inspire and manage creative people. To start, we chose a quiet, gray blind-debossed chipboard cover with a soft leather spine to provide a hint of the paradox within the book.

Once engaged, the reader finds a quirky combination of traditional text and page design interrupted by drawings, scribbles, and the use of unexpected materials. Intentionally, the design walks a fine line between clarity and contradiction, and somehow it all comes together.

Design Firm *Willoughby Design Group, Kansas City, MO*
Creative Directors *Ann Willoughby, Gordon Mackenzie, and Michelle Sonderegger*
Designer *Michelle Sonderegger*
Illustrators *Ann Willoughby, Meg Cundiff, Suzi Vanztos, Wendie Collins, and Gordon Mackenzie*
Photographer *Mike Regnier*
Printer *The Stinehour Press*
Paper *80# Starwhite Vicksburg Archival*
Publisher *OpusPocus Publishing*

Peruvian Connection Catalogue and Website

Peruvian Connection is a mail-order catalogue company that sells luxury knitwear. We originally designed the identity to reflect the utility, beauty, and luxury of Annie Hurlbut's handmade Peruvian knits. The catalogue and website are designed to provide a sensuous shopping experience while reinforcing the Peruvian brand image. Most of the photography is shot in Peru, which helps make the catalogue feel authentic.

Design Firm *Willoughby Design Group, Kansas City, MO*
Creative Director *Ann Willoughby*
Art Director *Deb Friday*
Designer *Nicole Satterwhite*
Photographers *John Goodman and Myron*
Typeface *Mrs Eaves*
Printer *Arandell Corporation*
Paper *Mead Web Dull*
Programmer *Cephas, The Lazarus Group*
Interface Designers *Derek Collins, Tracy Moore, and Trenton Kenagy*
Client *Peruvian Connection*

AIGA Communication
Graphics 20 Exhibition

Communication Graphics 20
September 29 – October 2, 1999

The Venetian Hotel, Las Vegas
Part of the "America: Cult and Culture"
AIGA Biennial National Design Conference

Exhibition Design Tom Wojciechowski,
Russell Design Associates, New York

Exhibition Photography
© 1999 Cava Photography, Las Vegas

After three intensive days of judging almost 4,000 entries in the *AIGA Communication Graphics 20* competition, a very mindful jury selected the 107 projects presented in this year's annual. In addition to the final selections, the most significant outcome of this process was the corresponding discourse that it generated. The banter ranged from the ridiculous to the sublime. For instance, we discussed the relevance of some of the competition's categories and how they related to the AIGA mission to advance excellence in graphic design. We also wondered why some of our respected peers chose not to enter their work. We recalled a time when posters were designers' "dream jobs" as we sifted through an uninspired pile of point-of-purchase materials. We even debated the value of a design annual that represented the best of 1998 but is not published until 2000. In retrospect, these debates made the experience worthwhile and assisted us in developing the appropriate criteria for our selections.

For me, the virtue of AIGA *Communication Graphics 20* is not only found in the selections but also in the aftermath of discussion the competition inspired. Our mission was to define this professional block of time by identifying solid design and strategic applications that provided clarity of thought in an age of excess. I will be the first to admit this was an ambitious and intimidating task. Ultimately, I hope you will question the final selections as meticulously as the judges did, for the most successful by-product of this competition will be more dialogue about the value of design.

As you review the excellent work included in AIGA *Communication Graphics 20,* you will notice some interesting selections. Some of the entries were included because their restrained elegance was universal in its appeal, like the work of Design: M/W. Other selections constituted excellent examples of information graphics. This category included the redesigned FedEx form, whose project statement succinctly asserted: "The new forms are easier to use than the old ones." The competition recognized pieces that demonstrated the intrinsic value of design in a brand-driven market: Target's whimsical Styrofoam deli cups and Martha Stewart's garden accessories for Kmart. There are also a few examples of design that appear to redefine a particular category by employing risky, yet reverent, strategy. See some of the annual reports produced by Bill Cahan & Associates.

When viewed holistically, AIGA *Communication Graphics 20* archives the expanding role design is playing in business and culture. It is encouraging to know that great design has the power to feed the hungry, deliver bottom-line results, create a branded environment, and sell bug spray that kills insects with an overdose of garlic. In 1998, designers had the opportunity to make something of our formidable status. We have begun to carve out an enviable professional niche for ourselves, and it is cheering to know that we are achieving this recognition without sacrificing our wit, dignity, and aesthetic dexterity.

Bill Grant

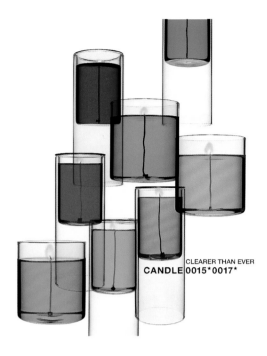

Design Firm / *Sayuri Shoji, New York, NY*
Art Director / *Sayuri Shoji*
Production Consultant / *David Seidler*
Photographer / *Takao Ikejiri*
Typeface / *Helvetica Neue*
Printer / *Pace Manufacturing, Inc.*
Client / *Sterling Development*

Candle 0015/0017

PROJECT STATEMENT

The first transparent solid wax candle ever on the market. This aromatic candle is targeted to anyone who appreciates a clean, modern style. "Clearer than ever" is the product/ packaging concept.

Design Firm / *Design Guys, Minneapolis, MN*
Creative Director / *Steven Sikora*
Designers / *Gary Patch and Scott Thares*
Photographer / *Jim Erickson*
Typefaces / *Avant Garde, Adobe Garamond*
Printer / *Hung Hing Printing Group, Ltd.*
Paper / *270 gsm Japanese CCNB and American E-Flute*
Client / *Target Stores*

Graves Packaging for Target Stores

PROJECT STATEMENT

In a mass-market environment, packaging, not a sales staff, informs the customer. This extensive line for Target says "simple, design, different." Isolating each item in a blue field is like placing it on display. Merchandised in 24-foot runs, the sea of blue boxes defines a Michael Graves shop in an otherwise wall-less space.

Design Firm / *Design Guys, Minneapolis, MN*
Creative Director / *Steven Sikora*
Designer / *Dawn Selg*
Photographers / *Darrell Eager and Lars Hansen*
Typefaces / *Avant Garde, Adobe Garamond*
Printer / *Heartland Graphics*
Paper / *Potlatch Vintage Velvet 80# Cover, 16 pt. Caroline*
Client / *Target Stores*

Graves January Press Kit for Target Stores

PROJECT STATEMENT

This press kit was developed for distribution at a press conference staged at the Whitney Museum of American Art. The kit was intended to be one of the takeaways at an event where the press was being introduced to a sizable share of the Michael Graves product line for Target Stores. The kit also reflects the sophisticated yet fun attitude with which the line was to be marketed.

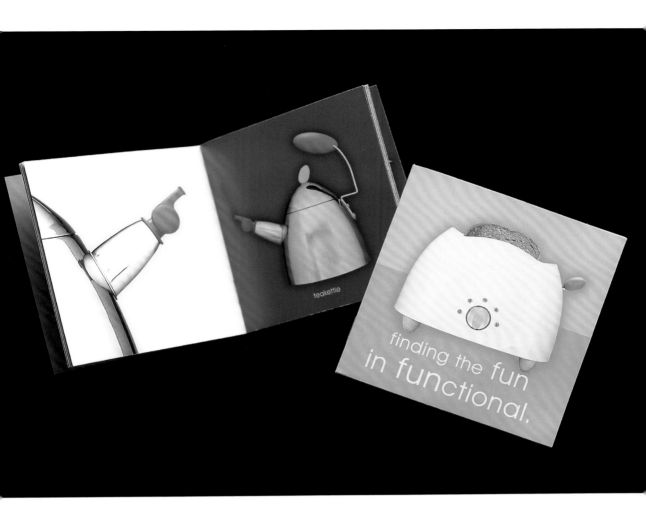

finding the fun in functional.

teakettle

Design Firm / *Design Guys, Minneapolis, MN*
Creative Director / *Steven Sikora*
Designer / *Dawn Selg*
Photographers / *Darrell Eager and The Studio*
Writer / *Jay Kaskel*
Typefaces / *Avant Garde, Adobe Garamond*
Printer / *Litho Inc.*
Paper / *Potlatch Vintage Velvet 100# Text*
Client / *Target Stores*

Graves Mini Catalogue for Target Stores

PROJECT STATEMENT

This point-of-sale catalogue was displayed on small Lucite fixtures and demonstrated a broad cross-section of the burgeoning Michael Graves product line at Target Stores. Its purpose was to cross-sell to other parts of the store and to make guests aware of "collections" in the event some items were out of stock. The catalogue represents an important element in a branding program that was consistent from packaging through fixtures, print collateral, and advertising.

Design Firm / *Coach (In-House)*
Creative Director / *Reed Krakoff*
Art Director/Designer / *Pamela Libonati*
Writer / *Patti Day*
Typefaces / *AT Sackers Heavy Gothic, Akzidenz Grotesk Light*
Printer / *Modern Arts Packaging Company*
Paper / *Custom Kraft Beater-Dyed Paper*
Client / *Coach*

Coach Brand Identity

PROJECT STATEMENT

The creative strategy behind our packaging program was to strengthen and refresh Coach's brand identity, communicating a sense of confidence, intelligence, and a contemporary point of view through elements that can only be Coach. The signature color hints at the richness of Coach's mahogany leather. A custom overall embossing cylinder was developed and applied to give the paper a tactile sense and the illusion of depth. The debossed registration stamp is consistent with the branded registration stamp on the inside of every Coach piece. The Coach wordmark was embossed and stamped in custom gold foil, while the classic lozenge logo was foil stamped on the sides, providing the final accent.

Design Firm / *Slaughter Hanson, Birmingham, AL*
Art Director / *Marion English*
Designers / *Jeanne Renneker, David Webb*
Typeface / *Humanist*
Printer / *Dickson's Engraving*
Client / *Olive Room*

Olive Room Promotion

PROJECT STATEMENT

The Olive Room is a late-night martini bar with an eccentric vibe, a Dean-Martin-meets-the-Jetsons kind of place. As a promotional piece, we produced a book of keepsake matches for them. We thought using an olive in their logo might be a tad obvious; instead, we used a crescent moon on an olive background to make the letter "O." We still wanted to slip in an olive someplace, so we had the match tip produced to look like an olive. The matchbook itself looks like an incense slipcase with a die-cut hole to hold a single match. The cover was matte engraving with white foil.

Design Firm / *Studio Archetype, San Francisco, CA*
Art Director / *Gregg Heard*
Designers / *Gregg Heard and Mark Ligameri*
Typeface / *Univers*
Client / *UPS*

UPS Packaging

PROJECT STATEMENT

Through the ups.com website, UPS customers can order their shipping supplies online rather than calling the UPS phone centers. This package design functions not only as the delivery vehicle for the supplies but helps to build awareness of the online supply-ordering capabilities. The bold graphics create an unmistakable UPS presence when delivered by the UPS driver.

Design Firm / *Doyle Partners, New York, NY*
Creative Director / *Stephen Doyle*
Designer / *Craig Clark*
Illustrator / *Suzanne Barnes*
Typeface / *Franklin Gothic Extra Condensed*
Client / *Martha Stewart Everyday/Kmart Corporation*

Martha Stewart Everyday Garden Line

PROJECT STATEMENT

The identity for Martha Stewart Everyday is composed of
a simple logo, executed in flexible colorways, and photography that is synonymous with Martha Stewart's brand —
that is, inspirational and informative. The logo and product
copy are printed in custom colors from the Martha Stewart
Everyday Colors line of paint, which is also sold at Kmart.
The program's bright, colorful packaging provides a cohesive,
unifying effect for products in many different categories. In
a fluorescent, mass shopping environment, the subtlety and
authority of these packages quietly shine out amid shelves
of screaming hot pink and turquoise packages.

Design Firm / *Studio d Design, Minneapolis, MN*
Creative Director / *Coco Connolly*
Art Director/Designer / *Laurie DeMartino*
Illustrator / *Paulina Reyes*
Printer / *Sweetheart*
Client / *Target Stores*

Target Stores Beverage Cups

PROJECT STATEMENT

These beverage cups were redesigned with one main objective in mind — to reduce printing costs. We also wanted to create something fun, refreshing, and memorable to express the unique flavor of Target Stores. The subject matter was drawn from the broad range of Target's customers. Keeping in mind the printing challenges, we told the story in a whimsical and quirky illustration style that lent itself to the irregularities of flexographic printing. The cups not only serve a distinct purpose, they continue to advertise Target once they have left the store.

Design Firm / *MTV Networks, New York, NY*
Creative Director / *Jeffrey Keyton*
Designers / *Tracy Boychuk and Todd St. John*
Typeface / *Akzidenz Grotesk*
Printer / *Dee Jay Litho*
Paper / *Finch Opaque 80# Text, Vellum Finish*
Client / *MTV Animation*

MTV Animation Kit

PROJECT STATEMENT

This campaign introduced a new look for MTV Animation. The new identity borrowed the fun aesthetic of animation in the burst shapes, but was packaged in an untraditional mailer.

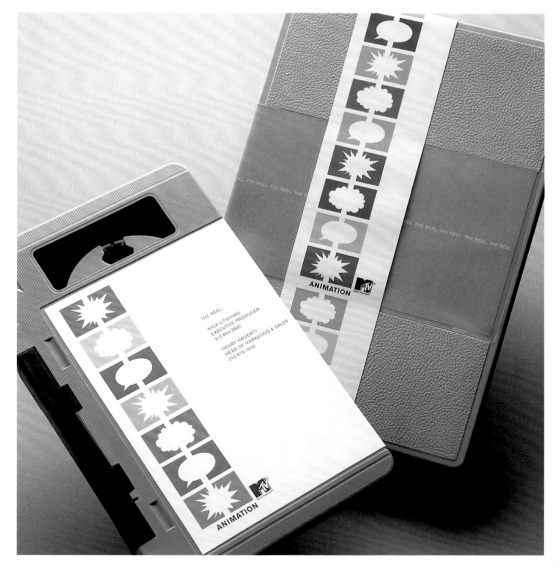

Design Firm / *James Victore, Inc., Beacon, NY*
Designer / *James Victore*
Typeface / *Tape*
Printer / *Rosepoint*
Paper / *French Butcher Paper*
Unofficial Client / *Times Square, NY*

"Disney Go Home" Poster

Design Firm / *James Victore, Inc., Beacon, NY*
Designer / *James Victore*
Typeface / *Tape*
Printer / *Rosepoint*
Paper / *French Butcher Paper*
Unofficial Client / *Times Square, NY*

"Just Say No" Poster

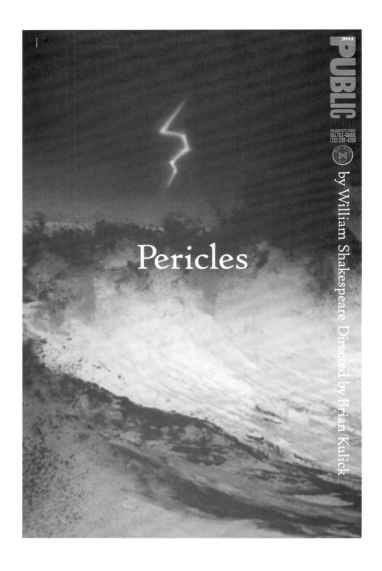

Design Firm / *Pentagram Design, New York*
Art Director / *Paula Scher*
Designers / *Anke Stohlmann and Keith Daigle*
Client / *The Joseph Papp Public Theater*

"Pericles" Poster

PROJECT STATEMENT

Now that most Broadway advertising attempts to duplicate
the bold, noisy look of the Public Theater graphics, typography in Pentagram's posters for the Public has grown quieter,
to stand out in the din. Shakespeare's play "Pericles"
features pirates, potions, shipwrecks, narrow escapes,
and miraculous resurrections.

Design Firm / *Pentagram Design, New York*
Art Director / *Paula Scher*
Designers / *Anke Stohlmann and Keith Daigle*
Client / *The Joseph Papp Public Theater*

"Stop Kiss" Poster

PROJECT STATEMENT

In "Stop Kiss," a couple's first kiss meets with violence on the streets of New York.

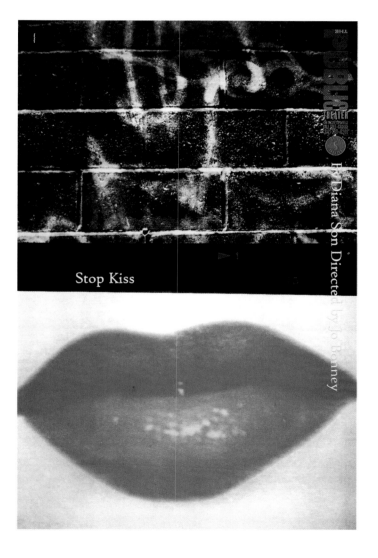

Design Firm / Pentagram Design, New York, NY
Designer / Michael Bierut
Typography / Michael Bierut
Printer / Solarz Bros. Printing Corporation
Paper / Weyerhaeuser Cougar Opaque Uncoated 80#
Client / Theatre S3

"American Dream" Poster

PROJECT STATEMENT

"The American Dream" is Edward Albee's absurdist farce set in a dysfunctional upper-class family. The play's themes of consumption and ambition inspire its poster, which impales the United States on the tines of an elegant fork. Typography was hand-lettered by the designer.

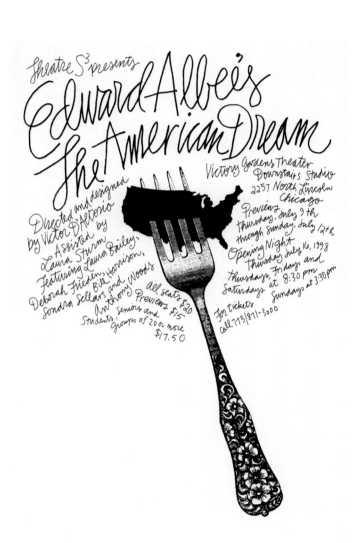

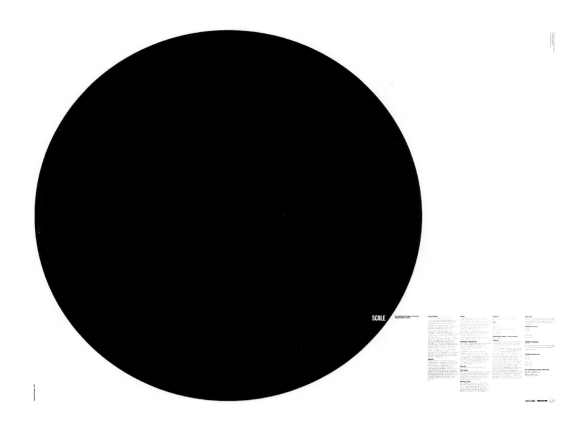

Design Firm / *Pentagram Design, New York, NY*
Art Director / *Michael Bierut*
Designer / *Kerrie Powell*
Typeface / *Franklin Gothic*
Printer / *Combine Graphics Corp.*
Paper / *Hammermill Accent Opaque 60# Vellum Finish*
Client / *The Architectural League of New York*

"Scale" Poster

PROJECT STATEMENT

This poster announced the Architectural League of New York's annual competition for young architects, with the chosen theme of "scale." Designer Michael Bierut said, given its subject, "I don't care how low the budget is or how high the mailing costs will be, or how limited the space on architects' bulletin boards, this poster is going to be big." The title of the show appears in 35-point type in a 35-inch diameter black dot. To save money, everything — rules of entry, mailing details, etc. — was printed on only one side of the poster sheet.

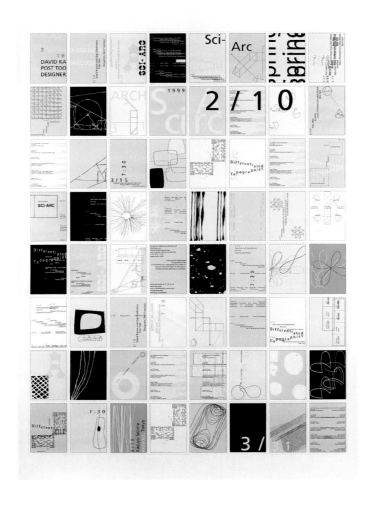

Design Firm / *Jennifer Sterling Design, San Francisco, CA*
Art Director/Designer / *Jennifer Sterling*
Illustrator / *Jennifer Sterling*
Copywriter / *Margi Reeve*
Printer / *A.B. Hirschfeld Press, Inc.*
Client / *Southern California Institute of Architecture*

Southern California Institute of Architecture Spring Lecture Series Poster

PROJECT STATEMENT

This piece is called "Differentiated Topographies" to reflect the nature of the lecture series. The SCI-Arc spring lecture series featured six architects of various fields including landscape, textile, traditional, and information architecture. Most people consider these fields to be very different and unrelated, but in fact they are all very related. The level of images on the poster represents the differentiated topographies and their interrelationships.

Design Firm / *Ziba Design, Portland, OR*
Creative Director / *Eike Wintzer*
Art Director / *Efrat Rafaeli*
Client / *IDSA*

IDSA 1998 Conference Signage

Design Firm / *Skidmore, Owings & Merrill, San Francisco, CA*
Art Director / *Lonny Israel*
Designers / *Lonny Israel and Jeremy Reginbogen*
Photographer / *Abby Sadin*
Typeface / *Meta*
Fabricator / *Thomas Swan Signs*
Client / *San Francisco Food Bank*

San Francisco Food Bank Donor Wall

PROJECT STATEMENT

The donor wall welcomes visitors and acknowledges the many individuals who funded the building project by providing services, materials, and labor as a donation or at cost, and those who generously gave money. The challenge was to design the donor recognition signage to suit its location with an economy of means.

The palette of materials includes tin cans, steel, and acrylic. Located at the main pedestrian entry, the donor wall is the focal point of the building lobby. Our intent was to remind the viewer, through the imagery of a simple tin can, that these contributors were "building against hunger."

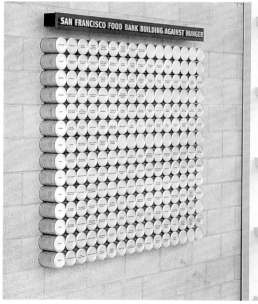

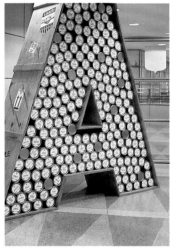

Design Firm / *Chermayeff & Geismar Inc., New York, NY*
Art Director / *Jonathan Alger*
Designers / *Jonathan Alger and Nina Katchadourian*
Photographer / *Mark Gulezian*
Fabricator / *Explus*
Client / *United States Agency for International Development*

USAID Visitors Center

PROJECT STATEMENT

Though the United States Agency for International Development is not well understood in this country, millions of people around the world know the United States only from the bold USAID shield emblazoned on a life-saving relief shipment tumbling from a truck. USAID's earnest spirit was evident nowhere in Pei Cob Freed's opulent new Reagan Building, of which USAID was the first major tenant. Accordingly, we gave this exhibit the appearance of a humanitarian shipment. The five main modules form the acrostic "USAID." Each letter heads a new topic sentence, such as "Assistance both public and private."

Design Firm / *i.e., design, Canton, GA*
Art Direction/Design / *i.e., design*
Photographers / *Maria Robledo, Steve Hell, Hedrick Blessing*
Fabricator / *EDE Corporation*
Client / *The Harbinger Company*

Harbinger Showroom

PROJECT STATEMENT

The Harbinger showroom in the Chicago Merchandise Mart was designed to showcase the company's high-end commercial carpets in an elegant, clean, and functional setting. The design was inspired by elements of haute couture fashion to emphasize the apparel-like detail of Harbinger's trend-setting colors, patterns, and textures.

The goal was to make the architecture of the showroom space disappear in relation to the product line, while incorporating strategic design elements of the recent brand repositioning. I.e., design took the bold step of incorporating neutral concrete floors with carpet insets to display new introductions in a series of "dressing rooms" equipped with full-length mirrors to show pattern repeats on smaller samples. A '50s carpet "cat walk" lures clients into the space alongside a series of large photo murals presented in heavy wooden frames. The space was designed to be open, clean, and inviting. It created a safe haven for designers to escape the excessive product proliferation, nose and marketing overload associated with NeoCon, the largest industry trade show.

Design Firm / *Spagnola & Associates, New York, NY*
Creative Director / *Tony Spagnola*
Designers / *James Dustin and Robert Callahan*
Photographer / *Peter Mauss/Esto*
Fabricator / *Creative Management Services*
Digital Video Producer / *Advanced Media Concepts*
Client / *Lucent Technologies*

Lucent Video Wall Display

PROJECT STATEMENT

Our challenge was to design a video display wall that would illustrate the products and services of Lucent Technologies to customers, in an exhibit format that would emphasize the international aspect of Lucent's business and would be easy to change and update.

We designed a display wall with eight video monitors in circular shapes behind back-painted glass panels. The silent twelve-minute video program (powered by the latest DVD technology) is made up of photographs and graphic imagery that communicate the Lucent message instantly, at a glance, without the use of words. Customers absorb brief moments of the program as they move from meeting to meeting within the center.

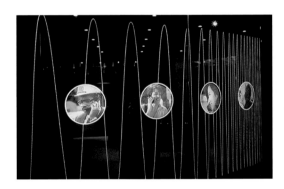

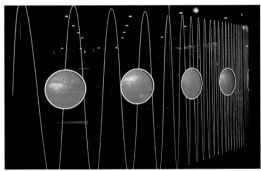

Design Firm / *Luke Hayman, New York, NY*
Designer / *Luke Hayman*
Project Manager / *Gabriela Mirensky*
Photographer / *Jennifer Krogh*
Typefaces / *Monotype Grotesque, Gateway*
Environmental Graphics / *Tim Hayden*
Client / *AIGA*

AIGA Communication Graphics 19 Exhibition Design and Graphics

PROJECT STATEMENT

The judges of *CG 19* were asked to look at the year's competition entries in a new way. Instead of considering, for example, whether an entry was a well-designed brochure, they asked themselves what the brochure did and how well it did it. The chair of the competition, Margo Chase, suggested that designers need to consider themselves in different roles, as problem solvers and business strategists rather than decorators and image makers.

The exhibition design and graphics of *CG 19* represented these ideas by using the visual language of engineering structures rather than façades. The main element was a lighting truss used as a shelf. Its clean steel grid informed the typography and feel of the exhibition.

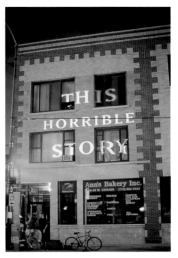

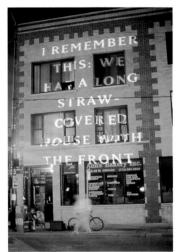

Design Firm / *Community Architexts, Chicago, IL*

Design Team / *B.J. Krivanek, Cynthia Perkin, Karla Roberts*

Site Director / *Jennifer Van Winkle*

Writers / *Halyna Boyko-Hrushetsky, Ivan Kolomayets,*
Lydia Kurylak, Lena Schrebetz-Skyba, Sinovi Turkalo

Photographer / *Edward Lines, Jr.*

Sponsor / *The Illinois Arts Council, Gaylord and Dorothy*
Donnelley Foundation

Witnesses

PROJECT STATEMENT

This multidisciplinary site involves the projection of large-
scale texts from and onto two buildings that face each other
across Chicago Avenue. These dynamic, historical billboards
suggest a dialogue between factions in the community —
elderly survivors of the 1932–1933 Ukranian famine (Us) and
outsiders such as Soviet officials and recent Latino immi-
grants (Them) represented by the voices of Soviet propagan-
da and local Chicago schoolchildren.

This site work explored the commodification of land,
crops, labor, real estate, and history itself, while drawing parallels between the historic genocide and the tenacious survival of urban children. The texts incorporated into this site
activation were created and collected during writing workshops conducted at the Ukranian Cultural Center (with elderly survivors of the famine) and at Ellen Mitchell Public School
(with ethnically diverse seventh-graders).

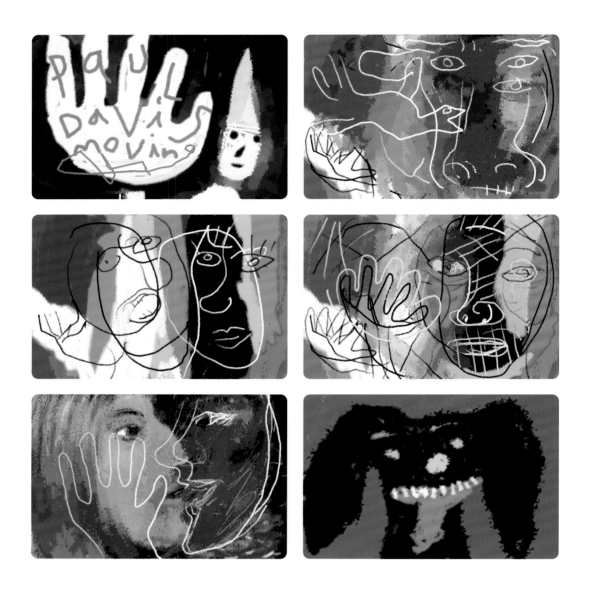

Design Firm / *Paul Davis Studio, New York, NY*
Illustrator/Animator / *Paul Davis*

The Masters Series at the School of Visual Arts Museum: Paul Davis Moving

Design Firm / *Slatoff + Cohen Partners, New York, NY*
Creative Director / *Jeffrey Keyton*
Art Directors / *Todd St. John, Tamar Cohen, and David Slatoff*
Designers / *Tamar Cohen and David Slatoff*
Photographer / *Guzman*
Typeface / *Avenir*
Programmer / *Ed Christensen*
Client / *MTV*

MTV 1998 Upfront CD-ROM

PROJECT STATEMENT

This is an interactive sales presentation that presents MTV's content and key marketing points to affiliates and potential advertisers. Its interactivity and modularity allows the presenter to tailor the presentation to specific audiences. MPEG video and an audio changer are used at the presenter's discretion to capture the essence and flavor of MTV Music Television.

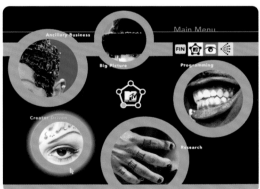

Design Firm / *Belk Mignona Associates, New York, NY*
Creative Director / *Hans Neubert*
Designers / *Hans Neubert and Jutta Kirchgeorg*
Executive Producer / *Alberta Jarane*
Lingo Programming / *Bryan Yee*
Database Programming / *Matt Anacleto*
Music / *Jarryd Lowder*
Photo Editors / *Susan Christenson and Deborah Dalton*
Producer / *Rupert Rogers*
Client / *Nonstøck Inc.*

Nonstøck.2 CD-ROM Catalogue

PROJECT STATEMENT

Nonstøck is a New York–based stock image company specializing in high-end photography and illustration, with twenty-seven international affiliates around the globe. BMA was asked to create Nonstøck's first interactive catalogue, Nonstøck.2, which has since been distributed in eighteen countries. The challenge was to redefine the marketplace by providing a level of design and technical sophistication unmatched by any of Nonstøck's competitors. The audiences are primarily designers, art directors, and art buyers with a low tolerance for junk mail, but a high sensitivity to design and its usefulness. Belk Mignona's approach was simple: to create a useful search tool that is easy to use, but entertaining and thought provoking at the same time. The result is a CD-ROM that works not unlike an application or a virtual desktop, where the experience of the search takes into consideration the way creative people think and play. It was our intention to strike a perfect balance between useful tool and playful toy.

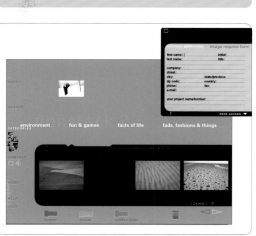

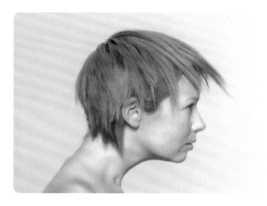

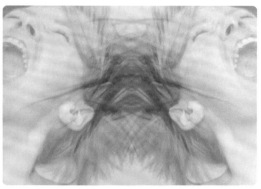
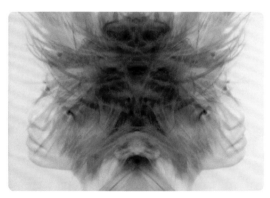

FASHIONABLY|LOUD MIAMI

Design Firm / MTV Networks, New York, NY
Art Director / Catherine Chesters
Designer / Catherine Chesters and Jenny Rask
Producer / Catherine Chesters
Photographer / Kenneth Willardt
Typeface / Helvetica
Music Composer / Amber Music

MTV "Fashionably Loud Miami"

PROJECT STATEMENT

Fashion in the '90s is more about image than style,
reflecting its fusion with the music world. This packaging is
for MTV's show featuring the hottest designers and musical
acts together, for viewers who love both.

ALL YOU HEAR IS THE SOUND OF PERFORMANCE

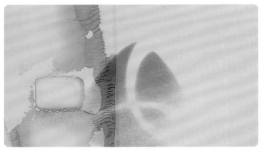

Design Firm / Jager Di Paola Kemp Design, Burlington, VT
Creative Director / Michael Jager
Designers / Herb George and Byron O'Neill
Design Directors / Jim Anfuso and Herb George
Producers / Leslie Dowe and David Mendelson
Director / Craig Champion
Film Production / Andy Mueller, Ohio Girl Film and Design
Editor / Katy Maguire, Optimus
Animators / Jon Keegan and Marko Markewycz
Photographers / Craig Champion and Dave Seaone
Client / Burton Snowboards

Burton "Jake" and "Silence" TV Spots

PROJECT STATEMENT

The creative concept for "Jake" was to present a fringe portrayal of Jake, the "original snowboarder," as a follow-up to the exposure snowboarding received in the winter Olympics and its sadly mainstream made-for-TV presentation to the world. The strategy was to communicate Burton's loyalty to the riders, and not the hype. A raw, honest, truthful documentary was the vehicle — all shot on 16mm in Switzerland and bathed in iodine.

A kino "film" spot for European theaters, "Silence" was created to capture the purity of riding. The concept was to communicate the feeling of freedom and escape that riders experience — to portray the harmony between the power of the mountains and the silent trust Burton product delivers. It was designed to run during the early season in movie theaters. "Silence" contrasted the booming rude voice of competing movie previews, allowing the audience to feel like they were riding.

Design Firm / *Brian Diecks Design Inc., New York, NY*
Creative Director / *Brian Diecks*
Designer / *Amanda Hayes*
Animator / *David Kelley*
Digital Video Producer / *Victoria Michael*
Client / *ESPN International*

SportsCenter International

PROJECT STATEMENT

The goal of this image campaign was to bring awareness of the popular domestic show ESPN SportsCenter to an international level while highlighting the wide range of sports that ESPN International covers. Initial style frames integrated photographic, scanned and Xeroxed tape, newspaper, and various paper elements with footage. These imperfect pieces, combined with 3-D wire frames, brought out the intensity of the competition of the sports and their athletes.

The frenetic pace was spontaneously brought to a halt by freezing the footage while the graphic elements continued to dart across the screen. This visual treatment gave ESPN SportsCenter International a look they could call their own to brand the show.

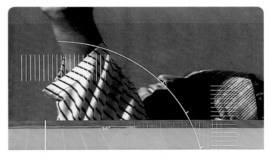

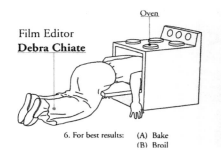

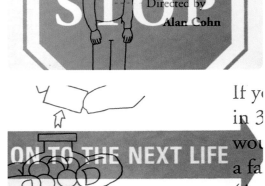

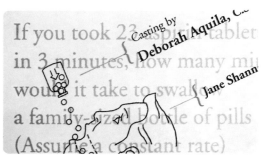

Design Firm / *Imaginary Forces, Los Angeles, CA*
Art Director / *Karin Fong*
Creative Director / *Peter Frankfurt*
Designers / *Karin Fong and Adam Bluming*
Illustrator / *Wayne Coe*
Head of Production / *Saffron Kenny*
Producer / *Maureen Timpa*
Editors / *Doron Dor, Kurt Mattila, Larry Plastrik*
Inferno Artist / *Jim Goodman*
Copywriters / *Adam Bluming and Karin Fong*
Typeface / *Adobe Garamond*
Client / *MTV Films, Paramount*

"Dead Man on Campus" Main Title Sequence

PROJECT STATEMENT

We wanted to introduce the black humor of the film in
the title sequence. The movie centers on the popular myth
that if your college roommate commits suicide, you are awarded straight A's for the semester. Using the standardized test
iconography, we devised our own SAT (suicide aptitude test).
The credits were woven into the text as part of the diagrams
and multiple-choice questions, each name getting a different
treatment. By setting the titles in a funny, unexpected format,
the sequence hinted at the dark comedy that follows. The
music, Marilyn Manson's cover of David Bowie's *Golden
Years,* provides one more ironic touch.

Design Firm / *Nike, Inc., Beaverton, OR*
Art Director/Designer / *Dan Richards*
Illustrator / *Dan Richards*
Writer/Director / *Neil Webster*
Typeface / *Clarendon*
Digital Video Producer / *Current Communications*
Client / *Nike Vision*

Vision Tech Video

PROJECT STATEMENT

The video was created as a technical training tool for Nike sales reps and accounts. It was designed to resemble educational films from the '60s. The challenge was creating such a comprehensive tool on a limited budget. The use of simple, crude animation was consistent with the concept and presented the technical features of Nike eyewear in an unexpected and entertaining way.

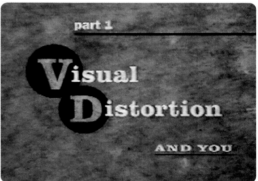

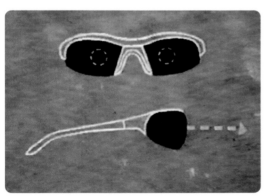

Design Firm / *MTV Networks, New York, NY*
Art Directors / *Todd St. John and Greg Hahn*
3-D Animator / *Pakorn Bupphavesa*
Producer / *Greg Hahn*
Typeface / *Helvetica Neue*
Music Composers / *Dust Brothers*

MTV Sports and Music Festival 2

PROJECT STATEMENT

The show combines two separate elements — sports and music. We made up an imaginary scientific facility where odd hybrids and mutant machines were being created, and designed around that concept. The stark white empty graphics tried to go in the opposite direction of how "extreme" sports are usually packaged.

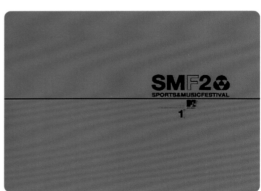

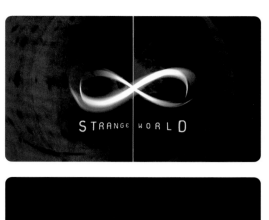

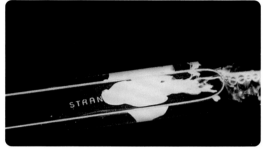

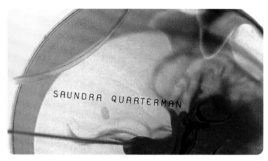

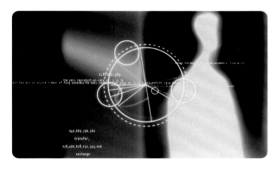

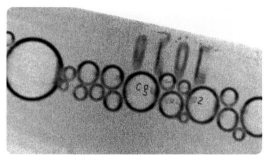

Design Firm / *Imaginary Forces, Los Angeles, CA*
Director/Art Director / *Karin Fong*
Creative Director / *Peter Frankfurt*
Designers / *Olivia D'Albis, Dana Yee, Karin Fong*
Producer / *Candy Renick*
Editors / *Mark Hoffman and Adrian Kays*
Inferno Artist / *Candice Scott*
2-D Animators / *Matt Cullen and Martin von Will*
Typeface / *Platelet*
Client / *Teakwood Land Productions/Fox Searchlight*

"Strange World" TV Open, Main Titles

PROJECT STATEMENT

The title introduces the theme of viral manipulation
using images of mitosis and lab equipment. Characters are
introduced as ambiguous shadows to heighten the sense
of alienation and intrigue the audience of this sci-fi show.

Design Firm / J.J. Sedelmaier Productions Inc.,
White Plains, NY
Art Directors / J.J. Sedelmaier and Jeff Hopfer
Designer / J.J. Sedelmaier
Animator / Brian Gaidry
Copywriters / J.J. Sedelmaier and Ron Henderson
Typeface / Rough House (title card at end)
Sound Editor / Reel FX
Client / Episcopal New Church Center

Episcopal New Church Center

PROJECT STATEMENT

In the style of a '50s or '60s instructional school filmstrip,
a father introduces the idea of going to church to his young
son. After hearing about the traditional churchgoing experience, the youngster opts for suicide instead of going to
church.

Design Firm / *J.J. Sedelmaier Productions Inc.,*
White Plains, NY
Creative Director / *J.J. Sedelmaier*
Designer / *Adrian Tomine*
Animator / *J.J. Sedelmaier*
Copywriters / *Adrian Tomine and J.J. Sedelmaier*
Digital Video Producer / *Rick Adams*
Sound Editor / *Tom Pompasello*
Client / *Art Directors Club*

Art Directors Club Awards Opening Title Segment

PROJECT STATEMENT

Adrian Tomine designed the opening segment for the 77th annual Art Directors Club awards. It demonstrates, in a humorous cartoon film noir style, an art director going to great lengths to steal an idea from another art director.

Design Firm / *Liska & Associates, Chicago, IL*
Art Director / *Steve Liska*
Designers / *Matt Raettig, John DeVylder, Nancy Anderson*
Photographer / *Steve Grubman*
Copywriter / *Matt Raettig*
Typeface / *Futura*
Client / *DryMartini.com*

DryMartini.com

PROJECT STATEMENT

Our goal was to create an e-commerce website that would be of interest to martini drinkers. Using a simple navigational button shaped like a coaster, we made it easy to view products as well as buy them. The copy helps support the breadth of products (glasses, shakers, etc.) offered on the site, while its humorous tone appeals to martini aficionados. We designed the site with web safe and web speedy elements, to ensure a simple and positive online shopping experience.

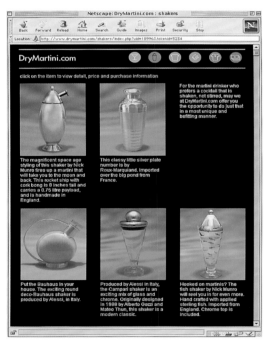

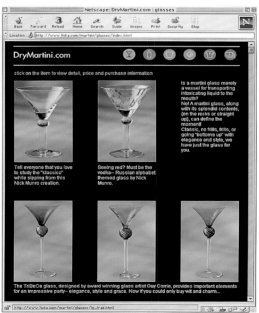

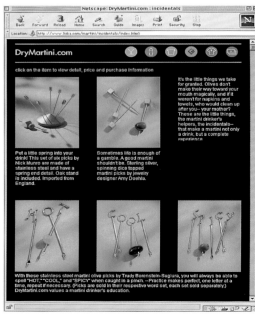

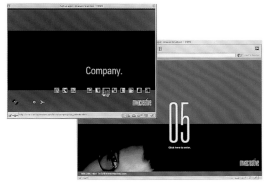

Art Director / *Corwin Stone*
Designers / *Corwin Stone and Michael Resenelli*
Photographers / *David Lowe and Corwin Stone*
Writers / *Dennis McKnew and David Lowe*
Programmer / *Roger Jennings*
Sound Editor / *Paul Godwin*
Client / *MWA Creative*

MWA Creative Website

PROJECT STATEMENT

MWA Creative, a full-service advertising and design agency,
needed a corporate website to reflect their new identity and
showcase their services and design talent. The website
needed to show users the range of services that MWA
offers, as well as the abilities of the design team. The interface was designed to be cool, yet accessible. The site
makes excellent use of music and interactivity with custom
sounds, roll-over buttons, and random page generation.
Inside the site, the agency's mission statement, client list,
and portfolio are presented in a way that any user can easily
and intuitively navigate. The portfolio is presented in a manner that does justice to the work and to the design team
that created it.

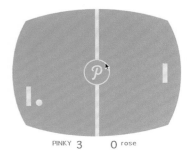

PINKY 3   0 rose

Big Pink, Inc.

Big Pink is a design company
specializing in broadcast and new media.
We're located in beautiful Manhattan at
37 West 20th Street, NYC 10011.
Phone: 212-367-9840. Fax: 212-367-9841.

Design Firm / *Big Pink, New York, NY*
Art Director / *Lisa Overton*
Graphic/Interface Designers / *Richard Eng and Lisa Overton*
Sound Effects / *Kwesi Collisson*
Writer/Programmer / *Richard Eng*
Typefaces / *Monoline Script, Avenir*
Client / *Big Pink, Ink*

Big Pink Website

PROJECT STATEMENT

Big Pink's website provides what's important to all of us —
a way to look busy while wasting time playing Pink Pong or
reading your Pink Horoscope. If absolutely necessary, you
can review Big Pink design work, staring intently should your
boss appear.

   This was a particularly satisfying project for Big Pink, in
that the client was delighted with our concept, and budget
requirements were never questioned.

   The Big Pink website was born in the year of the tiger,
and its fortune deems it will surprise you with its peculiari-
ties and will vent its wrath and express frustration if it must
(numerologists and competitive Pong players beware). And,
at times, indigestion may flare up if spicy foods are eaten.

Design Firm / *C3, New York, NY*
Creative Director / *Randall Hensley*
Designers / *Randall Hensley and Scott Williams*
Illustrators / *Scott Williams and Richard Madigan*
Writer / *Billie Harber*
Typeface / *Nueva Bold Extended*
Programmers / *Richard Madigan and Chris Ranch*
Client / *C3 Incorporated*

www.smallestsite.com

PROJECT STATEMENT

In a world increasingly obsessed with bigness, we thought it was time to celebrate the little things. So we created the world's smallest website. The smallest minimum browser size (100 pixels by 100 pixels) was used. Content includes features like "world's smallest" examples and tiny amusements like miniature online checkers. Fame is fleeting, since the features change daily.

No hard data is available yet, but the site is beginning to win awards. Let's hear it for the little guy.

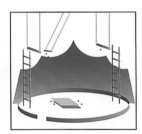

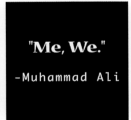

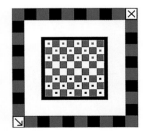

Design Firm / *Martha Stewart Living Omnimedia,
New York, NY*
Art Director / *Robert Fisher*
Designer / *Yong-Hern Soh*
Photographers / *Various*
Writers / *Amanda Straub and Laura Wallis*
Typefaces / *MSL Gothic, Garamond, Helvetica*
Programmers / *Justin Miller, Bill Vencil, Will Zirkle*
Client / *Martha Stewart Living Omnimedia*

marthastewart.com

PROJECT STATEMENT

The official Martha Stewart Living Omnimedia website, marthastewart.com, was designed as a virtual extension of the Martha Stewart brand. Translating the unique color palettes and photography of the brand proved to be a challenge, given the fluidity of the medium. Ultimately, the success of the site is due to its intuitive, simple-to-use interface. Martha Stewart has encouraged many new users to venture onto the web; these novices look for signs and metaphors from other media to help make the process of information-seeking, shopping, and community participation easy and enjoyable. Our users would expect nothing less.

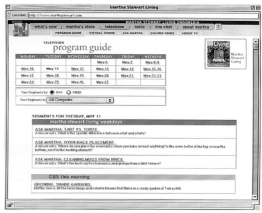

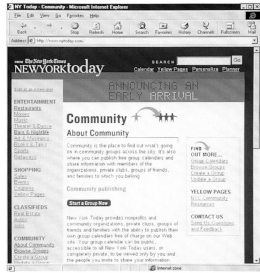

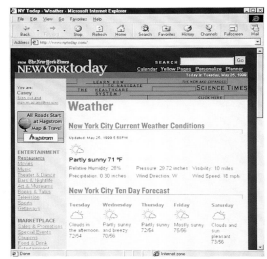

Design Firm / *Rare Medium, Inc., New York, NY*

Creative Directors / *Nam Szeto and Gong Szeto*

Designers / *Sara Golding and Casey Reas*

Production Designer / *Manny Tan*

Typeface / *Cheltenham and Champion*

Client / *The New York Times Electronic Media Company*

nytoday.com

PROJECT STATEMENT

The clear design challenges for this online city guide, nytoday.com, was to reflect the brand heritage and integrity of its originator, the *New York Times*, and at the same time showcase the depth and breadth of the *Times'* content in a user-friendly and entertaining way.

The resultant simple, clean design allows both natives and tourists to find everything from restaurant and theater reviews to traffic reports and nightclubs, all within two mouse clicks. The cool color palette and type choices were selected to convey the nighttime essence of the many events and to stay true to the brand identity of the *New York Times*.

Communicating this volume of information on a daily basis (all the happenings in New York City) required sophisticated information design that was more than just about color and typeface, however. It also meant visually prioritizing the content in a way that would be clear to even the newest user.

Design Firm / MetaDesign, San Francisco, CA
Design Director / Rick Lowe
Lead and Interaction Designers / Olivier Chetelat,
Shawn Hazen, Joseph Ternes
Screen Designers / Olivier Chetelat, Shawn Hazen,
and Eva Walter
Editors / Christopher Myers, Shel Perkins,
David Peters, Rhonda Rubenstein
Typeface / Interstate
Producer / David Peters
Technical Director / Joseph Ternes
Client / Fuse Conferences

FUSE98.com

PROJECT STATEMENT

FUSE98.com was created to provide logistical information
for the FUSE98 conference, "Beyond Typography," held in
San Francisco. The audience included potential attendees,
participants, organizers, the media, and the design community at large. More than simply an information resource, the
site was conceived as a "one-page wonder," an online home
base for the conference that would push the capabilities of
the web using DHTML. Besides layered typography and con-
cise navigation, a key element was the FUSE98 lab, a virtual
test site for digital experimentation. Designers who visited
the site were invited to contribute experiments for inclusion
in the lab. Submissions came from around the world and
ranged from a randomized business card generator to interactive poetry.

Design Firm / *MetaDesign, San Francisco, CA*
Design Directors / *Neville Brody and Rick Lowe*
Designer / *Mike Abbink*
Photographers / *Mike Abbink, Olivier Chetelat, Ligia Dias,*
Cornelia Frank, Melissa Guzman, Patrick Newbery,
Key Nothstein
Writers / *Jon Wozencroft and Christopher Myers*
Typeface / *Interstate*
Printer / *Bofors Fine Lithography*
Paper / *Gilbert Esse, Gilbert Gilclear*
Client / *FUSE98 Conference*

FUSE98 Program

PROJECT STATEMENT

With a slew of cutting-edge participants whose work
reached "Beyond Typography," the FUSE98 conference
presented a design challenge: a challenge of restraint.
Any materials created for FUSE called for a pure, almost
laboratory environment in which radical ideas about
communication could be expressed without trivializing
their significance. At the same time, we sought to bring
a human quality to the often heavy conference agenda.
Strips of locally shot images, as well as a satiric traveler's
guide, capture the naturally cinematic quality of the host
city, San Francisco.

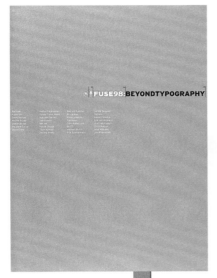

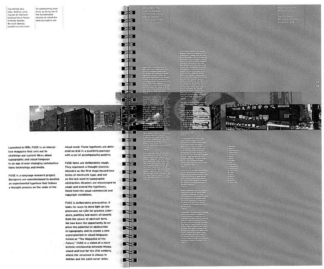

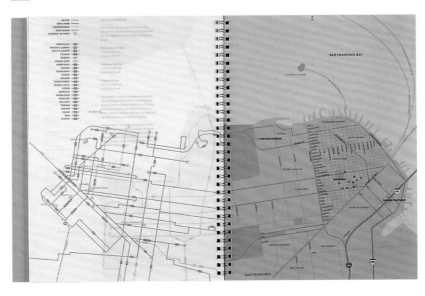

Design Firm / *Cahan & Associates, San Francisco, CA*
Creative Director / *Bill Cahan*
Designer/Illustrator / *Kevin Roberson*
Photographer / *Ken Probst*
Writers / *Kevin Roberson and Kim Sankaran*
Typefaces / *Trade Gothic, Bell Gothic*
Printer / *George Rice & Sons*
Paper / *Potlatch McCoy Velvet, Concord Matte*
Client / *Heartport*

Heartport 1997 Annual Report

PROJECT STATEMENT

Heartport develops minimally invasive cardiac surgery systems. Their revolutionary procedure, Port-Access, allows surgeons to perform many procedures through small openings between the ribs without cracking open the chest of the patient. The result is improved quality of life, quick recovery, and much less trauma than with conventional open-heart surgery. Because the past year saw a critical mass of patients having this new, minimally invasive procedure, we created a small book with many pages. The book explores the improved recovery process through personal photos and stories told by the patients.

Design Firm / Cahan & Associates, San Francisco, CA
Creative Director / Bill Cahan
Designer / Kevin Roberson
Photographer / Robert Schlatter
Writers / Kevin Roberson and Sylvia Wheeler
Typeface / Bembo
Printer / Lithographix
Paper / Potlatch McCoy Velvet
Client / Coulter Pharmaceutical

Coulter 1997 Annual Report

PROJECT STATEMENT

Coulter Pharmaceutical is developing Bexxar, a new drug
therapy to treat non-Hodgkin's lymphoma, the second
most fatal cancer. Most people afflicted with this disease
have a maximum of seven years to live. In clinical trials, 71
percent of patients using Bexxar have had their cancer go
into complete remission. Dramatic black-and-white portraits
and personal testimonials convey the drama of anguish,
recovery, and transformation many of these patients have
experienced. The small quote next to the date on the cover
reads, "I was supposed to die today." After turning the
cover, the reader sees a paragraph explaining the powerful
benefits of Bexxar and how it saved this patient's life.

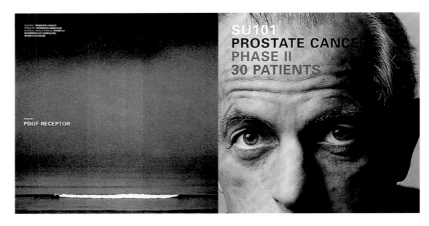

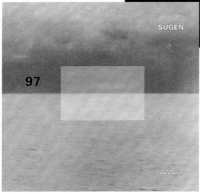

Design Firm / Cahan & Associates, San Francisco, CA
Creative Director / Bill Cahan
Designer / Sharrie Brooks
Photographers / Robert Schlatter and Various
Copywriters / Carole Melis and Sharrie Brooks
Typefaces / Univers, Bembo
Printer / Grossberg/Tyler
Paper / Fox River Starwhite Vicksburg, Potlatch McCoy Silk
Client / Sugen, Inc.

Sugen 1997 Annual Report

PROJECT STATEMENT

Sugen aims to broaden the alternatives for cancer treatment
by providing new drugs that use a mechanism entirely different from traditional chemotherapeutic agents. The hope is
that these new agents may bring us into a new era of living
with cancer as a long-term manageable disease, improving
patient survival and enhancing quality of life. The large photographic images carry this theme throughout the book, while
the text and smaller images illustrate Sugen's proprietary
drug discovery platform.

Design Firm / *Rigsby Design, Houston, TX*
Art Director / *Lana Rigsby*
Designers / *Thomas Hull and Jerod Dame*
Photographer / *Marc Norberg*
Writer / *JoAnn Stone*
Typefaces / *Didot, Helvetica Neue*
Printer / *H. MacDonald Printing*
Paper / *Appleton Utopia Premium*
Client / *American Oncology Resources*

American Oncology Resources Annual Report

PROJECT STATEMENT

Cancer. What are the odds? American Oncology Resources, the largest network of cancer doctors in the United States, asks this question poignantly, then offers a powerful response. The idea of the ubiquity of cancer frames the discussion in this annual report. Huge numbers — 1.3 million Americans diagnosed with the disease every year — are hard to grasp in the abstract. Comparing the odds of developing cancer to the odds that one will need glasses, or know how to swim, or own a television, helps convey the chilling message simply and effectively.

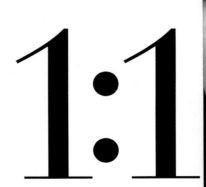

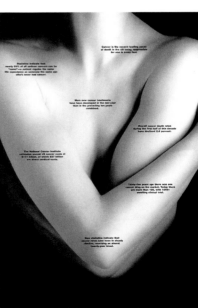

Design Firm / *Cahan & Associates, San Francisco, CA*
Creative Director / *Bill Cahan*
Designer / *Kevin Roberson*
Photographers / *Ken Probst and Various*
Copywriters / *Bob Giargiari and Kevin Roberson*
Typeface / *Trade Gothic*
Printer / *George Rice & Sons*
Paper / *French Dur-O-Tone, Vintage Velvet*
Client / *Molecular Biosystems.*

Molecular Biosystems 1998 Annual Report

PROJECT STATEMENT

A substantial portion of ultrasound images are unfit for diagnostic purposes because of poor contrast. Molecular Biosystems has created an *in vivo* contrast agent that dramatically increases the readability and clarity of ultrasound images. In order to capture the importance of this significant development, we presented a series of murky photographs, along with questions asking the reader to identify and "diagnose" the contents of each photo. Obviously, these questions are very difficult to answer. The quiz-like exercise is analogous to the physician's predicament in trying to make accurate diagnoses without clear images.

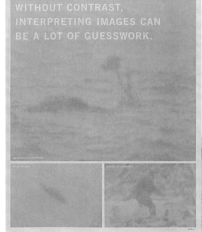

WITHOUT CONTRAST, INTERPRETING IMAGES CAN BE A LOT OF GUESSWORK.

IE TO THE NEW
ULTRASOUND
G. DEVELOPED
ECULAR
BIOSYSTEMS, OPTISON
CONTRAST ECHO
HELPS CARDIOLOGISTS
DIAGNOSE WITH
CONFIDENCE. NO
MORE FUZZ-O-GRAMS.

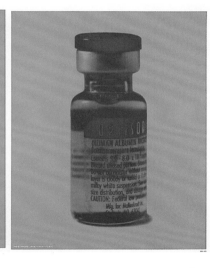

MARKET EXCLUSIVITY IN TWO
OF THE WORLD'S THREE
LARGEST MARKETS. OPTISON
IS ESTABLISHING ITSELF
QUICKLY AS THE CONTRAST
AGENT OF CHOICE.

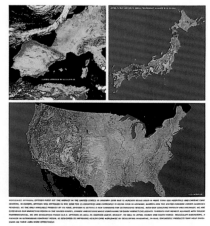

Design Firm / Cahan and Associates, San Francisco, CA
Creative Director / Bill Cahan
Designer/Illustrator / Bob Dinetz
Photographer / Jay Blakesberg
Copywriters / Carrie Wick and Bob Dinetz
Typeface / Helvetica
Printer / Lithographix
Paper / Warren Patina Matte
Client / Progenitor

Progenitor 1997 Annual Report

PROJECT STATEMENT

The intent of this annual was to convey Progenitor's unique approach to scientific research. The company's methods allow it to move from gene discovery to marketable product much faster than is expected in the biotech industry. The entire report was printed on one side of a single piece of paper to reflect the company's distinct character in a cost-effective way. The other side is a poster that brings out an emotional side of the science. The milestone chart and poster recall the hundreds of gene maps on the walls of Progenitor offices.

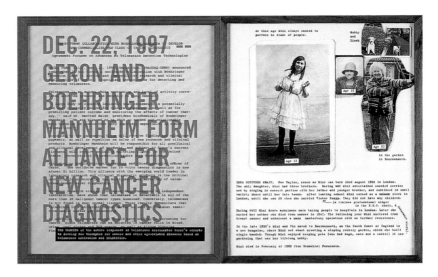

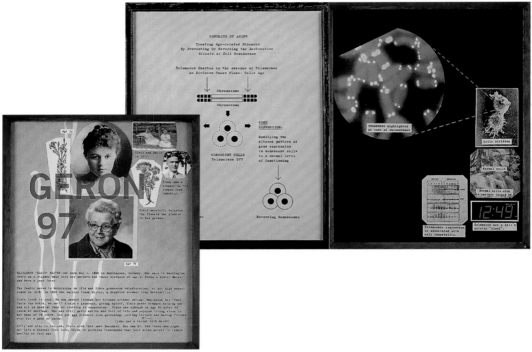

Design Firm / *Cahan & Associates, San Francisco, CA*
Creative Director / *Bill Cahan*
Designer / *Bob Dinetz*
Writers / *Carole Melis and Bob Dinetz*
Typefaces / *Trixie, Times, Courier*
Printer / *Color Graphics*
Paper / *Maker's Matte*
Client / *Geron*

Geron 1997 Annual Report

PROJECT STATEMENT

While presenting Geron's science in an understandable
format was a basic requirement, the intent was to highlight
the inescapable process of aging and how it affects the
quality of our lives as we grow older. Geron also wanted
to feature some of its employees and convey how disease
in their own families gives their work a personal perspective.
To support this theme, life stories, company milestones,
and science platforms are depicted in a hand-made, intimate
manner. The result is a message that disease is not fair or
predictable, and as we live our lives and grow older, we are
all vulnerable.

Design Firm / *Cahan & Associates, San Francisco, CA*
Creative Director / *Bill Cahan*
Designer/Illustrator / *Kevin Roberson*
Writers / *Kevin Roberson and Jennifer Schraeder*
Typeface / *Futura*
Printer / *George Rice & Sons*
Paper / *Fox River Starwhite Vicksburg, Weyerhaeuser Cougar, Champion Carnival*
Client / *Vivus, Inc.*

Vivus 1997 Annual Report

PROJECT STATEMENT

Vivus develops treatments for erectile dysfunction, more commonly known as impotence. Although this annual report contains primarily a straightforward business message, the use of bold diagrams, large oblique type, and a stiff hard cover hint at the end result of using their product. A cautionary cover band is a slight allusion to the explicit material contained in the book.

CAUTION:

**READING THIS ANNUAL REPORT
MAY CAUSE AN ERECTION**

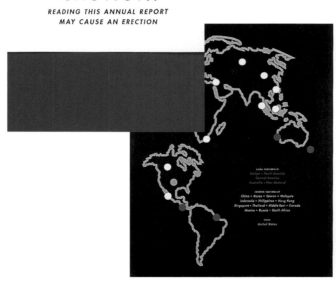

International Opportunities. With marketing authorizations issued by regulatory authorities on four continents, VIVUS will aggressively pursue international markets with a goal of making MUSE available around the globe. A key element of our international strategy is to collaborate with a premier pharmaceutical company in each region of the world. Astra AB and Janssen Pharmaceutica International are excellent examples of our success in implementing this strategy.

Astra's territory encompasses Europe, South and Central America, Australia and New Zealand. Janssen Pharmaceutica has distribution marketing rights for the rest of the world except Japan. VIVUS is actively pursuing a distribution partner for Japan.

To date, VIVUS and its partners have received international marketing authorizations for MUSE in Argentina, Brazil, South Korea, Switzerland and the United Kingdom. VIVUS will continue to be the exclusive manufacturer and supplier of MUSE to all international markets.

Design Firm / *Cahan & Associates, San Francisco, CA*
Creative Director / *Bill Cahan*
Designer / *Sharrie Brooks*
Writers / *Bennet Weintraub and Sharrie Brooks*
Typeface / *Bembo*
Printer / *Color Graphics*
Paper / *Weyerhaeuser Cougar*
Client / *Megabios*

Megabios 1998 Annual Report

PROJECT STATEMENT

Megabios is a leader in the field of gene therapy. It develops proprietary gene-based delivery systems and provides development expertise to create gene-based therapeutics for the treatment or prevention of genetic and acquired diseases. This year's annual report focuses on the company's strong base platform technology and, through the use of color and simple diagrams, explains the use of genes as therapeutics and their enormous potential.

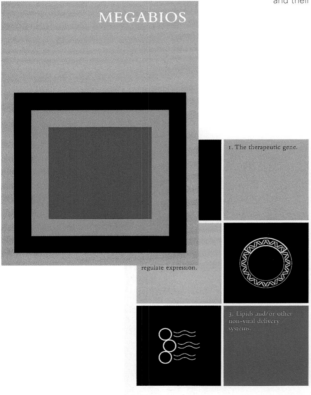

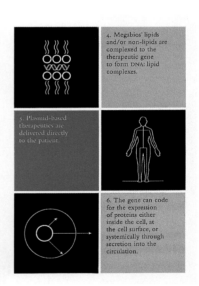

WE *leverage* our expertise by establishing corporate and academic partnerships.

Glaxo Wellcome plc. In April 1994, Megabios entered into a corporate partnership with Glaxo Wellcome to develop a gene-based therapeutic for the treatment of cystic fibrosis. Preclinical data demonstrate expression of the human form of the CFTR gene in the lungs of non-human primates, in the appropriate cell type, with no evidence of inflammation. In addition, approximately 20% of the target cells were shown to produce CFTR protein six weeks after a single aerosol administration, which exceeds the level believed to be required for achieving a therapeutic effect. Glaxo Wellcome commenced a Phase I/II clinical trial in cystic fibrosis patients using a Megabios gene delivery system, with encouraging results announced in the fourth calendar quarter of 1998.

27.

Design Firm / *Pentagram Design, New York, NY*
Art Director / *Michael Bierut*
Designer / *Brett Traylor*
Typefaces / *Sabon, Gill Sans, Bodoni Book Italic*
Printer / *Carton Craft*
Client / *March of Dimes*

March of Dimes Identity Manual

PROJECT STATEMENT

Originally founded in the 1930s to combat polio, a battle eventually won, the March of Dimes now works on all fronts to
ensure that every infant gets as healthy a start as possible.

The March of Dimes recently refocused its mission
from "fighting birth defects" to the slightly broader task of
advocating healthier babies. The organization's old mark
was geometric and corporate; the new identity needed more
warmth. Pentagram helped the March of Dimes settle
on the tagline "Saving babies, together" and the designers
developed a pictorial solution showing an adult cradling a
baby. Colors and typefaces were chosen to reinforce the
basic friendliness of the new logo.

The graphic standards manual for the new identity was
inspired by children's primers and laminated "chubby board"
books for babies and toddlers. The playful form of the manual helped make the introduction of the new mark memorable
and charming to the March of Dimes' many local chapters.
Since the MOD is a chapter-driven organization, it was
important that the new identity be welcome out in the field.

Design Firm / *Landor Associates, San Francisco, CA*
Creative Director / *Margaret Youngblood*
Art Director/Designer / *Jamie Calderon*
Photographer / *David Magnusson*
Writers / *Bruce McGovert, Laura Pickering, Susan Manning*
Typefaces / *Humanist 777, Classical Garamond*
Printers / *Paragraphics and Colormatch*
Paper / *Fox River Starwhite Vicksburg*
Client / *ITT Industries*

ITT Industries Identity Manual

PROJECT STATEMENT

Just as ITT Industries prides itself on building exceptional
products that are "Engineered for Life," the brand and all
its various applications need to be treated with the same
regard. Every element — the format, typography, materials,
photography, and illustration — used in the manual
contributes to the look and feel of ITT Industries, and helps
communicates the precision, strength, engineering, and
unity of the brand.

   Given the overall length of the manual, it was decided
that each section of the manual should be able to stand alone
as a separate book for ease of use. This approach posed
aparticular challenge in providing a final product with unique
parts that always felt unified as a whole. We also tried
not to make a dry and instructional identity standards manual,
instead creating a document that we hope provides both
content and inspiration to all who use it.

Design Firm / *Concrete, Chicago, IL*
Creative Director / *Jilly Simons*
Designers / *Jilly Simons and Kelly Simpson*
Typefaces / *Frutiger, FF Scala, Times New Roman*
Printer / *Rider Dickerson*
Paper / *Neenah Classic Crest*
Client / *Frankel Brand Marketing*

Frankel Style Guide

PROJECT STATEMENT

This style guide introduces a new image program to the employees of Frankel, a brand marketing agency in Chicago. The program included new identity graphics, along with a detailed account of business forms and printed communication vehicles used by the company. The format and uncoated stock are a deliberate choice, positioning the guidelines in a more colorful, user-friendly form than a traditional corporate identity manual.

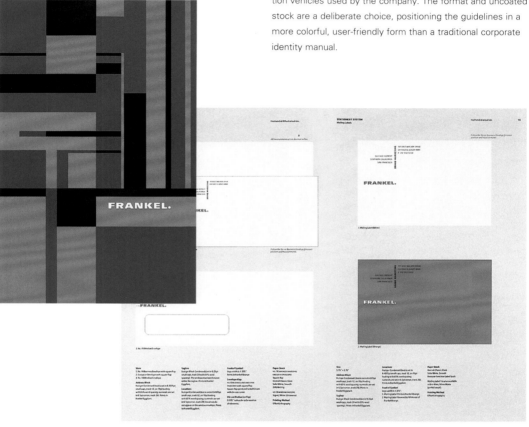

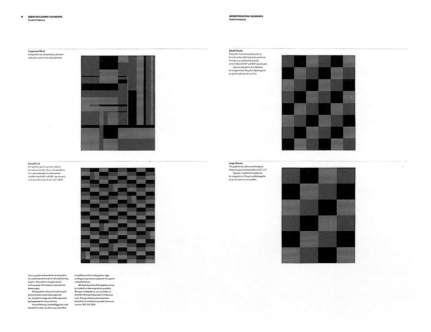

Design Firm / *Cahan & Associates, San Francisco, CA*
Creative Director / *Bill Cahan*
Designer / *Kevin Roberson*
Illustrator / *Tim Bower*
Writers / *Tim Peters and Kevin Roberson*
Typefaces / *Caslon, Clarendon*
Printer / *Digital Engraving*
Paper / *Fox River Starwhite Vicksburg*
Client / *InterWest Partners*

InterWest Partners Brochure

PROJECT STATEMENT
Most venture capital firms are perceived as "vulture capitalists" — only out for money. InterWest Partners, however, is known for being the nice guys of the business. Instead of bragging about their hefty capital resources or their long list of credentials, this annual report focuses on their keen ability to create and maintain relationships. Small line illustrations and short first-person biographical statements further differentiate our client's annual report from the slick approaches of most venture capital brochures. The entire brochure is letterpressed on French-folded paper to give it a personal, intimate feel.

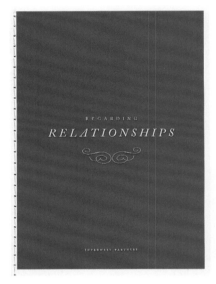

Our highest priority isn't finding good deals; it's earning the respect of an entrepreneur and building a relationship of trust and value.
AL CRITES

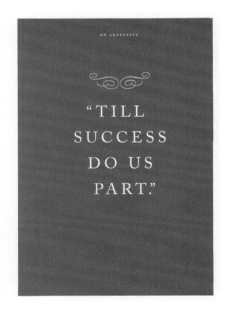

One of the most important things we do is help an entrepreneur build a high-performance team with the right mix of experience and the chemistry to work together effectively.
JOHN ZEISLER

Design Firm / *Oh Boy, A Design Company,*
San Francisco, CA
Creative Director / *David Salanitro*
Designer / *Ted Bluey*
Photographers / *Hunter L. Wimmer and Various*
Typefaces / *Trade Gothic, Bembo, Helvetica Neue*
Printer / *Colorgraphics*
Fabricator / *Compton Presentation Systems*
Paper / *Weyerhaeuser Cougar Opaque*
Client / *Charles Schwab and Company*

Increasing Visibility: A Tool Kit for Independent Investment Managers

PROJECT STATEMENT

Increasing Visibility provides public relations advice to
independent investment managers for Charles Schwab and
Company. Bold question-and-answer headlines depicting
opportunities for increased exposure divide each section.
With a screen-printed polyvinyl cover, spiral binding, and stock
photography as well as custom photography provided by
Oh Boy, the manual is an easy-to-use guide for those interested in increasing exposure and expanding their business.

Design Firm / *Slaughter Hanson, Birmingham, AL*
Art Directors / *Marion English and Jennifer Martin*
Photographer / *Sean Kernan*
Writer / *Laura Holmes*
Printer / *Ad Shop*
Paper / *Twin Rocker Handmade, Warren LOE Dull*
Client / *Ben Page Associates*

Ben Page Associates Catalogue

PROJECT STATEMENT

A landscape architect wanted a promotional piece that he could periodically customize to reflect the needs of a particular client. Drawing on his name, Ben Page, we developed the concept of "on page," which features photographs of Ben's landscaping work alternating with shots of an open book. The paper that Ben uses for sketching was used as flysheets between each project page. Handmade papers on the front and back were bound with silver grommets. The photos were printed in quadratones on dull coated paper. We bound 1,500 for the client and then provided his office with the materials to customize the rest to bind themselves.

Design Firm / *Renate Gokl, Urbana, IL*
Designer / *Renate Gokl*
Photographers / *Various*
Copywriter / *Peter Lindsay Schaudt*
Typefaces / *Gill Sans, Perpetua*
Printer / *Kingery Printing Company*
Paper / *Champion Benefit, Champion Pageantry*
Client / *Peter Lindsay Schaudt Landscape Architecture Inc.*

Schaudt Landscape Architecture Brochure

Design Firm / *Nesnadny & Schwartz, Cleveland, OH*
Creative Director / *Mark Schwartz*
Designer / *Michelle Moehler*
Photographer / *Frank Gohlke*
Writers / *David Bergholz and Deena Epstein*
Typefaces / *Interstate and Centennial*
Printer / *Fortran Printing, Inc.*
Paper / *Warren Strobe Gloss 100# Cover and*
Silk 100# Text, French Speckletone 70# Text
Client / *The George Gund Foundation*

The George Gund Foundation 1997 Annual Report

PROJECT STATEMENT

The George Gund Foundation is a private, nonprofit institution with the sole purpose of contributing to the well-being and progress of society. The annual report states the activities, achievements, and goals of the foundation by describing its grant-making in the past year to an audience of grant recipients and applicants, trustees, other foundations and corporations, and various governmental agencies.

The report contains a powerful photoessay that symbolizes the mystery and majesty of Lake Erie, to reflect the foundation's long-standing interest in the future of the lake and ever-growing awareness of the many roles the lake plays in the life of the community.

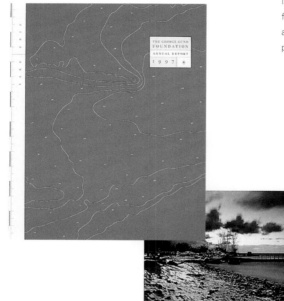

Design Firm / Design: M/W, New York, NY
Art Directors / Allison Muench Williams and J. Phillip Williams
Photographer / Gentl & Hyers
Typefaces / Grotesque, Bembo
Printer / Simon die Druckerei
Paper / Gmund
Client / Büttenpapierfabrik Gmund

Gmund Image Brochure

PROJECT STATEMENT

This corporate image brochure is used to introduce designers around the world to Büttenpapierfabrik Gmund. Since the audience speaks many different languages, multilingual text (in English, French, and German) was kept to a minimum and a photoessay was used to show the locale and factory. The first spread acts as a locator, describing the Gmund environment and facility. The brochure is packaged in the same signature "ream wrap" Gmund uses to package their paper. The cover shows the small paper lifts that Gmund paper is packaged in, while the back cover shows a stack of wrapped reams of paper.

The client asked us to show a range of techniques, such as engraving and letterpress, so these were incorporated on the caption page. Paper stocks were kept within a range of whites to show different types of stock with minimal interruption of the storyline.

Design Firm / *The Edison Group, Minneapolis, MN*
Creative Director/Designer / *Jo Davison*
Photographer / *Jake Armour*
Copywriter / *Chris Mihock*
Typeface / *Din Mittelschrift*
Printer/Client / *Trendex*

Trendex Directory of Solutions

PROJECT STATEMENT

Trendex packages information. They'll print it, stamp it,
bind it, and box it; they'll even sell equipment so customers
can do it themselves. Their challenge was illustrating their
capabilities so that single clients understood the breadth
of their business or the products and processes available.
The solution: an all-inclusive directory that demonstrates as
well as lists Trendex's capabilities.

Readers can see and touch die cuts, embosses, deboss-
es, foils, binding elements, tabs and cover stocks, as well
as peruse a range of finished pieces. The added value of the
book makes it a keeper, and positions Trendex as a knowl-
edgeable creative partner.

Design Firm / *Cahan & Associates, San Francisco, CA*
Creative Director / *Bill Cahan*
Designer/Illustrator / *Bob Dinetz*
Writers / *Joanna diPaolo and Bob Dinetz*
Typeface / *Helvetica*
Printer / *Lithographix*
Paper / *Exact Vellum Gray*
Client / *Mylex*

Mylex 1997 Annual Report

PROJECT STATEMENT

The purpose of this annual report was to answer, quickly and boldly, the three most important questions shareholders would ask Mylex after its disappointing year. In addition to the cost-effective one-color section, a full-color chapter was inserted into the middle of the report to highlight the areas in which Mylex's products have the greatest potential.

THINGS CHANGE:

LUXURY BECOMES NECESSITY.
INFORMATION GETS VALUABLE.
SPEED DOUBLES.
THE INTERNET IS EVERYWHERE.
EXPECTATIONS RISE.
MARKETS BECOME BROADER.

THE PIE GETS BIGGER.

**MORE
MORE
TA IS
OVED,
I/O HAS A
GREATER**

**AFFECT
ON SPEED
THAN
MICRO-
PROCES-
SORS.**

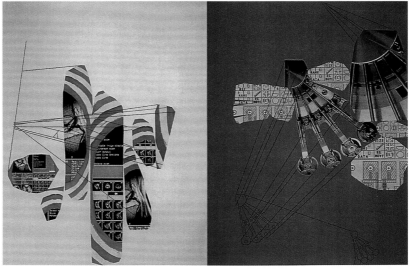

HEALTHCARE

MANUFACTURING

Design Firm / *Cahan & Associates, San Francisco, CA*
Creative Director / *Bill Cahan*
Designer/Illustrator / *Ben Pham*
Photographer / *Gallen Mei*
Typefaces / *Univers, Adobe Garamond*
Printer / *Alan Lithograph, Inc.*
Paper / *Mohawk Superfine*
Client / *ProBusiness*

ProBusiness Tax Brochure

PROJECT STATEMENT

ProBusiness distinguishes itself by the unparalleled level of service it provides clients, as well as through its innovative and flexible PC-based technology. The design of the brochure reflects both the personal service and the technological advantage by presenting photography that shows the human side of the company, and illustration that represents the technology.

IBM Benefits @ Work

Design Firm / *Stone Yamashita, San Francisco, CA*

Creative Director / *Keith Yamashita*

Art Director/Designer / *Jennifer Olsen*

Photographer / *George Lange*

Writer / *Jana Weatherbee*

Typefaces / *IBM Bodoni and Helvetica*

Printer / *Harperprints*

Paper / *Potlatch McCoy Silk*

Client / *IBM Corporate*

PROJECT STATEMENT

"One Team" and "@Work" are brochures given to new
IBM employees. "One Team" welcomes and motivates
new employees, outlines IBM's internal strategy of "Win,
execute, team," and sets expectations for working at IBM.
"@Work," a follow-up piece, clearly delineates the details
about IBM compensation and benefits packages.

Both pieces were designed to reflect "The New Blue"
— in the spirit of youth, intensity, and celebration — without
sacrificing content. Photos of IBM employees, a new and
consistent color palette, and straightforward language link
the pieces to each other, and to IBM's current advertising.

Design Firm / *Campbell Fisher Ditko, Phoenix, AZ*
Creative Director / *Steve Ditko*
Designers / *Mike Tomko and Steve Ditko*
Photographers / *Steve Ditko, Mike Tomko, and Mike Campbell*
Copywriter / *Susan Grapentine*
Typeface / *Univers*
Painter / *Imperial Litho and Dryography*
Fabricator / *Roswell Bookbinding*
Paper / *Potlatch, Strobe Dull*
Client / *CFD Design*

Thought Is the Potential for Everything

PROJECT STATEMENT

This piece is a beacon. With it, we seek to attract marketing
professionals who recognize the value of communicating
in original and unpredictable ways. Our design emerges as
much from human curiosity, experimentation, and social
exchange as it does from research and logic. This book is
our own exploration into how we think and the many
things we draw from in the process of changing ideas into
printed matter. It is a physical demonstration of how, by
mixing purpose with wanton creativity, we find an audience
far more willing to extend themselves into a message.

Design Firm / *Nike, Inc., Beaverton, OR*
Creative Directors / *Bob Lambie and Valerie Taylor-Smith*
Designers / *Valerie Taylor-Smith and Jenny Pelznek*
Illustrator / *Valerie Taylor-Smith*
Photographer / *Gary Hush*
Writers / *Bob Lambie and Stanley Hainsworth*
Typeface / *Avenir*
Printer / *Acme Printing*
Paper / *Mohawk Superfine 80# Text and Cover,*
Gilbert Gilclear 40# Vellum, Champion Carnival 70# Text
Client / *Nike, Inc.*

Nike Annual Report 1998

PROJECT STATEMENT

After a year filled with controversy in both foreign and domestic markets and low financial returns, Nike was challenged to produce an annual report that addressed our issues honestly at half the budget of prior years. Our approach was to reproduce actual customer feedback and to address the issues through their voices rather than our own, to get away from any perception of "corporate speak." The crossfire of opinions, suggestions, complaints, and praise were indicative of the mixed emotions that people were having about the brand. We wanted to address the company's issues head on and put "Big Corporate Nike" on the same playing field with our public (hence, Phil Knight's letter is placed amid other customer opinions.)

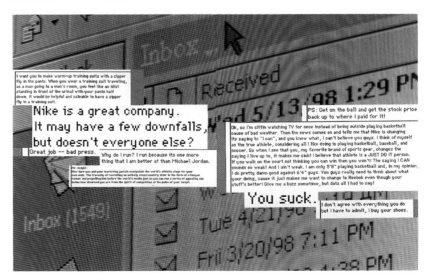

Design Firm / *CDC Communications and Design Consultancy, Inc., New York, NY*
Art Director / *Isabel Naegele*
Writer / *Michael Schwartz*
Typefaces / *Bell Gothic, Letter Gothic, Univers*
Printer / *Universitaets Druckerei Schmidt*
Paper / *Plano Plus Text, Strathmore Writing Cover*
Client / *CDC Communications and Design Consultancy, Inc.*

CDC Corporate Profile

PROJECT STATEMENT

The CDC Corporate Profile brochure communicates the corporate culture and philosophy of this leading design group. The color scheme is elegant and neutral, reflecting the architecture and interior of CDC's workplace, mostly gray, white, and black. The minimalism finds its balance of tension and creative energy. The thick, high-quality paper reflects our high standards, yet has a certain roughness, to give the feeling of a working atmosphere.

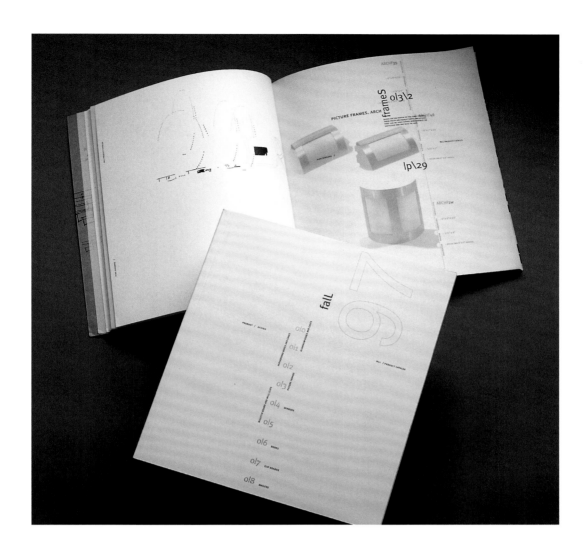

Design Firm / *Jennifer Sterling Design, San Francisco, CA*
Art Director/Designer / *Jennifer Sterling*
Photographer / *Dave Magnusson*
Illustrator / *Jennifer Sterling*
Copywriter / *Tim Mullen*
Printer / *Logos Graphics*
Client / *Pina Zangaro*

Pina Zangaro Spring Catalogue

PROJECT STATEMENT

The quality of the Pina Zangaro line created by Tim Mullen is due largely to the product design and quality control of his company. By designing a book that allowed the viewer to see Tim's initial doodles, sketches, and thoughts, we repositioned him as a product designer rather than a faceless company. While the summer catalogue resulted in a large number of orders of their products, it also unfortunately inspired several product knockoffs in retail stores.

Design Firm / *Jennifer Sterling Design, San Francisco, CA*
Art Director/Designer / *Jennifer Sterling*
Photographer / *Marko Lavrisha*
Illustrator / *Jennifer Sterling*
Writer / *Eric La Brecque*
Printer / *H. MacDonald Printing*
Client / *Marko Lavrisha*

Marko Lavrisha Photography Promotional

PROJECT STATEMENT

The objective was to create a portfolio of works that reflected five areas: fashion, location, product, concept, and miscellaneous. These were then divided into two slipcases, one for black-and-white images and the other for color. Each card contains a piece of a story that is told throughout a series of cards. The typography and design reflect the story line and the mood of the photography. The success of the volumes was achieved from a budgetary perspective, in that the book is modular and can be geared toward specific industries. Clients receive it as if it is a gift, and the beauty of the photography is more likely to make a lasting impression.

Design Firm / *studio blue, Chicago, IL*
Art Directors / *Kathy Fredrickson and Cheryl Towler-Weese*
Designer / *Cheryl Towler-Weese*
Image Research / *Matt Simpson and Kathy Fredrickson*
Typography / *Matt Simpson*
Writers / *Laura Letinsky, Elizabeth Bloom, and Various*
Typeface / *Akzidenz Grotesk, Scanned Plastic Letters*
Printer / *M&G Printing*
Paper / *Weyerhaeuser Cougar 80# Text*
Publisher / *University of Chicago Press*
Client / *The David and Alfred Smart Museum of Art*

Space/Sight/Self Exhibition Catalogue

PROJECT STATEMENT

This catalogue documents an exhibition whose work examines the role of portraiture and identity in contemporary art. In designing the book we sought to play off the notion of identity, making the book design as generic as possible. All titling type was scanned from the plastic letters used ubiquitously on changeable signs, from funeral parlors to discount carpet stores. The essays are typeset in large, straightforward Akzidenz Grotesk. We also inserted a distinct voice in the book that acts something like a Greek chorus: twenty-six concrete images of identity (such as fingerprints, passports, and DNA), which act as foils to the more fluid representation of identity proposed by the artworks.

Nina Levitt, Harbor, 1996. Courtesy of the artist. 7

2 Dawoud Bey, Laneisha II, 1996. Courtesy of the artist and Rhona Hoffman Gallery, Chicago.

Design Firm / *The Museum of Contemporary Art,*
Los Angeles, CA
Creative Director/Designer / *Anna Boyiazis*
Writer / *Cornelia H. Butler*
Typeface / *Franklin Gothic*
Printer / *B&G House of Printing*
Paper / *Potlatch McCoy Velour*
Client/Publisher / *The Museum of Contemporary Art,*
Los Angeles

Bronson Catalogue

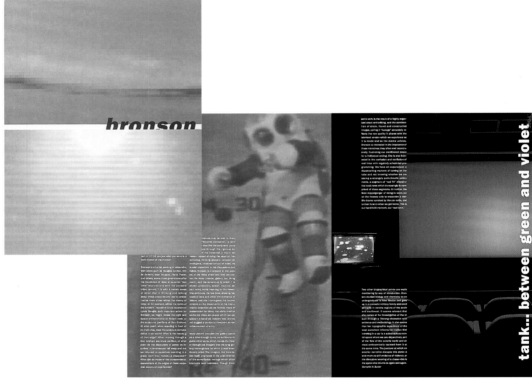

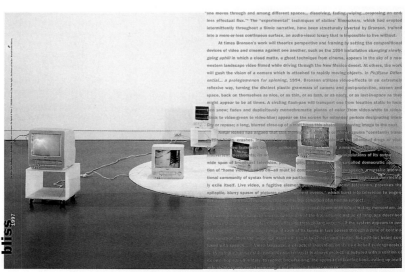

Design Firm / *The Attik Design Limited, New York, NY*
Creative Directors / *James Sommerville and Simon Needham*
Designers / *The Attik*
Photographers / *Mario Godlewski, Ben Jennings,*
Slater King, and Phil Balch
3-D Graphics / *Alex Rutherford*
Typefaces / *Enabler Thin, Univers, Stem/2C Stencil*
Writers / *Tim Watson and Alfredo Marcantonio*
Paper / *UK Paper Consort Royal Silk 135 gsm*
Printers / *Finchmark Limited and Fulmar PLC*
Client / *The Attik*

(Noise) 3.5: Analytical Experiments in Graphic Science

PROJECT STATEMENT

(Noise) 3.5 is the fourth in a series of promotional books
conceived, designed, and published by The Attik. The collection has become a catwalk for our work, enabling us to
express our style to clients, peers, and students. This latest
edition represents our evolving vision of design.

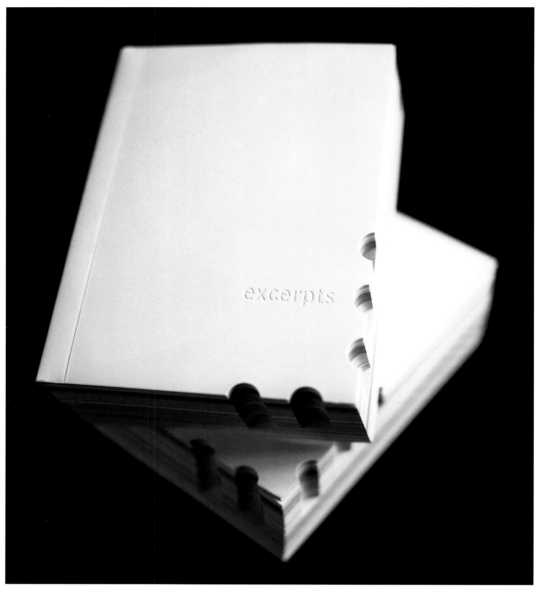

Design Firm / *Design: M/W, New York, NY*
Creative Directors / *Allison Muench Williams,*
Mats Hakansson, and J. Phillip Williams
Designers / *Allison Muench Williams and Mats Hakansson*
Printer / *Dickson's*
Paper / *Champion (Various)*
Client / *Champion International*

Excerpts

PROJECT STATEMENT

Each year, Champion does a promotion to make designers aware of the complementary colors and textures throughout its eight grades. Previously, Champion had made full-size dummy books and packaged them in bulky folders or bags, and the promotion often weighed several pounds. We streamlined the piece by creating one small but thick book of "excerpts" from their different grades, formatted to be reminiscent of a dictionary with tabbed chapters. The pages have perforated lines that can be used for writing, etc. The grades of paper are identified on the spine, which provided a design element that causes people to turn the book over and over in their hands — as well as a significant cost savings over printing the identifications on each page.

Design Firm / *Nesnadny + Schwartz, Cleveland, OH*
Creative Directors / *Mark Schwartz and Joyce Nesnadny*
Designers / *Joyce Nesnadny and Michelle Moehler*
Artists / *Marty Ackley, Donald Beachler, Linda Burnham,*
Jody Guralnick, Jane Hammond, David Humphrey, Sean Mellyn,
Amy Sillman, Elena Sisto, Megan Williams, and Andy Yoder
Photographers / *Ron Baxter Smith (cover) and Design*
Photography Inc. (artwork)
Writer / *Peter B. Lewis*
Typeface / *Trade Gothic*
Printer / *Fortran Printing, Inc.*
Paper / *French Construction Whitewash Cover, French*
Parchtone 60# Text, Warren Strobe Gloss #100 Text,
French Frostone Flurry 70# Text
Client / *The Progressive Corporation*

The Progressive Corporation 1997 Annual Report

PROJECT STATEMENT

For this annual report, "true stories" were included that
show how Progressive meets the needs of its customers and
is changing the face of auto insurance. Eleven artists were
commissioned to respond visually to each narrative. Their work
was published in the report and then became part of Progressive's art collection. Working within a very loose framework, in
which the possibilities for creative investigation and expression
were quite broad, we tried to create a publication that was
specifically relevant to Progressive.

Until our claim representative Robert Simon
arrived on the scene, a Progressive policyholder
in Garden City, Kansas was having a bad day.
First, some of his cows were missing. Then,
when he set off after them, his truck got stuck
in a field. Finally, while trying to get unstuck,
he inadvertently started a grass fire that almost
removed the garden from Garden City. It spread
for three miles destroying fields, fences and
equipment. How did our claim representative
react? Unable to assess the devastation from the
ground, he hired a pilot to fly him over the
scene, swooped down out of the clouds and
determined that the damage wasn't as bad as it
seemed. In the end, the claim was settled within
the property damage policy limits. Progressive's
claim representative Robert Simon may not
have saved the day entirely, but he certainly took
the edge off.

abOve   *and*   beyOnd

no. *3*

impressing a trOOper

On his way home one evening, a Progressive claim representative happened upon a minor auto accident
involving one of our policyholders. As
he was inspecting the damage to the
vehicle, the police arrived. "Well I
guess since you're here, I can leave,"
joked one of the troopers. Later, the
trooper asked if the claim representative wouldn't mind staying until
the police investigation was finished.

no. *8*

So our representative waited. What
did the trooper want? Just some information and a business card. He
was so impressed with our Immedi-
ate Response® claims service that he
wanted to become a policyholder!

Design Firm / *Helvetica Jones, Santa Monica*
Designer / *Garland Kirkpatrick*
Photographer / *Kim Yasuda*
Typefaces / *Scala, Scala Sans*
Printer / *Delta Graphics*
Publisher / *Japanese American National Museum*

Finding Family Stories Exhibition Catalogue

PROJECT STATEMENT

Projects like these are always in danger of being diluted by the bureaucracies that overshadow the work of the individual. This book negotiated these politics by giving primacy to the work of the artists. Putting the art forward certainly made for a more visually engaging book. It also suitably memorialized the efforts of many individuals involved in this three-year arts partnership project.

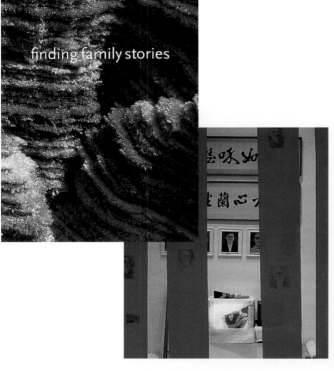

kim-chee kismet

five Korean-American artists look at the family
by Sarah Lee

*Like the dead-seeming cold rocks, I have memories within
that came out of the material that went to make me.*
—Zora Neale Hurston

For most of us, if we give it a chance, imagination can help us understand who we are. What we are is easy, but who we may be is far more difficult. Our public identities can be easily described. We are defined for the most part by what we do: salesman, dentist, storekeeper, housewife, lawyer, student, or artist. We are also defined to some degree by how we look and feel: young and athletic, middle-aged and professional, elderly and dependent. And, to be sure, we are categorized by our physical appearance: European, Latino, African, or Asian. Yet despite all these definitions, our true selves, our personal and essential identities, may still not be readily understood or appreciated. Identity is not a simple, linear equation but, rather, more like a calculus of variables that includes, among other things, language, ethnic values, spiritual beliefs, and complete perceptual cosmologies.

Who we really are is thus primarily a result of where we come from and what happened along the way. On the surface, our pasts seem simple enough and nearly irrelevant to our daily lives; yet so much of how we behave, what we believe, and how we perceive the world is determined by those

Heeyeon Chang, Untitled, 1994

25

of being or awareness of our Indianness is real when we participate in ceremony. As I have become more involved in traditional ceremonies and life-ways, I have a deeper understanding of my own spirituality and connectedness with the culture and language of my past.

Artist Frank LaPena conveys this connection in *Deer Spirit and Dance Spirit*. It reminds me of the first time I participated in sacred ceremony. As we danced and sang around the fire, the shadows reflected on the walls around us made me wonder how long ago my ancestors held ceremony in this sacred site. At that moment, I knew what it meant to be Indian. LaPena's work symbolizes that profound reconnection to the past in a modern world.

LaPena's *Earth Mother: Red Cap* is a ceremony to acknowledge the symbiotic relationship between humanity and earth. His *Blue Shadow Spirit* focuses on messages and symbols in rock art left by our ancestors thousands of years ago. The images are sacred and powerful. When we are in ceremony we feel their power and guidance. In *Blue Dog*, LaPena shows us an example of power and transformation. California Indians share similar stories about powerful people who carry medicine and can change into sacred animals. LaPena paints a spiritual ceremony conducted in his home after his father's death in *I Was Young When My Father Died: Sending the Spirit Home*. This work conveys a powerful ceremony conducted by many California Indians who are honoring traditions while living in a modern world.

Often there are conflicts between traditional native religions and contemporary western religions. The actual events that happen in our lives must always be balanced with our spiritual world on a daily basis. We must keep balance in our lives in a world that has not always been kind to us as a people. We must remember our connection to nature and the earth. We must listen, observe, and learn from our ancestors.

Susana C. Meza, Ph.D., is Associate Professor in the School of Education and Human Development at California State University, Fresno.

Frank LaPena / I Was Young When My Father Died: Sending The Spirit Home, 1993
When my father was killed I was five years old. It was devastating to me. I saw his ghost when I went to use the bathroom. The response was to have some feathers blessed and burned at the place I saw him in the house. The burning of the feathers was accompanied by singing. This ceremony was to help the spirit to break away from Earth and move on to the next dimension. The woman is my mother. The owl came and told us my father had died. Green is a sacred spiritual color associated with the Milky Way, the path to the above world. This painting is then a combination of my father's death and events that happened afterward.

92

93

Design Firm / *Slaughter Hanson, Birmingham, AL*
Designer / *Marion English*
Writer / *Laura Holmes*
Typeface / *Venetian*
Printer/Fabricator / *Ad Shop*
Paper / *Gilbert Esse, Mohawk Artemis*
Client / *Plain Clothes*

Plain Clothes

PROJECT STATEMENT

Plain Clothes is a small clothing store that caters to people who really care about clothing. Their selections are basically one-of-a-kind garments. For their tenth anniversary, the owners, a husband-and-wife team, wanted to produce a piece to thank their customers for their loyalty. Our concept was an intimate book of stories culled from their ten years of ownership. No photos or illustrations were used, just ten personal stores bound in book form and mailed in a tin box. Printed in two colors and bound in Japanese folded pages, the sewn book was a typography piece. The stories were so intriguing that we decided it would be best not to reveal their contents with anything illustrative. The finished piece conveyed the same one-of-a-kind aura as the shop itself.

Design Firm / *EAl/Atlanta, Atlanta, GA*
Creative Director / *Matt Rollins*
Designers / *Todd Simmons, Lea Nichols, and Matt Rollins*
Photographer / *Ken Schles*
Copywriter / *Matt Rollins*
Typeface / *Helvetica Neue, Franklin Gothic*
Printer / *Hennegan*
Paper / *Appleton Utopia One, Blue White Dull*
Client / *Appleton Papers, Inc.*

Appleton Utopia Promotion

PROJECT STATEMENT

In 1690, philosopher John Locke penned "An Essay Concerning Human Understanding," in which he established the idea of *tabula rasa.* Locke claimed (controversially, at the time) that ideas are not an innate part of our minds, but something gained only through experience. Using Locke's premise as the point of departure, we depicted the creative process as it often unfolds: unpredictably. The resulting piece, targeted at designers, positions Utopia as the only constant in the organic process of finding a great idea: a blank slate that offers infinite possibilities, a *tabula rasa* that dares one to begin.

Design Firm / *Cahan & Associates, San Francisco, CA*
Creative Director / *Bill Cahan*
Designer / *Bob Dinetz and Kevin Roberson*
Illustrator / *Riccardo Vecchio*
Photographers/Writers / *Bob Dinetz and Kevin Roberson*
Typeface / *Avenir*
Printer / *George Rice & Sons*
Paper / *Mohawk Options*
Client / *Mohawk Paper Mills*

Mohawk Options Paper Promotion

PROJECT STATEMENT

A quality printing paper should be open to interpretation. It should be flexible enough to enhance any project printed on it. The images in "Options Aug. 25 – Sept. 1" work the same way. There is more than one take on each photo or idea. On a variety of levels, the reader is asked to fill in the blanks, find the connections, and complete the stories. This narrative is one point of view on selected pages in the book.

Design Firm / *Cahan and Associates, San Francisco, CA*
Creative Director / *Bill Cahan*
Designer / *Sharrie Brooks*
Photographers / *Various*
Typeface / *Bauer Bodoni*
Printer / *DPI*
Paper / *Weyerhaeuser Cougar Text*
Client / *Sharpe & Associates*

Sharpe & Associates Sample Works

PROJECT STATEMENT

Sharpe & Associates represents one of the most uniquely focused and talented collections of photographers in the industry. This promotional campaign was designed to carve out a niche among clients from all categories of the creative industry who are looking for unique solutions to their creative needs. The design of the thirty-six-page sampling of work is meant to emphasize the work itself through the use of simple, classic typography and large-scale format.

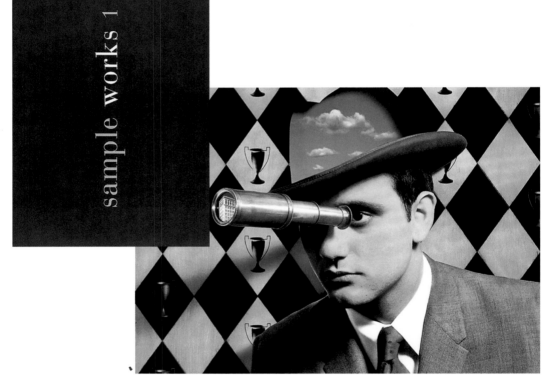

Design Firm / *Clifford Stoltze Design, Boston, MA*
Art Director / *Clifford Stoltze*
Designers / *Tammy Dotson and Clifford Stoltze*
Typefaces / *Calvino, Vitrina*
Client / *Hayhouse for Windham Hill*

Hayhouse CD — Happiness

PROJECT STATEMENT

One of a twelve-CD collection in which each CD explores a particular theme. These were designed to be sold in gift shops and bookstores, with an emphasis on the packaging materials and design. As a series they were designed to be held together by attitude, not format, allowing for greater individuality within the system. The Happiness solution combined quirky serif and script fonts with whimsical graphic forms and colors to create a package that suggests the mood of the music it contains.

Design Firm / *i.e., design, Canton, GA*
Art Direction/Design / *i.e., design*
Photographer / *Maria Robledo*
Typeface / *Futura*
Printer / *Lithographix*
Client / *Georgia-Pacific Papers*

Georgia-Pacific "Feel the Difference" Campaign

PROJECT STATEMENT

"Feel the Difference" was designed to focus on Nekoosa Solutions' features for "a new age of value and performance." A series of advertising inserts featured images of meditation, sleep, water, and music. Corresponding simple solutions for improving designers' quality of life, such as meditation and so on, were featured in each ad. Designers who responded to the ads received a special promotional item that also served as a fulfillment and incentive vehicle. The fulfillment piece asked designers to illustrate how Nekoosa Solutions allowed them to "feel the difference" with a personal case study of a project produced on the paper. The best case study was awarded a spa vacation for two.

I.e., design's image campaign for Nekoosa Solutions allowed Georgia-Pacific to dramatically increase sales of the product and enable users to perceive an average product in an above-average light. By the end of the campaign, Nekoosa Solutions had been transformed from "printer grade" to a legitimate text and cover choice.

Design Firm / *Design: M/W, New York, NY*
Art Directors / *Allison Muench Williams and Mats Hakansson*
Photographer / *Hans Gissinger*
Client / *Daeha Fashion*

EnC Image Book

PROJECT STATEMENT

EnC is a South Korean company that makes clothing for fourteen- to seventeen-year-old girls in Korea. This image book is targeted to girls who are a little bit rebellious, but still within the mindset of the Korean society (a less sexually forward point of view than their American counterparts). The androgynous look of many of the clothes is softened by the gentle photography.

write the softest words and
them that I may
my lips where you
I almost wish we were
but three summer days

three such days with
with more delight
years could ever count

Design Firm / *Concrete Design Communications, Inc.,*
Toronto, Ontario
Art Directors / *Diti Katona and John Pylypczak*
Designer / *Diti Katona*
Photographer / *Chris Nicholls*
Typeface / *Centaur Expert MT*
Printer / *Arthurs Jones*
Paper / *Utopia Premium Blue White Silk*
Client / *Lida Baday*

Lida Baday Fall 1998 Brochure

Design Firm / Design: M/W, New York, NY
Art Director / Allison Muench Williams
Photographer / Hans Gissinger
Writer / Laura Silverman
Printer / Active Graphics
Paper / Mohawk Satin and Vellum
Client / Mohawk Paper Mills

Mohawk Satin and Vellum "Beauty in Utility" Promotion

PROJECT STATEMENT

This piece takes a look at the simple things that are ubiquitous in our lives and asks us to consider them in a new light. The photography is deliberate, simple, and honest. These are not objects made beautiful by abstraction or styling techniques; rather, their intrinsic grace is laid bare. Even the black shape surrounding the light bulb comes from a utilitarian origin — to reflect a dark shadow and define the edge during photography. Sewing patterns, cardboard box graphics, and a topographic map are included as typographic parallels. The printer's color bars embedded in the gutter can be used to tell which photos are duotones, tritones, or four-color process. Industrial box staples and perforated scores are everyday finishing techniques that are actually quite beautiful. The die cut to the binding area makes decorative use of an area of the brochure that is usually unseen.

Design Firm / *Design: M/W, New York, NY*
Creative Director / *Allison Muench Williams*
Designers / *Allison Muench Williams and Mats Hakansson*
Photographers / *Gentl & Hyers, Geof Kern*
Writer / *Laura Silverman*
Typeface / *Helvetica Neue*
Printer / *Hennegan*
Paper / *Mohawk Superfine, Gmund Colors, Gmund Evers*
Client / *Takashimaya New York*

Takashimaya (Volume 6)

Design Firm / Concrete Design Communications, Inc.,
Toronto, Ontario
Art Directors / Diti Katona and John Pylypczak
Designer / Diti Katona
Photographer / Chris Nicholls
Typeface / Centaur Expert MT
Printer / Arthurs Jones
Paper / Utopia Premium Gloss
Client / Lida Baday

Lida Baday Spring 1999 Brochure

Design Firm / *Concrete Design Communications, Inc.,*
Toronto, Ontario
Art Directors / *Diti Katona and John Pylypczak*
Designer / *Nick Monteleone*
Illustrators / *Harry Bates and Paul Cox*
Photographers / *Ron Baxter Smith, Karen Levy,*
and Sheila Metzner
Writer / *Richard Hinzel*
Typefaces / *Trade Gothic, Bembo*
Printer / *Bowne of Canada*
Paper / *Luna Dull*
Client / *Harry Rosen*

Harry Direct Mail (Volume 1, Number 3)

There's a quiet elegance and orderliness to Gamla Stan, Stockholm's Old Town, that evokes a feeling of serenity as you walk along its narrow, winding streets. The tightly clustered web of simple 17th- and 18th-century buildings, painted in rich hues of ochre and sienna, hint at the wealth of the original owners through their ornate doorways. Lofty churches and an imposing royal palace represent the propriety of one of Europe's most peaceful nations. But with European history being notoriously bloody, even Stockholm has its story. In 1520, Stortorget, Gamla Stan's main square, was the scene of a three-day party hosted by Christian II upon his ascension to the Swedish throne to honour members of the Sturepartiet, the party in opposition to him. Unfortunately, after the third day the host forgot social etiquette and brought the party to a quick end by beheading all 100 of his elite guests. Today, Stortorget is lined with bustling cafés and antique shops that again welcome Stockholm's wealthy citizens, as well as an increasing number of tourists. As you watch elegantly dressed couples stroll hand-in-hand, it's difficult to imagine such violence ever occurred here. But then again, that's the charm of Europe.

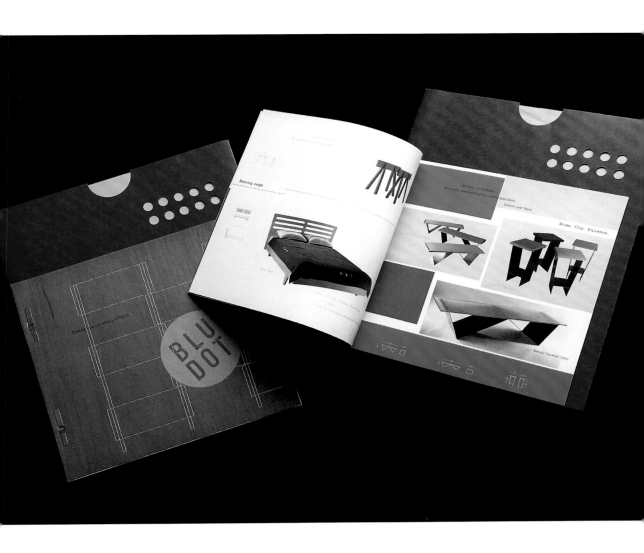

Design Firm / *Werner Design Werks, Minneapolis, MN*
Art Director / *Sharon Werner*
Designers / *Sharon Werner and Sarah Nelson*
Writer / *Blu Dot*
Typeface / *News Gothic, Univers Extended*
Printer / *Color Express*
Client / *Blu Dot Design & Manufacturing*

Blu Dot Catalogue

Design Firm / *Slatoff + Cohen Partners, New York, NY*
Creative Director / *Kim Rosenblum*
Art Directors / *Kenna Kay, Tamar Cohen, and David Slatoff*
Designers / *Tamar Cohen and David Slatoff*
Illustrators / *Chip Wass and Ed Fotheringham*
Writer / *Robert Leighton*
Typefaces / *Trade Gothic, Clarendon*
Printer / *Canfield Printing Inc.*
Paper / *National Velour Peachwrap,*
Champion Benefit Vertical Text, Hammermill Lustre
Client / *Acme Creative Group, Nickelodeon*

Nick at Nite Sales Kit

PROJECT STATEMENT

Nick at Nite shows comedy series from the '50s through
the '80s. They like to refer to their programming content as
"classic TV you can trust." We wanted to reflect their warm
and playful retro programming by using a fuzzy velour paper
stock and foil-stamped celebrity caricatures by Chip Wass
on the cover. The inside of the kit reveals an easy-to-organize
accordion file system that can be filled with single sheets
designed for each show and imprintable stationery that the
client can use to generate current marketing information.

Design Firm / *Liska & Associates, Chicago, IL*
Art Director / *Marcos Chavez*
Graphic Designer / *Susanna Barrett*
Photographer / *David Raccuglia*
Copywriters / *Terry Lane, Steve Seidl, Kurt Kueffner,*
Kim Rak, and Robin Albin
Typeface / *Swiss*
Printer / *Toppan*
Paper / *Mohawk Superfine Ultrawhite Eggshell Text,*
Silkscreened Ink on Chipboard Cover
Client / *Modern Organic Products*

MOP Product Launch Book

PROJECT STATEMENT

As part of the complete identity program designed for
MOP (Modern Organic Products), a brand owned by Revlon,
we created a comprehensive brochure to define the brand
and support the product launch. The brochure instantly
defines the MOP product line to encourage recognition
among salon owners, stylists, and patrons. A minimal image
style reduces the products to the most basic elements —
their natural ingredients. The brochure features models who
are intended to appeal to a targeted range of consumers
seeking products that are part of a healthy lifestyle.

mop modern organic products
for modern organic people

organic ingredients provide a direct,
intimate connection with nature

Design Firm / *Liska & Associates, Chicago, IL*
Art Directors / *Marcos Chavez and David Raccuglia*
Designer / *Aimee Sealfon*
Photographers / *David Raccuglia and Various*
Copywriters / *Kurt Kueffner, Terry Lane,*
Craig Hanson, and Various
Typefaces / *Helvetica Neue and Akzidenz Grotesk*
Printer / *Tanagraphics, Inc.*
Paper / *Warren Strobe*
Client / *American Crew*

American Crew Menswork Magazine, Premier Issue

PROJECT STATEMENT

Our intent with *Menswork*, a biennial magazine published by American Crew, was to give salon professionals, their clientele, and the general public a look at the brand's current attitude. The magazine features educational editorials, innovations in hair care, related fashion reports, and the new American Crew grooming products. The premiere issue is sixty pages, oversized and perfect bound.

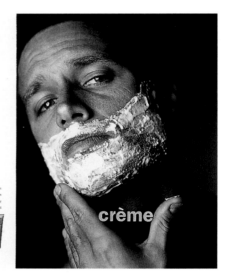

Design Firm / *MTV Networks, New York, NY*
Creative Director / *Jeffrey Keyton*
Art Director / *Todd St. John*
Designers / *Todd St. John and Jennifer Barone*
Photographer / *Guzman*
Writers / *James Wood and Soo-Hyun Chung*
Typeface / *Avenir*
Printer / *Dee Jay Litho*
Paper / *Fox River Starwhite Vicksburg*
Client / *MTV*

MTV Media Kit

PROJECT STATEMENT

The media kit compiles informational statistics and key selling points about the MTV channel for various media buyers. Close-up shots of musicians were used to answer the theme "What does music look like?" The binder fabric was made out of the same material that is used for amplifiers and deejay cases.

Design Firm / *Pattern, San Francisco, CA*
Creative Director / *Koichi Hara*
Designer / *Christopher Lawrence*
Photographers / *Mamoru Minamiura and Ian Reeves*
Writers / *Koichi Hara, Michael G. Lemle,*
Robert Fulgrum, Izumi Masatoshi
Typefaces / *Centaur, Helvetica Neue Condensed*
Paper / *Starwhite Vicksburg Archiva 65# Cover*
Client / *Japonesque, Inc.*

Form of Spirit

PROJECT STATEMENT

This project was done for Japonesque Inc. in San Francisco,
a gallery of the Japanese aesthetic reflected in antiques
to contemporary artwork and furnishings. Japonesque on
the Pier, an annex, exhibits the large stoneworks of Izumi
Masatoshi. The owner of the gallery wanted a printed piece
that captured the startling and simple qualities of Izumi's
stones. Working together on the project, the owner and
the designer were able let go of all their preconceived ideas
about the design of the piece. They were then able to see
what was truly there: the quiet energy supported by these
stones, the large scale, the old and the new, reflected in letterpress and offset printing. These things became the form
of this light spirit. The piece was then sent as a promotion
to artists, collectors, and corporations. It is also on display at
the gallery.

"In one's short life, it is a joy to face the Stone which brings
back the distant past and gives hint of the future."
— Izumi Masatashi

Design Firm / *The New York Times Magazine,*
New York, NY
Art Director / *Janet Froelich*
Designers / *Jennifer Morla and John Underwood*
Typefaces / *Helvetica, Stymie Extra Bold*
Publisher / *The New York Times*

The New York Times Magazine "Shock of the Familiar" Cover

Design Firm/Client / *@radicalmedia, New York, NY*
Art Director/Designer / *Rafael Esquer*
Typeface / *Interstate*
Printer/Fabricator / *Bright Star Industries*

New Year's Laundry Bag

PROJECT STATEMENT

Instead of giving clients a gift for the holidays, we asked them to donate clothing to those who are truly in need. In a bicoastal effort, we coordinated all pickups and deliveries of the donations to the chosen charities. Most clients, however, chose to keep the laundry bags and to send their donations in plain bags and boxes.

Design Firm / *Sagmeister Inc., New York, NY*
Art Director / *Stefan Sagmeister*
Designers / *Stefan Sagmeister and Hjalti Karlsson*
Illustrator / *Martin Woodtli*
Photographer / *Tom Schierlitz*
Typefaces / *Custom Type, Highway Gothic*
Printer / *Jae Kim Printing Company*
Paper / *Newsprint, Corrugated Board*
Client / *Anni Kuan Design*

Anni Kuan Brochure

PROJECT STATEMENT

This is a fashion brochure for New York designer Anni Kuan, celebrating New York laundromats.

We really only had the budget to print a postcard, but a friendly designer told us about a really cheap newspaper printer who could do the entire run for under $500. We then bought wire hangers (2 cents apiece) and corrugated board (12 cents apiece). We got a shrinkwrap machine ($500) and the client hired a student to put it all together.

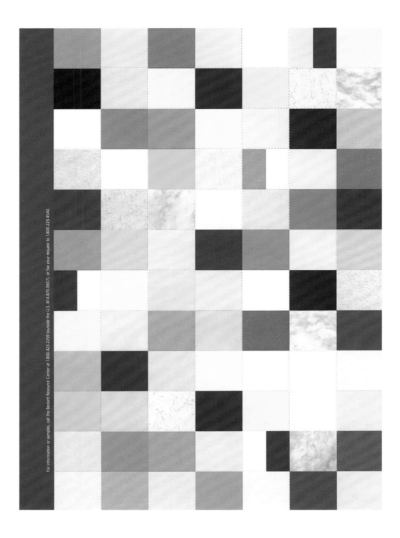

For information or samples, call the Beckett Resource Center at 1.800.433.2259 (outside the U.S. 814.870.9657), or fax your request to 1.800.229.4540.

Design Firm / *Petrick Design, Chicago, IL*
Art Director / *Robert Petrick*
Designers / *Robert Petrick and Dave Wozniak*
Typefaces / *Frutiger, Perpetua*
Printer / *Lithographix, Inc.*
Paper / *Beckett Super Smooth Expression Iceberg 65# Cover*
Client / *Beckett Papers*

Beckett Advertisement

Design Firm / *Landor Associates, San Francisco, CA*
Creative Director / *Eric Scott*
Designer / *Kirsten Tarnowski*
Typefaces / *Univers Condensed, ITC Century Condensed*
Client / *FedEx*

Redesign of FedEx Forms

PROJECT STATEMENT

Our assignment was to develop a worldwide airbill system that would simplify, for customers, the process of filling out the form and streamline, for FedEx employees, the process of tracking packages. We had to use the existing paper size and create a system in which information-entry areas would remain consistent even when the form was printed in different languages. Our creative strategy was to emphasize the clear organization of information in an easy-to-read format.

Design Firm / *Delessert & Marshall, Lakeville, CT*
Art Director/Designer / *Rita Marshall*
Typeface / *Bodoni Old Face*
Printer / *Corporate Graphics*
Paper / *Crane's Crest 100% Cotton*
Client / *Delessert & Marshall*

Delessert & Marshall Stationery

PROJECT STATEMENT

The project was to design business papers for Delessert
& Marshall, an international design and illustration studio.
The concept was to use the graphic elements of measure-
ments in centimeters and inches to represent the work
of the two partners — one European, one American.
The result is a simple, yet arresting solution that functions
graphically, humorously, and intelligently.

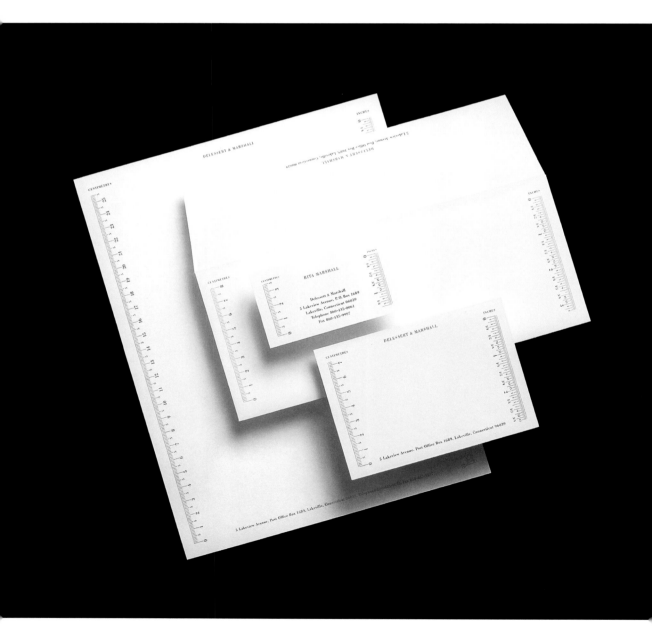

Design Firm / *Beth Singer Design, Washington, DC*
Art Director / *Beth Singer*
Designer / *James Rhoades*
Client / *American Israel Public Affairs Committee*

American Israel Public Affairs Committee Anniversary Logo

PROJECT STATEMENT

On the occasion of Israel's fiftieth anniversary, this logo was commissioned by the American Israel Public Affairs Committee, American's pro-Israel lobby, to celebrate the relationship between the United States and Israel.

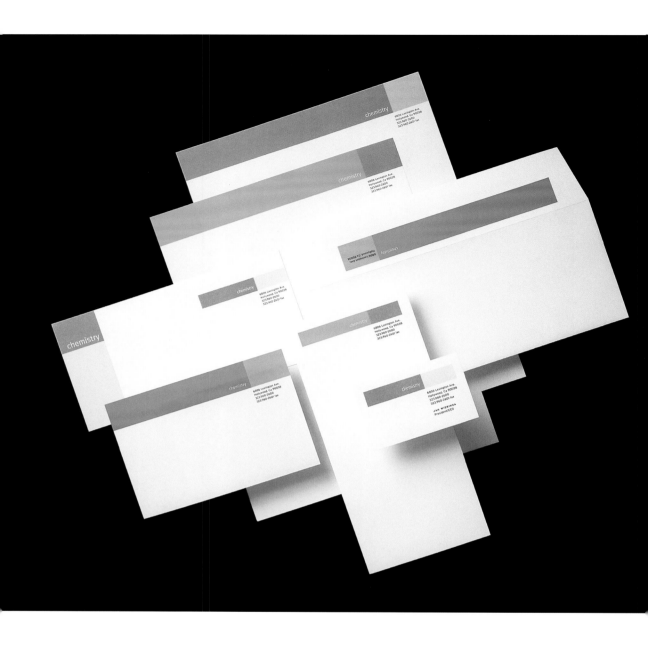

Design Firm / *Ph.D., Santa Monica, CA*
Art Directors / *Clive Percy and Michael Hodgson*
Designer / *Clive Percy*
Typefaces / *Meta, Interstate*
Printer / *Foundation Press*
Paper / *Mohawk Superfine Text and Cover*
Client / *Chemistry*

Chemistry Stationery

PROJECT STATEMENT

This particular commercials production company had strug-
gled to come up with a name that would help to reposition
an existing company, Harmony Pictures, and reveal the
new direction in which it was headed. Chemistry — and all
that the word suggests — was chosen. The graphic identity
needed to be stylish, charming, and open ended. In remem-
bering what we thought was magical about the name, we
came upon the notion of evoking the simplest, most wonderful chemistry experiment: the litmus test.

Design Firm / *Signal Communications, Silver Spring, MD*
Art Director/Designer / *J.J. Chrystal*
Typeface / *Bodoni*
Client / *Jon Dennis*

Dennis Photography Logo

PROJECT STATEMENT

The client's initials are used to depict the process of exposing an image in this logo for Dennis photography.

Design Firm / *D. Collins Art for Industry, Denver, CO*
Art Director/Designer / *Dana Collins*
Client / *Boom Boom Records*

Boom Boom Logo

PROJECT STATEMENT

Boom Boom Records is a small start-up company that specializes in making 12-inch vinyl records for dance club disk
jockeys. Boom Boom prides itself on heavy bass mixes. I
hand cut the type out of black paper, put the letterforms
down on a stereo speaker, and created a horrific bass sound
from the speaker. I continued this process until the letters
vibrated themselves into a position the client approved of.

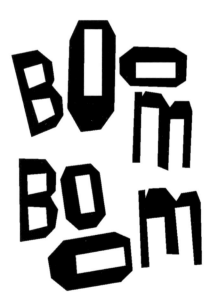

Design Firm / *Studio d Design, Minneapolis, MN*
Art Director / *Laurie DeMartino*
Designers / *Laurie DeMartino and Zack Custer*
Typefaces / *News Gothic and New Baskerville*
Printer / *Atlantic Press*
Paper / *French Frostone Flurry*
Client / *Park Avenue United Methodist Church*

Park Avenue United Methodist Church Stationery

PROJECT STATEMENT

Park Avenue Church wanted a redesign of their stationery with two objectives in mind. They wanted to include their mission statement on each stationery component, and they also wanted an identity that would be unique to this particular church — something that would spark interest in and create awareness about Park Avenue to potential members.

Creating a logo for a church was a challenge, considering that most religious imagery is applicable to all churches. The leaf was chosen not only to represent "Park," but also to symbolize life, constant growth, and renewal. Various colors were used to reinforce the theme of growth, by representing the changing of the seasons. The hand is brought together with the leaf to represent the hand of Jesus, as well as their racially and culturally integrated congregation.

169

Design Firm / *Skout, San Francisco, CA*
Art Director/Designer / *Ed Anderson*
Typefaces / *Trade Gothic and Minion Expert*
Printer / *Logos Graphics*
Paper / *Champion Benefit and Fox River Rubicon*
Client / *Skout*

Skout Stationery

PROJECT STATEMENT

Skout's name suggests exploration and discovery. The stationery was designed to illustrate these concepts through both layout and construction. Instead of the typical #10, a unique envelope was designed to "package" the letterhead. Its construction offers the recipient a more tactile and therefore more memorable experience. Considerations such as perforated folds and printed salutation on the letterhead ensure a consistent look in an unconventional way.

AIGA *Communication Graphics 20* exhibition at America:
Cult and Culture, the AIGA biennial design conference.

50 Books
50 Covers
of 1998

Traditionally, book design has been a rich, special territory for graphic designers. This does not mean that all books have been designed in a traditional manner, but rather that designers of all types have sought refuge in the art of the book. Books are to designers what buildings are to architects; we seek to build that worth building, to find information and stories worth preserving, and to create some vestige of permanence. Even as we seek to reinvent the book — as a relevant form and as a vehicle of communication — the impulse to design books is a valuable tradition within our profession.

We have expanded the jury to include both designers and professionals involved in book production and publishing. The goal of these efforts, and our hope, is that this competition will acquire greater credibility among designers, relevance among publishers, and awareness among the general public. In this light, we encourage your participation.

William Drenttel
Eric Madsen

Co-Chairs

the board of directors of the
american institute of graphic
arts invites you to enter
communication graphics 20
and **50 books/50 covers 1998.**
the quality of the profession
depends upon participation.
enter competitions early and
often. **it's your profession;
make something of it.**

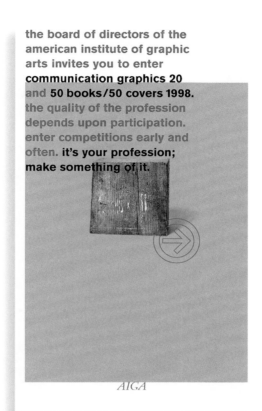

AIGA

Eric Madsen, co-chair, is president of The Office of Eric Madsen, a full-service Minnesota-based graphic design firm specializing in all aspects of corporate identity and brand development, marketing and capability materials, and editorial design for clients in the United States, Europe, and Japan. His work has been recognized nationally and internationally by the AIGA, Applied Arts (Canada), the Society of Typographic Arts, the Society of Publication Designers, *Communication Arts, Idea* (Japan), *Graphis,* and *Print,* as well as the Art Directors Clubs of New York, Dallas, Houston, Los Angeles, and Minneapolis. Madsen is a current member of the AIGA's national board and a trustee of the College of Visual Arts, St. Paul. He is a past vice president and founding board member of AIGA / Minnesota and has served as chair of the AIGA national nominating committee.

Wildlife as Canon Sees It
Design Firm *The Office of Eric Madsen, Minneapolis, MN*
Creative Director/Art Director *Eric Madsen*
Designers *Eric Madsen and Amy Van Ert*
Illustrator *Dugald Stermer*
Photographers *Various*
Typeface *Garamond*
Printer *Watt/Peterson, Inc.*
Paper *Potlatch Quintessence Dull*
Publisher *Canon Inc.*

Visions of the People
Design Firm *The Office of Eric Madsen, Minneapolis, MN*
Creative Director/Art Director *Eric Madsen*
Designers *Eric Madsen and Kim Feldman*
Typefaces *Garamond, Latin Condensed*
Printer *Watt/Peterson, Inc.*
Paper *Potlatch Quintessence Dull*
Publisher *The Minneapolis Institute of Arts*

VISIONS OF THE PEOPLE

A Pictorial History of Plains Indian Life

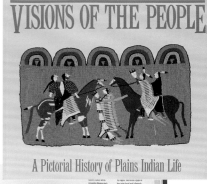

Michael Carabetta

Michael Carabetta is creative director of Chronicle Books, a San Francisco–based publisher. Chronicle Books projects he has directed have received recognition from the AIGA and have appeared in many design publications, including *Graphis, Communication Arts, Critique,* and *I.D.,* and have received awards from the San Francisco Ad Club, New York Art Directors Club, and the Western Art Directors Club.

Before joining Chronicle Books in 1991, he worked for ten years with Landor Associates, directing corporate identity projects in their San Francisco, London, and Hong Kong offices. He is an occasional contributor to the *AIGA Journal,* has guest lectured on design at California State Chico and San Jose State universities, and currently teaches design at California College of Arts and Crafts.

Fat Tire
Design Firm *Amici Design*
Creative Director *Michael Carabetta*
Designers *Lee Jakobs and Roberto Carra*
Typeface *Interstate*
Paper *157 gsm Matte Art*
Printer *Excel*
Publisher *Chronicle Books*

The Blues Album Cover Art
Design Firm *Chronicle Books, San Francisco, CA*
Designers *Sarah Bolles and Michael Carabetta*
Typeface *Bell Gothic*
Paper *360 gsm Gloss Art Stock, 110 gsm Matte Art*
Printer *Dai Nippon*
Publisher *Chronicle Books*

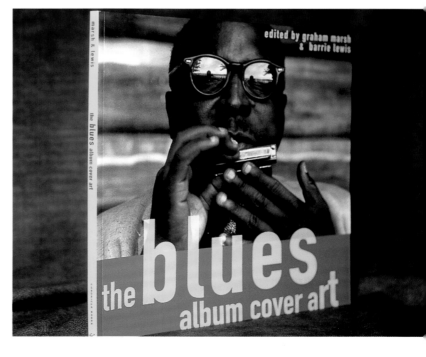

Since 1979, Richard Hendel has been design and production manager for the University of North Carolina Press, a position he has also held at Yale University Press, the University of Massachusetts Press, and the University of Texas Press. He has taught graphic design and book design at RISD, London College of Printing, the University of Massachusetts, and the Radcliffe Publishing Program.

Hendel has been a juror for most national and regional book shows and his work has often been selected for those shows. A past winner of the National Book Award for typographic design and the silver medal at the Leipzig Book Fair, Hendel is the author of *On Book Design* (Yale University Press) and co-author of *Glossary of Typesetting Terms* (University of Chicago Press).

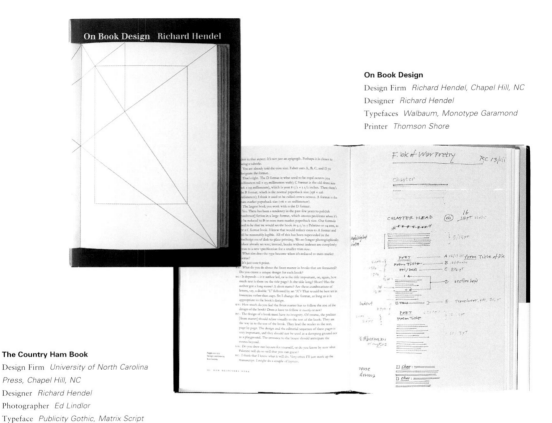

On Book Design

Design Firm *Richard Hendel, Chapel Hill, NC*
Designer *Richard Hendel*
Typefaces *Walbaum, Monotype Garamond*
Printer *Thomson Shore*

The Country Ham Book

Design Firm *University of North Carolina Press, Chapel Hill, NC*
Designer *Richard Hendel*
Photographer *Ed Lindlor*
Typeface *Publicity Gothic, Matrix Script*
Printer *John Pon*

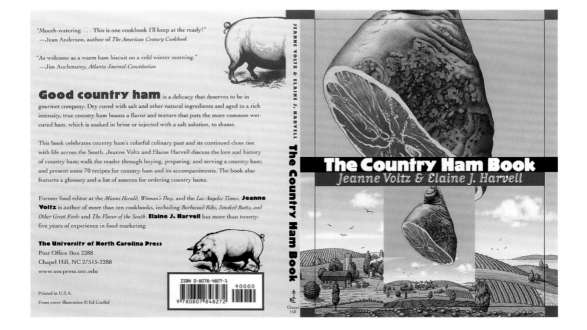

Raquel Jaramillo

Raquel Jaramillo is a vice president and creative director of Henry Holt and Company in New York. In the ten years since she joined Holt, Jaramillo has designed jackets for such literary heavyweights as Salman Rushdie, Paul Auster, Stephen Dixon, Thomas Pynchon, John Fowles, Robert Olen Butler; best-selling authors such as Sue Grafton and Martha Grimes; nonfiction, poetry, and classic backlist titles. Having worked on such a diverse range of titles, Jaramillo has a healthy respect for the non-glamorous jacket treatments that might not win awards but are the bread-and-butter of the industry. She has also published two board books for children, which she wrote and photo-illustrated, and is working on a coffee-table picture book, which she plans to publish next year. Jaramillo lives in Brooklyn with her husband, who is also an art director, and their son.

Timbuktu
Design Firm *Henry Holt, New York, NY*
Creative Director/Graphic Designer
Raquel Jaramillo
Photographer *Ann Giordana*
Typeface *Beowolf*
Printer *Phoenix*
Publisher *Henry Holt*

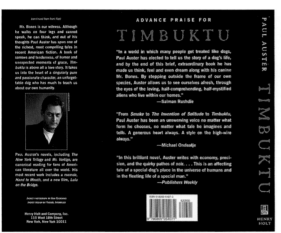

30 Pieces of a Novel
Design Firm *Henry Holt, New York, NY*
Creative Director/Graphic Designer
Raquel Jaramillo
Printer *Phoenix*
Publisher *Henry Holt*

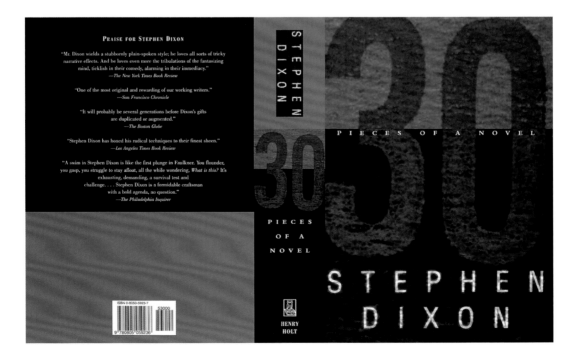

After working in advertising agencies in Denver for many years, Rita Marshall moved to Switzerland in 1981 and began designing books for children and adults. She continues to work for many European and American publishers and is the creative director of The Creative Company, a children's book publisher in Mankato, Minnesota. She has received international acclaim for her work, including gold and silver medals from the New York Art Director's Club and the Society of Illustrators, and has been awarded the Bologna Book Fair Premio Grafico four times. Her work has been featured in *Graphis*, *Print*, and *Communication Arts*. Marshall now lives in Connecticut with her husband, the illustrator Etienne Delessert, and their son.

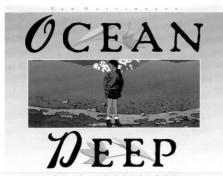

Ocean Deep
Design Firm *Delessert and Marshall, Lakeville, CT*
Art Director/Designer *Rita Marshall*
Illustrator *Yan Nascimbene*
Typefaces *Kennerly, Opti Morgan, Opti Packard*
Printer *Proost International*
Paper *150 gr Ideal Premier Matte*
Publisher *Creative Editions*

Chased by the Light
Design Firm *Delessert and Marshall, Lakeville, CT*
Art Director/Designer *Rita Marshall*
Photographer *Jim Brandenburg*
Typefaces *Phaistos Roman, Classic Roman*
Printer *Grafiche AZ*
Paper *150 gr Gardamatt*
Publisher *Creative Editions*

Deenie Yudell

Since becoming the design manager of the Los Angeles–based J. Paul Getty Trust in 1990, Deenie Yudell has art directed more than one hundred books and other print materials — garnering Getty publications 125 awards — and has developed the overall look of the Getty's environmental graphics. She has also gained much recognition for earlier work in both the public and private sectors, including the Boston Children's Museum, the Boston Redevelopment Authority, the Mayor's Office of Boston, the design firms Design & Devices (Boston) and John Follis & Associates (Los Angeles), and the Los Angeles County Museum of Art. Yudell has taught design at Boston University's School of Fine & Applied Arts, and at Otis / Parsons Art Institute in Los Angeles. She is the author and designer of *Make a Face*.

American Arts & Crafts: Virtue in Design
Designer *Deenie Yudell*
Photographers *Peter Brenner and Barbara Lyter*
Typefaces *Fournier, Exposition*
Printer *Westerham Press Ltd.*
Paper *Consort Royal Matt 150 gsm*
Publisher *The Los Angeles County Museum of Art*

German Expressionist Prints and Drawings, Volumes 1 and 2

The Robert Gore Rifkind Center for German Expressionist Studies
Designer *Deenie Yudell*
Photographer *Peter Brenner*
Typefaces *Caledonia, Franklin Gothic Condensed*
Printer *R. Oldenbourg GmbH*
Paper *150 gsm Scheufelen VBS dull coated*
Publisher *The Los Angeles County Museum of Art*

179

At the end of the last century, as mechanized type composition began to replace hand-set type in the book printing trade, typesetting was commonly divided between "straight" and "fat" work. Straight work was standard columns of text set without decoration or ornament, while fat work included headlines, ads, and labels that featured elaborate typographic contortions. While the majority of work was straight, the fat was a plum given to the experienced craftsmen to showcase their skill. (Straight work was often performed by female machine-compositors, while fat work was always done by men and by hand.) The most challenging fat work was a practice known as "rule-bending," which involved the manipulation of the lead slugs — usually used for printing lines and underscores — to create elaborate curves and frames that defied the limitations of letterpress technology. Rule-bending was the ultimate test of a compositor's talent and numerous contests were initiated, the results published in the trade journals.

As I watched the judges pore over the 930 entries in the *50 Books* competition this summer, I was reminded of those desperately inventive compositors, perfecting their craft in the face of the imminent annihilation of their trade. I wonder whether we late twentieth-century book designers are in a similar spot. Of course old-tech never completely disappears. In fact, once displaced, old technology often becomes a luxury reserved for rarefied conditions that demand, and can afford, Old World craftsmanship. (For instance, once the duty to produce readable texts had been ceded to the machines, those nineteenth-century typesetters refashioned themselves as typographic artists supplying the humanity the machines lacked.) Trades and professions undergoing the process of technological anachronization are forced to find new functions and values to justify their existence.

Predicting the demise of the book is a common, albeit risky, game, but the argument that the book is a more popular form than ever is no assurance that it is eternal. The traditional role of the book is under assault. There can be no argument that the process of printing a book is slow, expensive, and environmentally untenable. The distribution, warehousing, retailing of printed information is another enormous burden. The speed of modern media contradicts the time it takes to produce a decent book and new theoretical discourse has destabilized the notion of a single, authoritative text. Designing books is hardly a profitable venture and most designers take them on as a labor of love or some kind of duty to culture. Television, radio, instant copying, computers, and networks all take their toll and each surpasses in some important manner the limited nature of printing on paper.

It might be that the book is a medium without a future. (Where can it go?) Rather than eulogize the book, however, it is more interesting to speculate on the way in which the loss of a future has changed books, and book design, and has set designers desperately scrambling for ways to make it relevant. (The condition left the judges of this competition grappling with basic questions like "What is a book anyhow?") That sense of working in a medium in flux seemed to generate two basic strategies, both of which were recognized by the *50 Books* jury.

The first strategy accepts the impossibility for books to engage the future and falls back on traditional notions of typography, page composition, materiality, and form. (I see this as a new "Book Beautiful" movement driven by the packaging and the gift book phenomena.) The objects produced under this strategy tend to be either exquisite volumes that refer to and twist traditional forms, or things that are not books — brochures, annual reports, agendas, personal portfolios —that adopt the physical characteristics of "real" books in order to tap into the unique cultural authority books possess. The alternate strategy borrows from the flexibility and latitude of the so-called New Media and deploys them in the pages of a traditional book form. Both strategies are rule-benders, a new kind of fat work. The book becomes a site for a whole range of narrative and typographic experiments that attempt to rethink the conventions of the form or to adopt a multi-narrative, web-structured, de-centered, networked philosophy and give it some tangible, printed form.

The interesting thing about both strategies is that each engages as its subject the book form itself. By embracing the historical notion of a proper book or willfully rejecting the constraints of those traditional forms, the designer reinforces the undergridding Inherent Goodness of Books and all the powerful social connotations that grand myth carries with it: value, longevity, culture, worthiness. Despite the great destabilization technology has wrought, that basic notion as a central conceit, as a great clarifying convention, remains remarkably intact. The books we see in these kinds of competitions are not so much books about things but books about books. In the way that those old-time typesetters bent rules and set them in place with puddles of plaster or chewed paper to defy the constraints of their limited technology, book designers manipulate their pages to reject the limitations made all too obvious by new technologies. The results are often beautiful, fascinating objects that demonstrate unquestionable levels of skill and are all the more poignant in that they seem to signal the end of something.

Susan Sellers *2 x 4, New York*

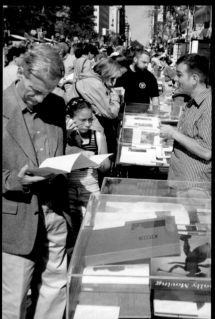

50 Books / 50 Covers of 1998
September 26, 1999

At "New York Is Book Country"
New York, New York

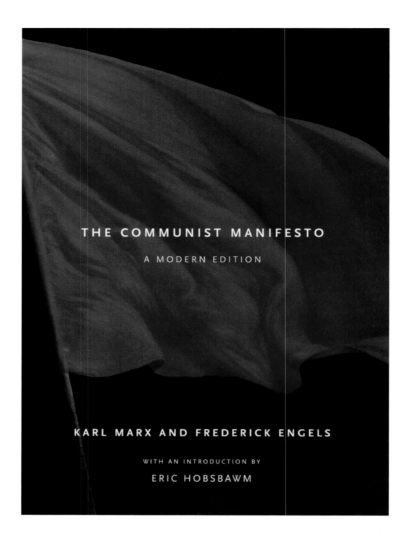

THE COMMUNIST MANIFESTO

A MODERN EDITION

KARL MARX AND FREDERICK ENGELS

WITH AN INTRODUCTION BY
ERIC HOBSBAWM

Authors / *Karl Marx and Frederick Engels*
Publisher / *Verso*
Design Firm / *Lisa Billard Design, New York, NY*
Designer / *Lisa Billard*
Illustrators / *Vitaly Komar and Alexander Melamid*
Typeface / *Scala Sans*
Printer / *White Quill Press*

The Communist Manifesto

PROJECT STATEMENT

To celebrate the 150th anniversary of the first English
publication of *The Communist Manifesto*, a new introduction
was commissioned and the twenty-three-page pamphlet
was reissued as an upscale edition. With Vitaly Komar and
Alexander Melamid's *The Red Flag* painting on the new
cover, the *Manifesto*, according to Verso's plan, is being
"self-consciously marketed toward sybarites." The sophistication achieved by the simplicity of image and typography
makes the topic more accessible to an audience generally
unaccustomed to reading political works.

Author / *Giles Foden*

Publisher / *Alfred A. Knopf, Inc.*

Design Firm / *Alfred A. Knopf, Inc., New York, NY*

Art Director / *Carol Devine Carson*

Designer / *John Gall*

Photograph / *Archival*

Typefaces / *Alternate Gothic, Clarendon, Century Schoolbook*

The Last King of Scotland

PROJECT STATEMENT

With a title like this, you would not immediately think that this was a novel about Idi Amin. I thought the best thing to do was to juxtapose these two incongruous elements on the cover as a prelude to the bizarre story told within.

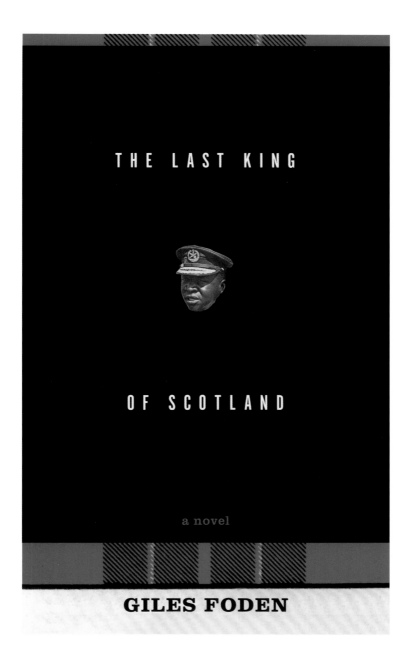

Author / *Henry Mayer*
Publisher / *St. Martin's Press*
Design Firm / *St. Martin's Press, New York, NY*
Art Director/Designer / *Henry Sene Yee*
Typefaces / *Opti Morgan One and Two,*
Poster Bodoni, Mrs Eaves, Caslon 224
Printer / *Phoenix Color*

All on Fire

PROJECT STATEMENT

All on Fire is the National Book Award Finalist in Nonfiction for the biography of William Lloyd Garrison, a great political agitator and abolitionist. For thirty-five years, Garrison edited and published *The Liberator*, an influential weekly abolitionist newspaper. His innovative use of various typefaces, point sizes, rules, and ornaments to draw attention to his message had a lasting influence on graphic design, even to this day.

My urgent headline approach for the book jacket reflects that period of newspaper design through the use of distressed type, treatment of art, and choice of paper stock.

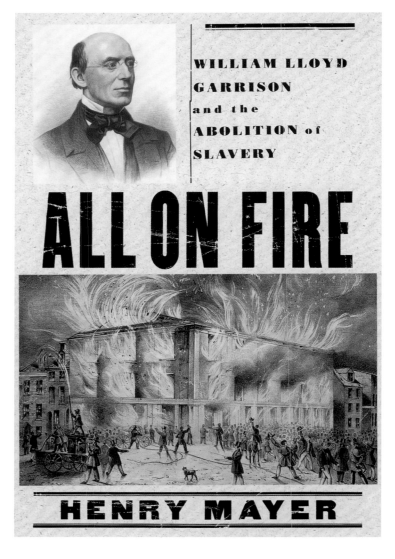

Cities
of the Plain

Cormac McCarthy

Author / *Cormac McCarthy*
Publisher / *Alfred A. Knopf, Inc.*
Design Firm / *Alfred A. Knopf, Inc., New York, NY*
Art Director/Designer / *Chip Kidd*
Illustrator / *Larry Schwarm*

Cities of the Plain

PROJECT STATEMENT
Cities of the Plain is the third in McCarthy's magnificent Border trilogy, following *All the Pretty Horses* and *The Crossing*. This design makes the most sense when viewed next to the other two — the first is stark black-and-white, the second a sepia duotone, and now this, in full color. The title's reference to Sodom and Gomorrah was not lost on me, and it's a good thing, because that's all I had to go on — there was no manuscript. But having read the first two, I had a fairly good idea of where the story was going, and it wasn't anyplace nice. When I finally got to read it (long after the jacket had been put to bed), I had one of those "Hold me" moments — there actually was a scene where one of the characters talks of a wild prairie brush fire.

"Jim Thompson is the best suspense writer going, bar none."
—*The New York Times*

THE
NOTHING
MAN

author of The Grifters and The Killer Inside Me

JIM
THOMPSON

Author / *Jim Thompson*
Publisher / *Vintage Books*
Design Firm / *Vintage Books, New York, NY*
Art Director / *John Gall*
Designer / *Chin-Yee Lai*
Photographer / *Aleksandr Rodchenko*
Typefaces / *Helvetica Neue Extended A, Letter Gothic*

The Nothing Man

PROJECT STATEMENT

A cropped black-and-white photo and the sharp red block
on the top are a variation of other Jim Thompson book cover
designs. The confusion and anxiety in the man's eyes also
echo the main character's yearning for the missing element
in his life.

Author / *James Agee*
Publisher / *Vintage*
Design Firm / *Vintage Books, New York, NY*
Art Director / *John Gall*
Designer / *Megan Wilson*
Photographer / *John Vachon*
Typeface / *Engravers Gothic*
Printer / *Coral Graphics*

A Death in the Family

PROJECT STATEMENT

I always assumed that this photograph was taken by Walker Evans. How fitting it would be, then, to reunite Walker Evans with his literary collaborator, James Agee. As it turned out, the photograph was actually taken by a lesser known WPA photographer named John Vachon. At least it looks like a Walker Evans.

Author / *Jon Stewart*
Publisher / *Rob Weisbach Books/William Morrow*
Art Director / *Richard Aquan*
Designer / *Archie Ferguson*
Photographer / *Frank Ockenfels III*
Typeface / *Copperplate*
Printer / *Coral Graphics*

Naked Pictures of Famous People

PROJECT STATEMENT

Abraham Lincoln is perhaps one of the last public figures one would expect — or want — to see naked (except for a good friend of mine). His likeness is undeniable, making it a joke to think that placing the "bar" over his eyes could possibly conceal his identity.

I was given a large pile of expensive and disappointing photographs and asked to come up with something tasteful, witty, and both historical and current. The solution is a bit of a shock (if only mildly so) and timely. It acts as a social commentary on the exercise of the public exposé — is nothing sacred? — while also making you chuckle (I think).

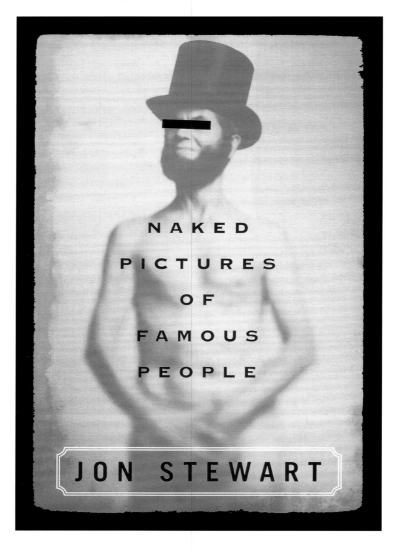

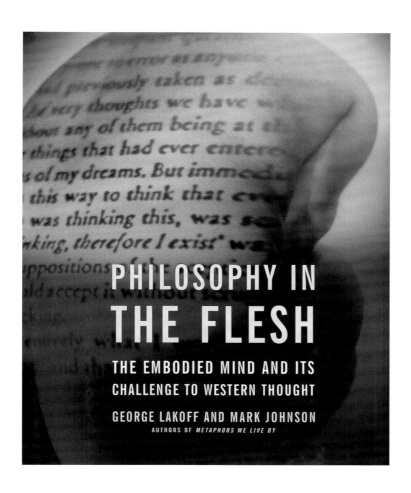

PHILOSOPHY IN THE FLESH

THE EMBODIED MIND AND ITS
CHALLENGE TO WESTERN THOUGHT

GEORGE LAKOFF AND MARK JOHNSON
AUTHORS OF *METAPHORS WE LIVE BY*

Authors / *George Lakoff and Mark Johnson*

Publisher / *Basic Books*

Design Firm / *High Design, New York, NY*

Art Director/Designer / *David J. High*

Photographer / *Marc Tauss*

Typeface / *News Gothic Bold Extra Condensed*

Printer / *R. R. Donnelley*

Paper / *R. R. Donnelley Light Matte with
Aqueous Coating and Spot Varnish*

Philosophy in the Flesh

ben neihart

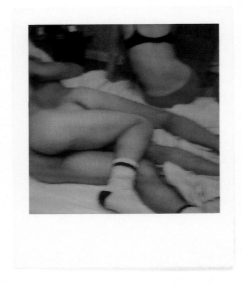

burning girl

a novel

Author / *Ben Neihart*
Publisher / *Rob Weisbach Books/William Morrow*
Art Director / *Rob Weisbach*
Designer / *Michael Ian Kaye*
Photographer / *Jack Louth*
Typeface / *Distressed Helvetica*
Printer / *Coral Graphics*
Paper / *100# Whitesheet C/1/S*

Burning Girl

PROJECT STATEMENT

The Polaroid refers to a box of seedy images kept in a shoe-box under the bed of the main character of this provocative novel. I was asked to make the sexiest book jacket possible and was forced to use the least sexy of all the photos commissioned. I guess sex doesn't sell.

Author / *Robert R. Provine*
Publisher / *Little, Brown and Company*
Design Firm / *Little, Brown and Company, New York, NY*
Creative Director/Designer / *Michael Ian Kaye*
Photographer / *Daniel Bibb*
Typeface / *Helvetica*
Printer / *Phoenix Color*
Paper / *80# Phoenix Truewhite C/1/S*

Laughter

Author / *Gerald Coles*
Publisher / *Farrar, Straus & Giroux*
Art Director / *Susan Mitchell*
Designer / *Anne Fink*
Photographer / *Yuji Shiba/Photonica*
Typefaces / *Quandary, Letter Gothic*
Printer / *Phoenix*

Reading Lessons

PROJECT STATEMENT

In designing *Reading Lessons,* I placed myself back in first grade tackling what seemed like an insurmountable puzzle. How do I make sense of these forms? Combining phonics, word recognition, and sheer will, many of us are able to become literate. The book focuses on those who are not and why.

The jacket is designed to make us remember and pay attention to the process of learning how to read. It uses what are at first unrecognizable letter forms to have us re-experience the process and the self-acknowledgment that comes when one literally and mentally understands what one has read.

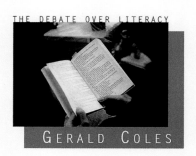

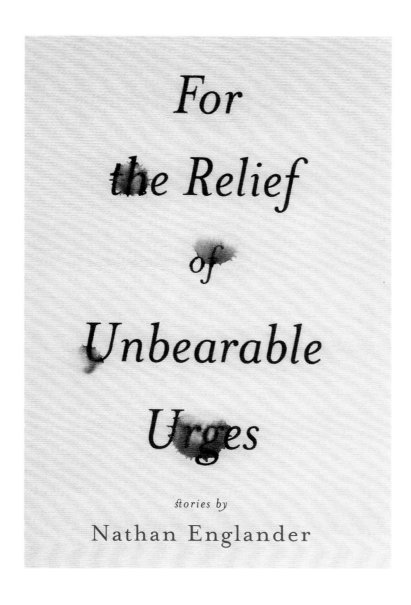

For
the Relief
of
Unbearable
Urges

stories by

Nathan Englander

Author / *Nathan Englander*
Publisher / *Alfred A. Knopf, Inc.*
Design Firm / *Alfred A. Knopf, Inc., New York, NY*
Art Director / *Carol Devine Carson*
Designer / *Barbara de Wilde*
Typeface / *Mrs Eaves*
Printer / *Coral Graphics*
Paper / *Tomahawk*

For the Relief of Unbearable Urges

PROJECT STATEMENT

The title story of this collection refers to the unbearable urge that a married, Orthodox Jewish man has to make love to his wife, who won't let him. In the larger view of the entire volume of stories, the unbearable urge is to weep, to weep over human sorrow, which the author lightly brushes up against in each piece. So the stains are really caused by tears.

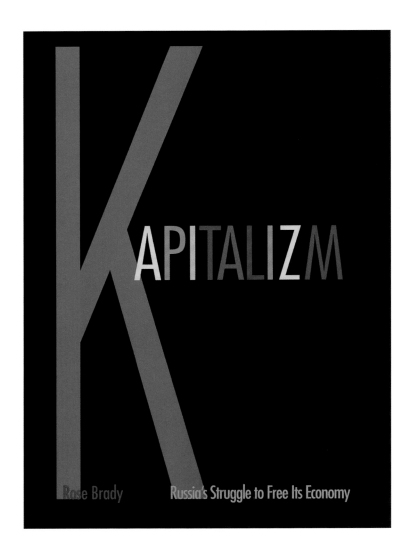

KAPITALIZM

Rose Brady   Russia's Struggle to Free Its Economy

Author / Rose Brady
Publisher / Yale University Press
Design Firm / Yale University Press Design Department,
New Haven, CT
Designer / Nancy Ovedovitz
Typeface / Futura Condensed
Printer / Jaguar Advanced Graphics
Paper / 100# Silverado

Kapitalizm

Author / *William G. Hyland*
Publisher / *Yale University Press*
Design Firm / *Yale University Press Design Department,*
New Haven, CT
Designer / *Nancy Ovedovitz*
Photographer / *Corbis/Bettmann*
Typeface / *Meta Plus Normal*
Printer / *John P. Pow Company*
Paper / *S.D. Warren 100# White Enamel*

Richard Rodgers

Author / Craig Arnold
Publisher / Yale University Press
Design Firm / Yale University Press Design Department, New Haven, CT
Designer / Sonia L. Scanlon
Typeface / Bodoni
Printer / John P. Pow Company
Paper / S.D. Warren Lustro Gloss 100#

Shells

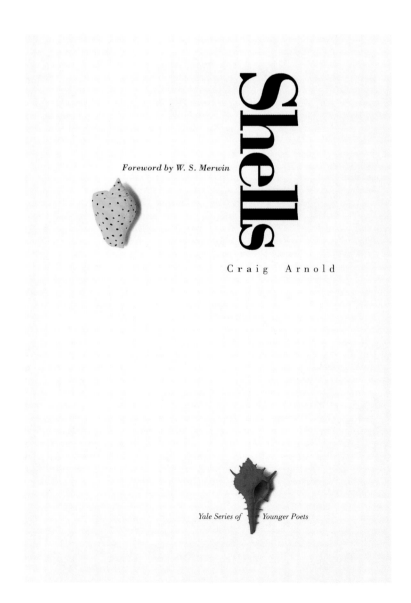

JAMES WILCOX | PLAIN AND NORMAL

A NOVEL BY THE AUTHOR OF
MODERN BAPTISTS AND SORT OF RICH

Author / *James Wilcox*
Publisher / *Little, Brown and Company*
Design Firm / *Little, Brown and Company, New York, NY*
Creative Director / *Michael Ian Kaye*
Designer / *Rymn Massand*
Photographer / *Mauritius/Nawrocki*
Typeface / *Helvetica*
Printer / *Phoenix Color*
Paper / *80# Phoenix Truewhite C/1/S*

Plain and Normal

PROJECT STATEMENT
Plain and normal it's not.

Authors / *James Steele and David Jenkins*
Publisher / *Phaidon Press*
Design Firm / *Phaidon Press, New York, NY*
Art Director / *Alan Fletcher*
Photographer / *Julius Schulman*
Typeface / *Neue Helvetica Ultra Condensed*

Pierre Koenig

PROJECT STATEMENT

The cover of *Pierre Koenig* features a vintage photograph that epitomizes the architect's Modernist style. The panoramic nighttime view of Los Angeles through his signature glass walls reflects the leisurely lifestyle of which Koenig's houses were emblematic. The cover design reflects the transparency of Koenig's buildings, a recurring theme, as well as placing his name firmly within the now iconic image of Case Study House 22.

Authors / *Ezra Pound and Dorothy Pound*
Editors / *Omar Pound and Robert Spoo*
Publisher / *Oxford University Press*
Design Firm / *Oxford University Press, New York, NY*
Art Director / *Kathleen Lynch*
Designer / *Julie Metz*
Typeface / *Hand lettering*
Printer / *Jaguar Advanced Graphics*
Paper / *100# C/1/S*

Ezra and Dorothy Pound: Letters in Captivity 1945–1946

Ezra and Dorothy Pound letters in captivity 1945-1946

OMAR POUND AND ROBERT SPOO

Author / Ben Elton
Publisher / St. Martin's Press
Design Firm / St. Martin's Press, New York, NY
Creative Director/Designer / Steve Snider
Illustrator / Steve Snider
Typeface / Hand Lettering and Brush Script
Printer / Phoenix Color
Paper / Mohawk Superfine White 80# Text

Popcorn

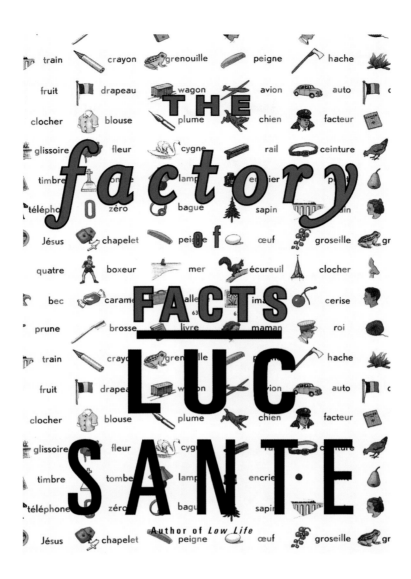

Author / Luc Sante
Publisher / Pantheon Books
Design Firm / Pantheon Books, New York, NY
Art Directors / Marjorie Anderson and Barbara de Wilde
Designer / Barbara de Wilde
Typefaces / Univers, Mrs Eaves
Printer / Coral Graphics

The Factory of Facts

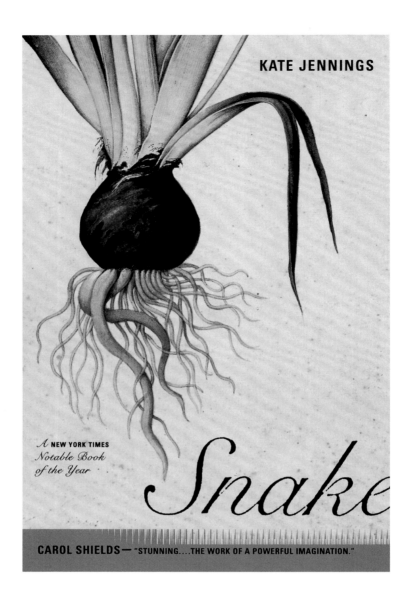

KATE JENNINGS

A **NEW YORK TIMES** *Notable Book of the Year*

Snake

CAROL SHIELDS — "STUNNING....THE WORK OF A POWERFUL IMAGINATION."

Author / *Kate Jennings*
Publisher / *Back Bay Books/Little, Brown and Company*
Design Firm / *Little, Brown and Company, New York, NY*
Creative Director / *Michael Ian Kaye*
Designer / *Leslie Goldman*
Photographer / *Scala/Art Resource*
Typeface / *Univers and hand lettering*
Printer / *Phoenix Color*
Paper / *10 pt. Phoenix C/1/S*

Snake

PROJECT STATEMENT

Snake is a sad, gritty story about a dysfunctional family in Australia. The cover is symbolic: the roots represent the family, Down Under; the blossoms (growth, beauty, happiness) are nowhere to be seen; the type is gritty. The palette is dry and the overall feeling is somewhat compelling and slightly disturbing at the same time.

Author / *Henry Mitchell*
Publisher / *Houghton Mifflin*
Art Director / *Michaela Sullivan*
Designer / *Carol Devine Carson*
Typefaces / *Bulmer, Orator*

Henry Mitchell on Gardening

PROJECT STATEMENT

Henry Mitchell, the gardening expert and essayist, was no refined dilettante. He had no fear of dirtying his hands and could be earthy in his writing style as well. For reality's sake, I borrowed the gardening gloves of a friend who is a hard-working gardener, Andy Hughes, to get the masculine spirit across. They were scanned as they were, with dirt and grass fresh from his weekend efforts.

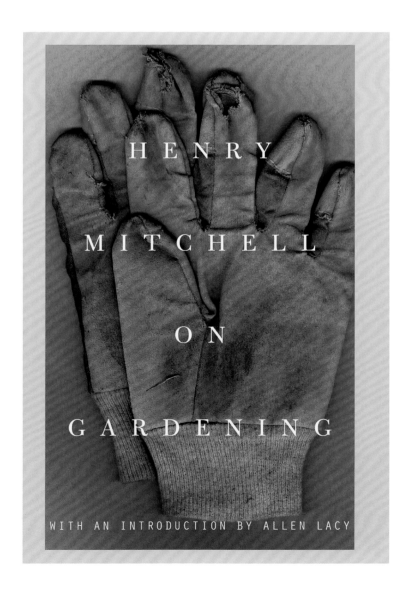

Authors / *Jacques T. Godbout and Alain Caillé*
Publisher / *McGill–Queen's University Press*
Design Firm / *David Drummond, Malone, NY*
Art Director/Designer / *David Drummond*

The World of the Gift

PROJECT STATEMENT

The author argues that, contrary to the assumption that our society functions on the basis of the pursuit of self-interest, the gift still constitutes the foundation of our social fabric. A gift can take many forms, from blood, organs, and charitable donations to small acts of kindness. The concept for the cover was to make the book itself a gift, and to convey the gesture and spirit of giving.

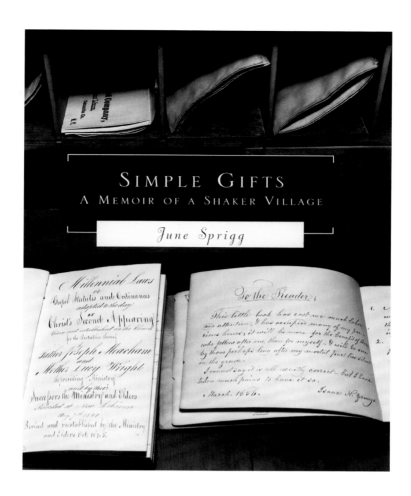

Author / *June Sprigg*

Publisher / *Alfred A. Knopf, Inc.*

Design Firm / *Alfred A. Knopf, Inc., New York, NY*

Art Director / *Carol Devine Carson*

Designer / *Susan Carroll*

Photographer / *Linda Butler*

Typefaces / *Serlio, Dorchester Script*

Simple Gifts

PROJECT STATEMENT

Linda Butler's photography depicts the intimate aspects of Shaker life, thereby making the people individuals, not just a group. The beauty in her photography conveys the beauty in everyday Shaker life.

20th century the columbia his
century the columbia history
the columbia history of the 20
columbia history of the 20th c
history of the 20th century the
of the 20th century the colum
the 20th century the columbia
20th century the columbia his
century the columbia history
the columbia history of the 20
columbia history of the 20th c
history of the 20th century the
of the 20th century the colum
the 20th century the columbia
20th century the columbia his
century the columbia history
richard w. bulliet, editor the 20
columbia history of the 20th c
history of the 20th century the

Editor / Richard W. Bulliet
Publisher / Columbia University Press
Design Firm / Columbia University Press, New York, NY
Art Director / Linda Secondari
Designer / Peter Grant
Typeface / Gothic 720 (Bitstream)
Printer / Coral Graphics

The Columbia History of the Twentieth Century

PROJECT STATEMENT

How to illustrate the twentieth century? That was the problem facing the designer of this jacket. He chose to ignore
the obvious mushroom cloud or test-tube baby and use the
title itself to represent our unrepresentable time. The use of
sans serif letterforms and metallic inks suggests Modernism
and the machine age. The repetition of the title across the
black field conveys the movement of film, mass production,
and the passage of time. The lack of color acknowledges the
contribution of black-and-white documentary photography
and film to our present view of this century.

Authors / *Michelle Fine and Lois Weis*
Publisher / *Beacon Press*
Design Firm / *Beacon Press, Boston, MA*
Art Director / *Sara Eisenman*
Designer / *Elizabeth Elsas*
Photographer / *Tom Arndt/Swanstock*
Typeface / *Alternative Gothic No. 2*
Printer / *Coral Graphics*
Paper / *100# Coated One Side*

The Unknown City

PROJECT STATEMENT

The Unknown City is a scholarly book about a forgotten generation of working-class urban Americans. The design nearly fizzled when Elizabeth had to switch photographs mid-job because of permission difficulties. She managed to find another with exactly the same fissure to accommodate the type and still succeed thematically. For a nanosecond, editorial felt that the new photo looked too much like Wall Street; fortunately, good design prevailed. The typography has this amazing interaction with the photo. If the title were in Russian, you would still get it.

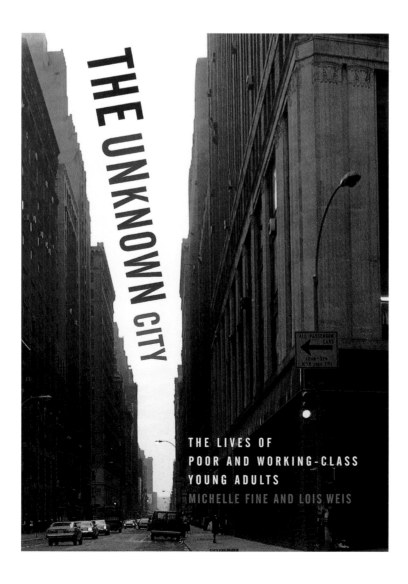

Author / *David Foster Wallace*

Publisher / *Little, Brown and Company*

Design Firm / *Little, Brown and Company, New York, NY*

Creative Director / *Michael Ian Kaye*

Designer / *John Fulbrook III*

Photographer / *Karen Beard*

Typeface / *Trade Gothic*

Printer / *Phoenix Color*

Paper / *80# Phoenix Truewhite C/1/S*

Brief Interviews with Hideous Men

PROJECT STATEMENT

I've always been a fan of David Foster Wallace's unique voice. He has the ability as a writer to take the reader into worlds of emotional complexity and comic power. I wanted something striking and strange for this jacket to represent Wallace's wild mind. The silkscreened bag over the head seemed straightforward yet powerful and funny. Mixed with Karen Beard's photography and gritty hand-lettering, it created a total package I was very pleased with.

Or, I just read the title of the book before I started designing...

THE ARCHIVIST

MARTHA COOLEY

A NOVEL

"COOLEY HAS GIVEN US SOMETHING VALUABLE AND RARE."
—NEW YORK TIMES BOOK REVIEW

Author / *Martha Cooley*
Publisher / *Back Bay Books/Little, Brown and Company*
Design Firm / *Little, Brown and Company, New York, NY*
Creative Director / *Michael Ian Kaye*
Designer / *Amy Goldfarb*
Printer / *Phoenix Color*
Paper / *10 pt. Phoenix Color C/1/S*

The Archivist

PROJECT STATEMENT
Without getting too caught up in deep meanings, put simply,
this is a book about an archivist and the library he maintains
(along with a history lesson and a love story). I think this
cover is successful because it clearly yet subtly conveys the
subject matter.

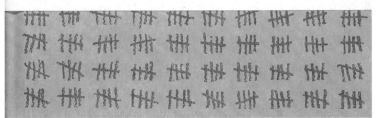

THE YEAR

1000

WHAT LIFE WAS LIKE AT THE
TURN OF THE FIRST
MILLENNIUM

AN ENGLISHMAN'S WORLD

ROBERT LACEY
AND DANNY DANZIGER

Authors / *Robert Lacey and Danny Danziger*
Publisher / *Little, Brown and Company*
Design Firm / *Little, Brown and Company, New York, NY*
Creative Director / *Michael Ian Kaye*
Designer / *John Fulbrook III*
Typeface / *Fairfield*
Printer / *Phoenix Color*
Paper / *Strathmore Renewal Spackle Vellum*
Case / *Rainbow A Arctic Antique by Ecological Fibers*

The Year 1000

PROJECT STATEMENT

Hatch marks seemed an appropriate way to mark time
before A.D. 1000, the year the abacus was invented. The
1,000 marks covering the case are juxtaposed with classic
typography on the belly band to suggest the authoritative
quality of Lacey's book.

Author / *Jorge Luis Borges*
Publisher / *Penguin Putnam Inc.*
Design Firm / *Penguin U.S.A., New York, NY*
Art Director/Designer / *Paul Buckley*
Photographer / *Unknown*
Typefaces / *Merlot, Didot*
Printer / *Coral Graphics*
Paper / *100# Ultrawhite*

Selected Poems

PROJECT STATEMENT

Selected Poems is number two in a three-book series compiling much of the work of this multifaceted author. Borges was obsessed with labyrinths of all kinds — physical or worlds within worlds of his own making. Having no illusions of being capable of coming up with a design that could encase the essence of his writings, I opted for a look that hinted at the cerebral quality of his work and at how important a figure he was to twentieth-century literature. It is also a grid design that with minor changes works whether it is a volume of his fiction, poetry, or essays.

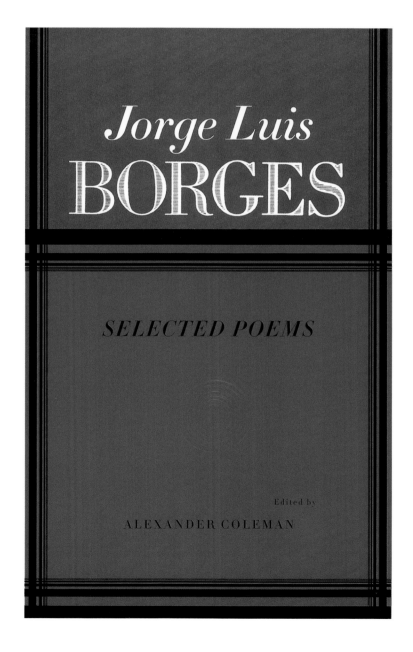

Author / Julián Ríos
Publisher / Vintage Books
Design Firm / Vintage Books, New York, NY
Art Director/Designer / John Gall
Photographer / Deborah Samuel/Photonica
Typefaces / Didot, Engravers Gothic

Loves That Bind

PROJECT STATEMENT

This novel is a bit of an intellectual game in which the author runs through his various sexual conquests alphabetically and each of his twenty-six girlfriends resembles a different famous literary heroine. I thought this would be a great opportunity to get some big beautiful letterforms on a cover that have nothing, editorially speaking, to do with the cover copy.

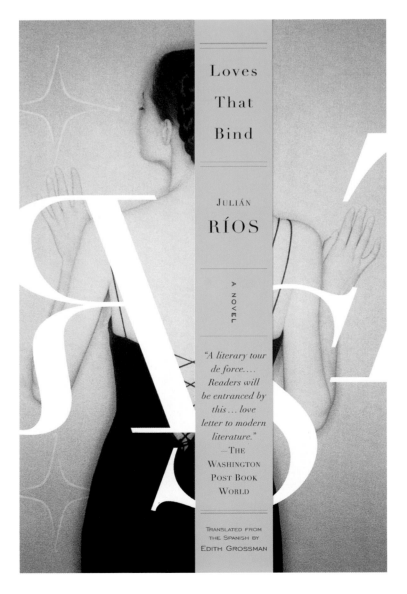

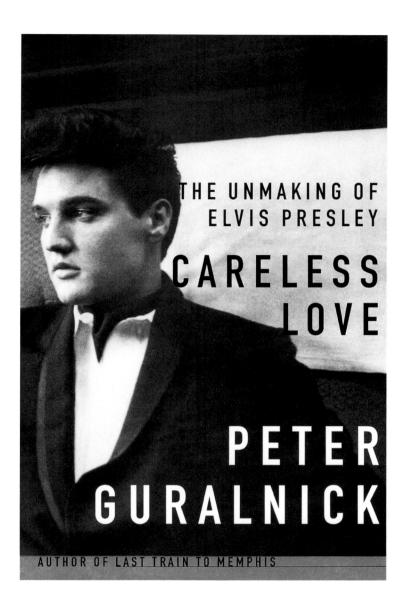

THE UNMAKING OF
ELVIS PRESLEY

CARELESS
LOVE

PETER
GURALNICK

AUTHOR OF LAST TRAIN TO MEMPHIS

Author / *Peter Guralnick*
Publisher / *Little, Brown and Company*
Design Firm / *Little, Brown and Company, New York, NY*
Creative Director/Designer / *Michael Ian Kaye*
Photograph / *From the Lynn Goldsmith Collection*
Typeface / *DIN Engschrift Alternate*
Printer / *Phoenix Color*
Paper / *100# Phoenix Truewhite C/1/S*

Careless Love

PROJECT STATEMENT

A major music biographer writes about the later years
of Elvis's life. Using the image of Elvis looking out the train
window captured the uncertain future of this musician at
the beginning of his self-destruction.

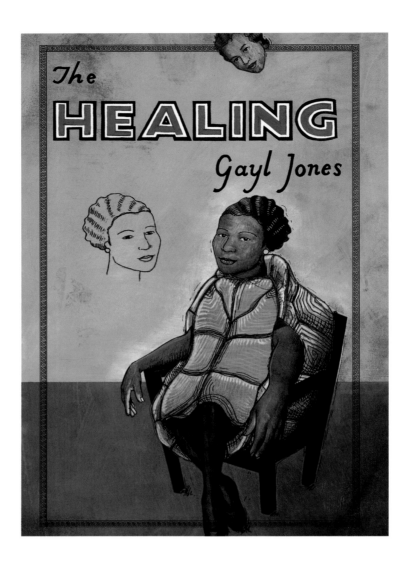

Author / *Gayl Jones*
Publisher / *Beacon Press*
Design Firm / *Beacon Press, Boston, MA*
Art Director / *Sara Eisenman*
Designer/Illustrator / *Leigh Wells*
Type / *Hand drawn by Leigh Wells*
Printer / *Coral Graphics*
Paper / *100# Coated One Side*

The Healing

PROJECT STATEMENT

Since Beacon Press is a publisher known for nonfiction, illustration was the best way to signal the transition to fiction. I chose Leigh Wells because her samples showed a down-home, magic otherness with collage, line drawing, oil, and watercolor that matched the book stylistically. She sent in three ideas. Though the editor originally preferred another sketch, she agreed to the turtle lady, loved it, and heroically defended it to the author. The turtle lady achieved national recognition and thank God we didn't have to conform to some trite idea of what African American books have to look like.

Author / *Amit Chaudhuri*
Publisher / *Alfred A. Knopf, Inc.*
Design Firm / *Alfred A. Knopf, Inc., New York, NY*
Art Director / *Carol Devine Carson*
Designer / *John Gall*
Photographer / *William Gedney*
Typefaces / *Mrs Eaves, Meta*

Freedom Song

PROJECT STATEMENT

What I like best about this design is how beautifully it reflects the languorous, gem-like quality of the writing contained inside. What I like second best is that I was able to use a classic horrible book cover printing effect (foil stamping) in a way that is conceptual, subtle and still eye catching.

Author / *David Mas Masumoto*
Publisher / *W.W. Norton & Company*
Design Firm / *W.W. Norton & Company, New York, NY*
Art Director / *Timothy Hsu*
Designer / *Barbara de Wilde*
Typeface / *Hiroshima*
Printer / *Courier Companies Inc.*
Paper / *Glatfelter Sebago Antique Cream 55#*

Harvest Son

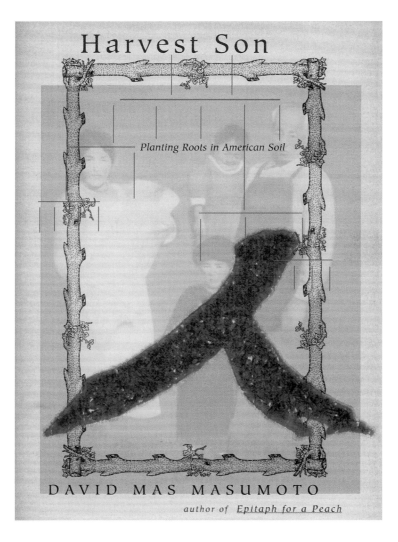

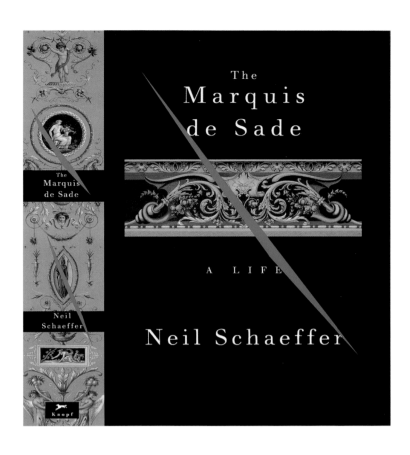

Author / Neil Schaeffer
Publisher / Alfred A. Knopf, Inc.
Design Firm / Alfred A. Knopf, Inc., New York, NY
Art Director/Designer / Chip Kidd

The Marquis de Sade

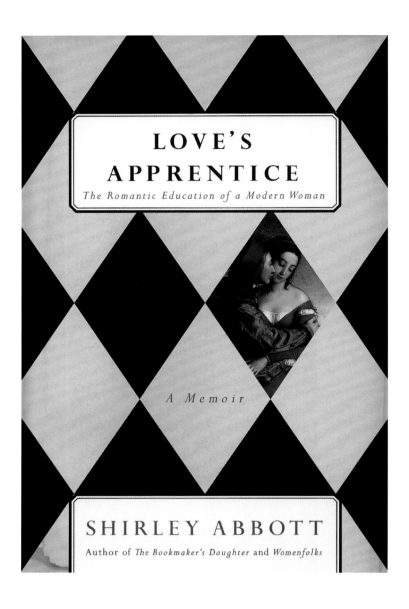

Author / *Shirley Abbott*
Publisher / *Houghton Mifflin Company*
Design Firm / *Houghton Mifflin Company, Boston, MA*
Art Director/Designer / *Michaela Sullivan*
Illustrator / *William Dyce*
Typeface / *Perpetua*
Printer / *Henry Sawyer Company*
Paper / *Lustro Gloss 80# Coated*

Love's Apprentice

PROJECT STATEMENT

For this memoir of a Southern girl's romantic education,
the painting and "aged" background on the cover were used
to suggest the author's affinity with Casanova.

Author / *Anne Fadiman*
Publisher / *Farrar, Straus & Giroux*
Design Firm / *Farrar, Straus & Giroux, New York, NY*
Art Director/Designer / *Susan Mitchell*
Illustrator / *Rockwell Kent, from the library of Elnita Straus, Council House*
Typeface / *Copperplate 32bc, Matrix Script*
Printer / *Phoenix*
Paper / *80# Hammermill Alpine White, Lustre Regalia*

Ex Libris

PROJECT STATEMENT

With *Ex Libris* as the title, an updated bookplate concept seemed a natural fit for this jacket. The Rockwell Kent illustration and the author's "Confessions of a Common Reader" subtitle were a good match as well. But how to give oomph to a spare design? I selected a very smooth uncoated stock and an uncommon color. The green shade required two passes through the printing press.

Author / *Robert Musil*
Publisher / *Basic Books*
Design Firm / *High Design, New York, NY*
Art Director/Designer / *David J. High*
Typeface / *Pixymbols FARmarks*
Printer / *R. R. Donnelley*
Paper / *R. R. Donnelley Light Uncoated with Belly Band*

Diaries

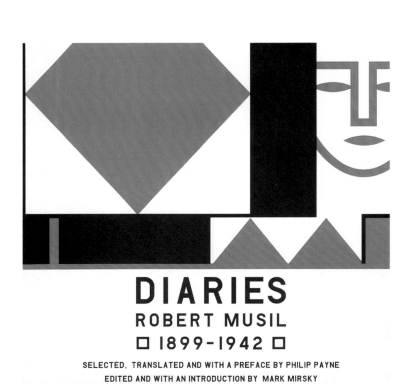

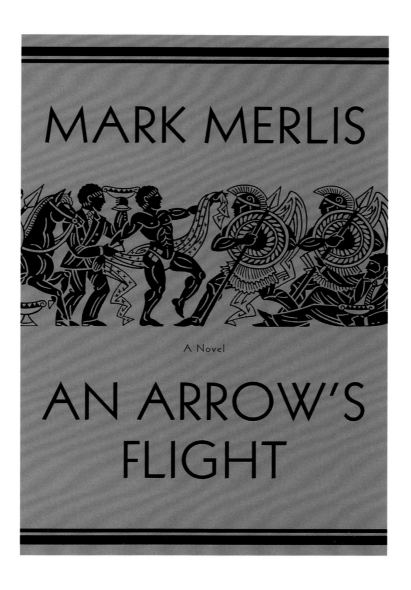

MARK MERLIS

A Novel

AN ARROW'S
FLIGHT

Author / *Mark Merlis*
Publisher / *St. Martin's Press*
Design Firm / *St. Martin's Press, New York, NY*
Art Director/Designer / *Michael Storrings*
Illustrator / *Jill Korla Schwartz*
Typeface / *Kabel*
Printer / *Phoenix Color*
Paper / *80# Tomahawk White*

An Arrow's Flight

PROJECT STATEMENT

In this novel, Mark Merlis magically blends ancient head-lines with modern myth. The jacket combines them visually, with contemporary figures cleverly sharing the space with ancient Greeks in a classic motif inspired by early Greek vases. The two-color graphic simplicity and homoerotic narratives of those ancient vessels combine modern sensibilities with historical significance. Color, paper stock, and type choice contribute to the intent of the overall design.

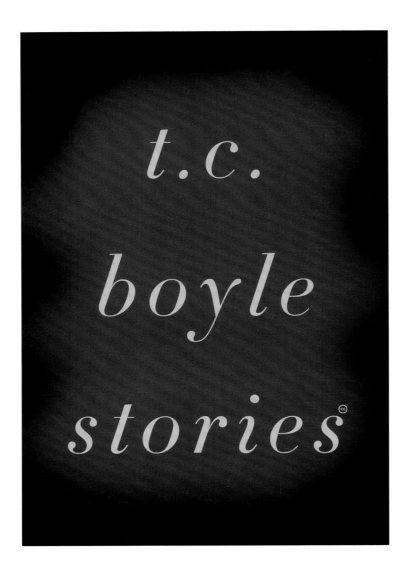

Author / *T.C. Boyle*
Publisher / *Penguin Putnam Inc.*
Design Firm / *Penguin U.S.A., New York, NY*
Art Director/Designer / *Paul Buckley*
Photographer / *Alan Arkaway*
Typeface / *Didot*
Printer / *Coral Graphics*
Paper / *003 Ultra White*

T.C. Boyle Stories

PROJECT STATEMENT

T.C. Boyle is as talented a writer as many of publishing's biggest stars, yet major commercial fame has eluded him. The packaging needed to make this collection of short stories as "big looking" and impressive as possible. I was asked to use a photo of the author on the cover, which I did not feel would help sell the book or make a good cover. I talked the powers that be into an elegant all-type treatment for the front cover that has a simple, yet bold quality and used a full-bleed portrait of Boyle on the back, which presented him as an important author but in a much more confident and tactful manner.

Author / *Allegra Goodman*
Publisher / *The Dial Press*
Creative Director / *Michael Ian Kaye*
Designer / *Barbara de Wilde*
Typefaces / *Mrs Eaves, Engravers Gothic*
Printer / *Coral Graphics*

Kaaterskill Falls

PROJECT STATEMENT

The painting referred to in this book is of the locale of the story. It was an obvious choice to show it in some way, but the challenge was to relate it to the story's main character, an Orthodox Jewish woman who has many children but yearns for more from life. She reads, and this seemed like the natural way to show both things. The image was made on the scanner so the color is very saturated and warm. The type relates to the caption that might appear under the plate of an old illustrated book.

Author / *Evelyn Waugh*
Publisher / *Little, Brown and Company*
Design Firm / *Little, Brown and Company, New York, NY*
Creative Director / *Michael Ian Kaye*
Designer / *Rymn Massand*
Illustrator / *Bill Brown*
Printer / *Phoenix Color*
Paper / *80# Mohawk Superfine White Smooth*

The Complete Stories of Evelyn Waugh

PROJECT STATEMENT

I wanted the jacket to feel like the stories: on the surface, very pretty, very dainty, very English dandy; upon further inspection, an underlying dark humor.

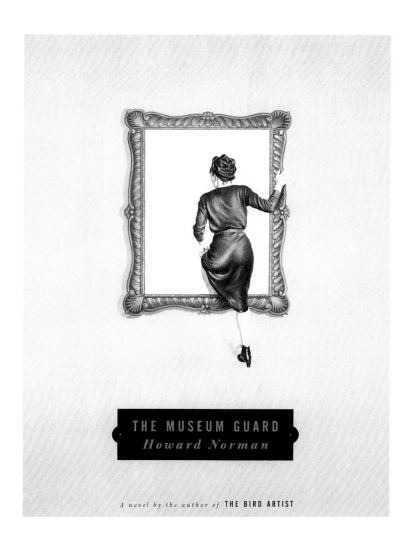

Author / *Howard Norman*
Publisher / *Farrar, Straus & Giroux*
Design Firm / *Farrar, Straus & Giroux, New York, NY*
Art Director/Designer / *Susan Mitchell*
Illustrator / *Ruth Marten*
Typeface / *Alternate Gothic 2, Bulmer*
Printer / *Phoenix*
Paper / *Mohawk 80# Cool White Vellum*

The Museum Guard

PROJECT STATEMENT

I care as much about the physical, tactile properties of the jacket as I do about the visuals. I created the black label motif to refer to the nameplates on museum frames and complement Ruth Marten's beautiful illustration for the jacket. Selecting the right paper stock on which to print this design was of the utmost importance. I wanted to final jacket to have texture, feel good to the touch, without sacrificing the color or detail of the art. The shiny black stamping materials for the label was chosen to contrast with the paper surface — a play of light against a matte blue-gray background.

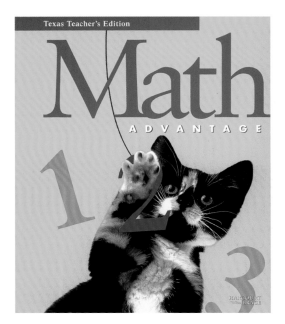

Publisher / *Harcourt Brace*
Design Firm / *Hornall Anderson Design Works, Seattle, WA*
Art Director / *Debra McCloskey*
Designers / *Debra McCloskey, Sonja Max, and Taro Sakita*
Photographer / *Stock*
Printers / *Various*

Harcourt Brace Math Textbook

PROJECT STATEMENT
The client, Harcourt Brace, needed a series of book covers
for their math textbooks. There were three essential criteria
for the design process: animals had to be used for the lower
grades; bold colors were deemed essential for getting the
readers' attention; and numbers had to be incorporated in
with the animal graphics in the overall design. In addition,
large, embossed, reader-friendly type was also used. These
books are sold at educational trade shows. The benefit of
these boldly designed book covers is that it makes the books
seem less technical, more fun and appealing to children.

Author / *Justin Chin*
Publisher / *St. Martin's Press*
Design Firm / *High Design, New York, NY*
Designer / *David J. High*
Typeface / *Bundesbahn Pi3, Helvetica Heavy and Light, Zapf*
Printer / *Coral Graphics*
Paper / *10 pt C/1/S*

Mongrel

MONGREL

essays, diatribes + pranks

✳ justin chin

Author / Stanley Aronowitz
Publisher / Houghton Mifflin Company
Design Firm / Houghton Mifflin Company, Boston, MA
Art Director / Michaela Sullivan
Designer / Martha Kennedy
Illustrations / Modified clip art
Typeface / Eseventeen
Printer / Henry Sawyer Company
Paper / 80# Mohawk Vellum

From the Ashes of the Old

PROJECT STATEMENT
This book examines the recent reemergence of the labor movement as a major political and economic force. The jacket was inspired by the leaflets and posters of the original movement — the use of bold typography printed in an unsophisticated, inexpensive way. To achieve this look, unfused color laser printouts were smudged and distressed for the final art, which was printed one color on uncoated stock.

From the Ashes ! of the Old !

AMERICAN LABOR AND
AMERICA'S FUTURE

STANLEY ARONOWITZ

Author / *Lorrie Moore*

Publisher / *Alfred A. Knopf, Inc.*

Design Firm / *Alfred A. Knopf, Inc., New York, NY*

Art Director / *Carol Devine Carson*

Designer / *Barbara de Wilde*

Typeface / *Steinway*

Printer / *Coral Graphics*

Birds of America

PROJECT STATEMENT

Though I think the title refers more to a field guide, and the idea of a field guide of characters and personalities instead of birds, I decided to pursue this from an innocent child's view... more of a second-grader's paper, so well written that it gets a sticker. There are three stickers that were printed and the books varied in appearance so slightly that most bookstore owners didn't even notice. I know some devoted Lorrie Moore fans who had to buy all three versions — I am one of those fans. This author collects characters and literary images the way people collect objects at flea markets.

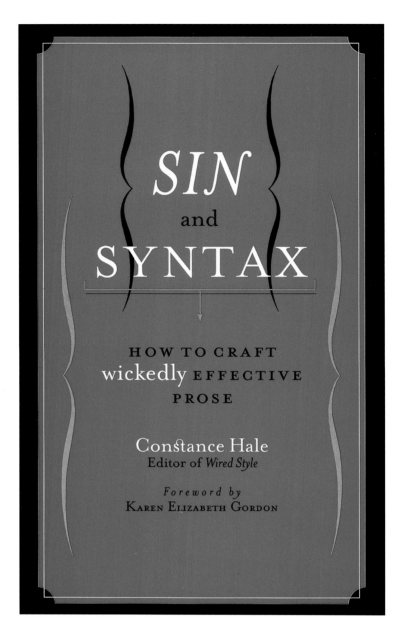

SIN
and
SYNTAX

HOW TO CRAFT
wickedly EFFECTIVE
PROSE

Constance Hale
Editor of *Wired Style*

Foreword by
KAREN ELIZABETH GORDON

Author / *Constance Hale*
Publisher / *Broadway Books*
Design Firm / *Broadway Books, New York, NY*
Creative Director / *Roberto de Vicq de Cumptich*
Designer / *Angela Voulangas*
Typefaces / *Mrs Eaves, Edison Brackets*
Printer / *Coral Graphics*

Sin and Syntax

PROJECT STATEMENT
This is meant to be a typographic interpretation of the
fact that, as most graphic designers know, sin is so easy to
commit and syntax is so hard to follow.

Author / *Jock Reynolds*
Publisher / *Phillips Academy/Addison Gallery of American Art*
Design Firm / *Phillips Academy, Andover, MA*
Art Directors / *Ellen Hardy and Jock Reynolds*
Designer / *Ellen Hardy*
Photographers / *Frank Graham, Jock Reynolds,*
Julie Berson, Cici Mendez, Tony Costanzo
Typeface / *Trade Gothic*
Printer / *LaVigne, Inc.*
Fabricator / *New Hampshire Bindery*
Paper / *110 point Eska Binder Board,*
8 point Mark V C/1/S Cover

New Ceramic Sculpture

PROJECT STATEMENT
Robert Hudson and Richard Shaw were artists in residence
at Phillips Academy for one trimester and this collaborative
body of work is the result of their time together. I felt each
artist made a significant contribution, and to put two images
on the front was not as desirable to me. Half of the books
had a Hudson image on the front and Shaw image on the
back; the other half vice versa.

Authors / *Charles Stainback, Mark Alice Durant, and Vik Muniz*
Publisher / *Arena Editions*
Design Firm / *Arena Editions, Santa Fe, NM*
Creative Directors / *Bethany Johns with Elsa Kendall*
Designer / *Bethany Johns*
Typefaces / *New Baskerville, Trade Gothic*
Printer / *Editoriale Bortolazzi Stei*
Paper / *Gardamatt Art 250 gsm*
Client / *International Center of Photography*

Vik Muniz: Seeing Is Believing

PROJECT STATEMENT

Seeing Is Believing is the first retrospective monograph
of this very singular artist. Designed to accompany a major
traveling exhibition of the same title, the book is sectional-
ized by series to reveal the working process of this latter-day
illusionist. Muniz works with unusual materials in his photography — thread, sugar, chocolate, wire, tomato sauce —
and draws from a host of visual influences from popular
culture, film, art history, and photography. Accordingly, many
illustrations were used within the extensive texts to illumi-
nate the plate section of the book. The cover image plays off
the nature of illusion and the title of the exhibition.

Authors / *Denise Miller et al.*
Client / *The Museum of Contemporary Photography, Chicago*
Design Firm / *studio blue, Chicago, IL*
Art Director / *Kathy Fredrickson and Cheryl Towler Weese*
Designers / *Cheryl Towler Weese and Todd Nossek*
Typography / *Matt Simpson*
Typefaces / *Helvetica, Bodoni, Metro, Vag, Gridnik*
Printer / *Meridian Printing*
Paper / *Aberdeen Coated*

Photography's Multiple Roles

PROJECT STATEMENT

A catalogue documenting a museum's permanent
collection is often a parade of similarly presented but unrelated greatest hits — where design plays a minimal role in
clarifying content. In *Photography's Multiple Roles*, our team
structured the presentation of a contemporary photography
museum's collection by usage — art, document, market, and
science — in an effort to enrich the reader's understanding
by grouping and connecting the works.

The design and typography of the book reinforce this
structure. Helvetica, the museum's house font, is used
for all general texts, while fonts with a more specific persona
are used in the four lead essays. A four-square grid structures the book, making its way into the front matter, chapter
openers, and essays.

Author / *Mark Alice Durant*
Publisher / *Arena Editions*
Design Firm / *Arena Editions, Santa Fe, NM*
Art Director/Designer / *Elsa Kendall*
Typeface / *Perpetua*
Printer / *Editoriale Bortolazzi Stei*
Paper / *Gardapatt 150 gsm*

McDermott & McGough: A History of Photography

PROJECT STATEMENT

This project is a retrospective of the photography of
David McDermott and Peter McGough, the artist duo who
have found immense inspiration from the nineteenth
century. *A History of Photography* is the first collection of
their photographs using archaic, non-silver printing processes. The book was designed to evoke the look and feel
of early illustrated books, while allowing these unique photographic images to speak on their own terms. The paper
selection, cover design, and overall layout reflect the duo's
aesthetic point of view, and yet the book is a very modern
object, using some of the best printing and binding available
in the world.

Editor / *Mari Carmen Ramirez*
Publisher / *Jack S. Blanton Museum of Art,*
Fondo Nancional de las Artes, Argentina
Design Firm / *Henk Van Assen, New York, NY*
Creative Director/Designer / *Henk Van Assen*
Typefaces / *Interstate, Stamp Gothic, FF Scala, FF Scala Sans*
Printer / *Hill Graphics*
Paper / *Mohawk Options, Champion Carnival,*
French Construction

Cantos Paralelos

PROJECT STATEMENT

Cantos Paralelos is an art catalogue investigating the work
of nine Argentinian artists produced between 1960 and
1997. The most important element uniting the work is the
use of parody to criticize art and politics.

   The book is structured untraditionally in a mixture of
essays, artists' writings, and newspaper articles interspersed
with color plates of the exhibited works. As many of the
selected artists were not part of the art establishment,
several of the images are printed as screenbacks to indicate
a sub-narrative. The high-end, glossy paper commonly
used for art catalogues was avoided here, to reflect the fact
that many of these artists were forced to work with cheap
and found materials and to reflect the idea that newspapers
were an important and active medium for artists.

Author / *Lynn Geesaman*
Publisher / *Umbrage Editions/New York*
Design Firm / *Paul Carlos and Urshula Barbour, New York, NY*
Art Director / *Paul Carlos*
Designers / *Paul Carlos and Urshula Barbour*
Photographer / *Lynn Geesaman*
Typeface / *Mrs Eaves*
Printer / *Amilcare Pizzi*

Poetics of Place

PROJECT STATEMENT

Lynn Geesaman's photographs deal with human interaction and intervention with nature. Her subject matter is the formal gardens and parks created in the seventeenth and nineteenth centuries. The design and especially the typography evoke the feeling of the formality and rationality by upending some common, traditional book formats. The size of the book and page format are arranged so that there is a lot of open space. The photographs and text columns sit low on the page. The large leading makes the line lengths read as abstract lines. Within these lines, however, are the fascinating organic ligatures that Mrs Eaves — a reinterpretation of the eighteenth-century typeface Baskerville — beautifully affords. But the most important aspect is to reproduce the photographs as faithfully as possible with just two colors and a tinted varnish. All the factors that add up to make a good photography book — good photographs, good printing, good design — were all in register in producing this book.

Author / *Philippe Halsman*
Editors / *Jane Halsman Bello and Steve Bello*
Publisher / *Little, Brown and Company*
Designer / *J. Abbott Miller*
Photographer / *Philippe Halsman*
Typefaces / *Akzidenz Grotesque, Bureau Grotesque*
Printer / *Meridian Printing*
Paper / *Mead Signature Dull 100# Text*

Halsman: A Retrospective

PROJECT STATEMENT

The images of the great portrait photographer Philippe
Halsman are brimming with playfulness, wit, and beauty.
We wanted these qualities to be reflected in this retrospective. The designer caught the mood and innovative nature
of Halsman's work perfectly with his fanciful alphabetical
tour of Halman's subjects. Reproduction quality was also
of supreme importance — vintage prints were scanned at
the Halsman studio and much care was taken to make
the duotone printing reflect the richness of the prints, with
round-the-clock scrutiny by the authors and publisher.
Seldom, in my experience, has the graphic design of a book
so well reflected the spirit of the work it presents.

Author/Publisher / *Canada Post Corporation*
Design Firm / *Malcolm Waddell, Toronto, Ontario*
Creative Director / *Iain Baines*
Designers / *Bryan Canning, Gary Mansbridge,*
Malcolm Waddell
Typefaces / *Monotype Walbaum, Matrix*
Printer / *Litho Acme*
Separations / *Imaginex Inc.*
Paper / *Purity Super Matte 230 gram*

Collection Canada 1998

PROJECT STATEMENT

Collection Canada contains all the stamps issued by
Canada Post in 1998 and the stories behind them. In addition
to the hobbyist, this bilingual book is intended for a general
audience. One hundred thousand copies are produced annually, which sell out over three years. The major design and
production problem involves incorporating throughout the
book plastic mounts of differing sizes to hold the stamps,
which also must be arranged to minimize bulking problems.

Authors / *Pierre Hermé and Dorie Greenspan*
Publisher / *Little, Brown and Company*
Design Firm / *Little, Brown and Company, Boston, MA*
Creative Director/Designer / *Julia Sedykh*
Photographer / *Hartmut Keifer*
Typeface / *Didot HTF, Bodoni Antiqua*
Printer / *KHL Printing*
Paper / *130 gsm Tjiwi Matt, 120 gsm IKKP*

Desserts by Pierre Hermé

PROJECT STATEMENT

The book is set in the modern version of a classic French typeface, Didot. Unusual photography, where exquisite desserts are combined with props like plastic forks and paper plates, inspired the playful treatment of the recipe titles. The basic recipes and dictionary of ingredients are printed on uncoated stock to emphasize their utilitarian function and to draw more attention to the featured recipes.

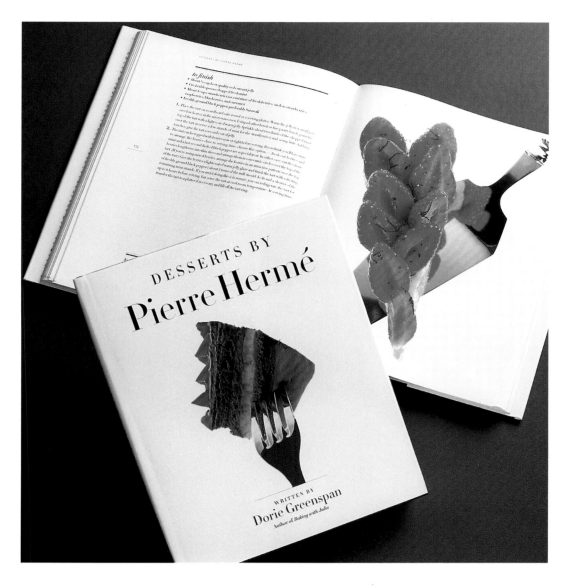

Author / *Bob Kolar*
Publisher / *Dutton Children's Books*
Design Firm / *Dutton Children's Books, New York, NY*
Art Director / *Sara Reynolds*
Designers / *Sara Reynolds and Richard Amari*
Illustrator / *Bob Kolar*
Typeface / *Gill Sans, Gillies Gothic*
Printer / *South China Printing Co.*
Paper / *128 gsm Japanese Matte*

Do You Want to Play?

PROJECT STATEMENT

Bob Kolar's wonderfully quirky book features two friends
and a large cast of supporting characters. Written as an
ongoing dialogue, the text required that each character have
its own typographic voice, distinctive enough to guide the
reader through the packed sideshow of visual and verbal
asides. The typeface became an integral part of each composition, with placement and scale critical in complementing
the art. Since the art is so densely textured and detailed,
one typeface was used for the main text to avoid cacophony.
The idiosyncratic shapes and variety provided by Gill Sans
engage with the art playfully, echoing the subject of the book.

Author / *David Schiller*
Publisher / *Workman Publishing*
Design Firm / *Workman Publishing, New York, NY*
Art Director/Designer / *Paul Gamarello*
Illustrator / *Marc Rosenthal*
Typeface / *Publicity Gothic, Century Expanded*
Printer / *Pearl East Printing Co., Inc.*
Paper / *157 gsm Matte Art*

The Runaway Beard

PROJECT STATEMENT
The Runaway Beard is an illustrated storybook for children
age three to seven that comes with an object that's both
irreverent and irresistible — a fake beard — and a sensibility,
in design and illustration, that appeals to the nostalgia
of parents. Showcasing the beard, while also protecting it,
became the central design and production challenge, leading
to the die-cut see-through cover with plastic pouch. The
result is a cover that makes strong eye contact while also
working as a visual joke, showing the character with and
without the beard.

Author / *Charles R. Smith, Jr.*
Publisher / *Dutton Children's Books*
Design Firm / *Dutton Children's Books, New York, NY*
Art Director / *Sara Reynolds*
Designer / *Ellen M. Lucaire*
Photographer / *Charles R. Smith, Jr.*
Typefaces / *Scala, Autotrace*
Printer / *Jade Productions*
Paper / *128 gsm Japanese Matte*

Rimshots: Basketball, Pix, Rolls, and Rhythms

PROJECT STATEMENT

The jazzy onomatopoetic prose and poems were the
driving force behind the design of *Rimshots*. Inspired by their
most infectious energy and the powerful photographs of
Charles R. Smith, Jr., I found myself playing with colors and
letterforms, as a player struts his stuff on the court. Two
typefaces reflect the duality of street ball: Scala evokes its
choreographed elegance, Autotrace its bold improvisation.
A distinct personality was given to each story by combining
these fonts for maximum effect. The placement of the
images further underscores the spontaneity of a pick-up
game. Basketball fans will notice that many of the color com-
binations correspond to the colors of professional teams.
We set out to make *Rimshots* an open and energetic book
that would invite all young people into the text — even those
who would normally rather play than read — like players
joining in a game.

Author / *Isabelle Beaudin*
Publisher / *Les 400 Coups*
Design Firm / *Andrée Lauzon, Montréal, Québec*
Art Director/Designer / *Andrée Lauzon*
Illustrator / *Isabelle Beaudin*
Typefaces / *Spectrum MT, Letter Gothic, and Kunstler*
Printer / *Litho Mille-îles*
Fabricator / *Reliure Gratton*
Paper / *Cornwall 12 pts, Gardamatte 200 gsm*

Abécédaire de Antonio à Zéphirin

PROJECT STATEMENT

Abécédaire means "alphabet primer" — the ideal subject
for a typographic cover design, I thought at first. But in the
end, I built the cover around the little Zeppelin illustration
that was my favorite. The academic connotation of the word
"Abécédaire" inspired the schoolbook-like design. The hand-
writing on the inside covers was provided by the illustrator's
son David, then six years old, who refused to write the
alphabet in lower case and insisted on using a terribly dam-
aged piece of onion paper.

Author / Carol Payne
Publisher / Canadian Museum of Contemporary Photography
Design Firm / Robert Tombs Studio, St. Lambert, Québec
Art Director/Designer / Robert Tombs
Photographer / Thaddeus Holownia
Typefaces / Adobe Walbaum, Akzidenz Grotesk Extended
Printer / Herzig Somerville Ltd.
Fabricator / Beck Bindery Services Ltd.

Extended Vision: The Photography of Thaddeus Holownia 1975–1997

PROJECT STATEMENT

The design of this publication had two governing principles. First was to achieve the best possible photographic reproduction available, hence the stochastic film. The second was to attempt to treat the bilingual display type of the catalogue differently, which was done by setting the English in Akzidenz Grotesk Bold Extended (an allusion to the book title) and the French in Walbaum Italic, an unusual but successful solution. The intersection of the form with the content has proved very dynamic.

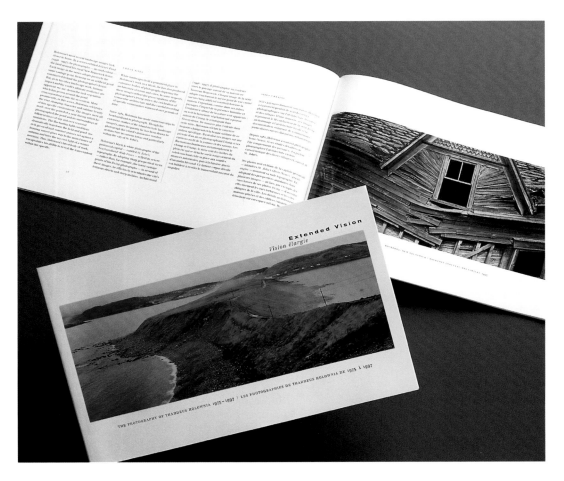

Author / *Raghubir Singh*
Publisher / *Phaidon Press*
Design Firm / *Phaidon Press, New York, NY*
Art Director / *Alan Fletcher*
Designer / *Stuart Smith*
Photographer / *Raghubir Singh*
Typeface / *Bell Gothic*

River of Colour: The India of Raghubir Singh

PROJECT STATEMENT

River of Colour: The India of Raghubir Singh comes as close
as any book could to capturing the photographer's remarkable skill with color and light. The book's straightforward
cover introduces the wealth of rich colors that Singh saw as
the most important aspect of his native India. The image
quality and large scale of the book combine to successfully
portray Singh's dynamic and profound photographs.

Publishers / *High Museum of Art, Harry N. Abrams, Inc.*
Design Firm / *John T. Hill, Bethany, CT*
Creative Directors/Designers / *John T. Hill and Dorothy Hill*
Typeface / *Walbaum*
Printer / *Palace Press International*
Paper / *140 gsm Matte Hi Q*

Walker Evans: Simple Secrets

PROJECT STATEMENT

For this museum catalogue of privately collected vintage
Walker Evans prints, which was printed in both soft and
hardcover for a large audience, the physical properties
of this body of work suggested both format and production
choices. Like several artists working with limited means
in the 1920s and 1930s, Evans produced many powerful
yet small prints. The number of these in the collection, plus
Evans's preference for modest format, helped indicate the
choice of size.

Also, characteristic of this and other collections of early
silver gelatin prints, there is a subtle and rich patina that can
best be approximated with four-color printing. It was worth
the effort to show this diversity in what may first appear to
be black-and-white images.

Authors / *Susan Fletcher Witzell, Jane A. McLaughlin,*
Mary Lou Smith

Publisher / *Woods Hole Historical Collection*

Design Firm / *Diane Jaroch Design, Rockford, IL*

Art Director/Designer / *Diane Jaroch*

Photographer / *Baldwin Coolidge*

Typeface / *Minion*

Printer / *Toppan Printing Co.*

Paper / *86# New Age Matte Coat*

New England Views

PROJECT STATEMENT

This book is a retrospective of the work of Baldwin Coolidge,
a photographer who opened his studio in Boston in 1878
and worked for four decades capturing images of New
England. Duotone printing was essential in order to replicate
the sepia tones of the originals, but this limited the page
count to 200 because of its expense. How to organize all of
the material into these 200 pages was the biggest part of
the design challenge, the luxury of one image per page being
impossible. Photographs of similar content were paired,
making room for the most dramatic ones to be featured in
full-page bleeds, adding variety and contrast to the layout.
Keeping the trim size to a modest 10.5 x 9 inches gave
the book a more intimate, photo album feeling and made the
volume extremely easy to hold and enjoy. Ultimately, the
design simply sought to enhance the beauty and historical
value of these wonderful photographs.

Authors / *Deborah Rothschild, Ellen Lupton,*
and Darra Goldstein
Publisher / *Yale University Press*
Design Firm / *Cooper-Hewitt, National Design Museum,*
New York, NY
Art Director/Designer / *Ellen Lupton*
Illustrators / *Stenberg Brothers*
Photographer / *Jim Frank*
Typeface / *Bureau Grotesque, Airport Gothic, and Scala*
Printer / *Studley Press*
Paper / *Gilbert Esse, Mead Moistrite*
Client / *Cooper-Hewitt, National Design Museum and*
Williams College of Art

Graphic Design in the Mechanical Age

PROJECT STATEMENT

This is a catalogue for the exhibition of the same name,
organized by Williams College Museum of Art in association
with the Cooper-Hewitt. The book is directed at a general
audience, with special interest for designers and art histori-
ans. The special edition jacket was made by reproducing
a poster from the exhibition and folding it down to become
the jacket. The jacket is thus literally a wrapper, a piece
of material folded around an object. Flat posters were sold
in the museum shops.

Author / Anthony J. Labbé
Publisher / American Federation of Arts and the University
of Washington Press
Design Firm / Doyle Partners, New York, NY
Creative Director / Stephen Doyle
Designer / Craig Clark
Typefaces / Trade Gothic, FF Scala, Rockwell, Craw Modern,
Bureau Grotesque, Matrix Script, Modern, News Gothic,
Lucida Sans, Engravers, CG Devine, Falstaff, Grotesque,
Spartan, Mrs Eaves
Printer / South China Printing

Shamans, Gods, and Mythic Beasts: Colombian Gold and Ceramics in Antiquity

PROJECT STATEMENT

The American Federation of Arts sponsored this traveling
exhibition and the accompanying catalogue. An exhibition of
such artifacts risked, they thought, the danger of being perceived as a lackluster academic exercise. Their brief to us
was, "Help!"

Our first contribution to the editorial process was to refuse
to design the book if they called it *The Gold of El Dorado*
(a title that was eventually squelched). Second, we blotted out
all the maroon and cobalt velvet backgrounds against which the
artifacts had been photographed. The rest was easy, devising
a color palette from the artwork and printing in stochastic so
that minuscule type could be rendered in 4/c. The bright white
pages sometimes looked too stark against this ancient art,
so we ground some pre-Colombian dirt into some of the pages
for a modern antiqued look.

Author/Publisher / *The Minneapolis Institute of Arts*
Design Firm / *Larsen Design & Interactive, Minneapolis, MN*
Creative Director / *Richelle Huff*
Designers / *Todd Nesser and Elizabeth Kaney*
Photographers / *Gary Mortensen, Robert Fogt, and Alec Soth*
Typeface / *Centaur*
Printer / *Diversified Graphics*
Binding / *Midwest Editions*
Paper / *Sappi Warren Lustro Dull*

Treasures from the Minneapolis Institute of Arts

PROJECT STATEMENT

Treasures from the Minneapolis Institute of Arts was
commissioned to salute the Institute's 115-year history and
celebrate its collection. Larsen added a qualifier: we would
not permit the book design to interfere with the art. *Treasures* succeeds on those terms: Each page isolates a master-
piece, and special care was taken to reproduce each work
in its original colors. Working with existing transparencies,
many of them over thirty years old, was a challenge, but the
printer brought proofs to the institute, and color was
checked alongside the original art. It was this attention, this
detail, along with the collection's vibrant pieces, that gives
the book its richness.

Authors/Artists / *Various*
Publisher / *North Carolina State University*
Art Director/Designer / *Beth Clawson*
Photographer / *Beth Clawson*
Typefaces / *Minion Regular, Minion Italic, Bell Gothic,*
Frutiger 67, Warehouse
Printer / *Theo Davis Sons, Inc.*
Paper / *Mohawk Superfine 80# Text and Cover*

Windhover

PROJECT STATEMENT

Windhover is North Carolina State University's visual arts
and literary publication. Inspired by the famous war recruitment posters of J.M. Flagg, I incorporated the "I Want You"
message into the process through which submissions were
collected and chosen for the journal. This edition utilizes
an army figurine as an abstract representation of the submit-
ters, the reader, and myself. I found words in each of the
written entries to further support the visual language I developed for the book.

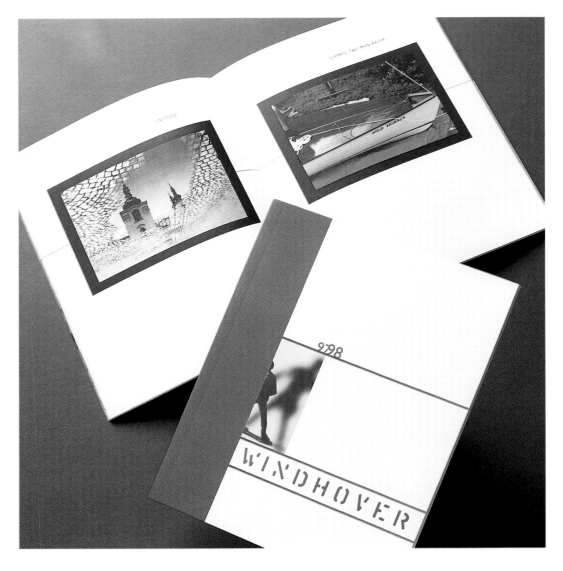

Editors / *Michael Bell and Szetsung Leong*
Client / *The Future Project*
Design Firm / *reasonsense,® South Pasadena, CA*
Art Directors/Designers / *Rebeca Méndez and Szetsung Leong*
Photographers / *Various*
Typeface / *Franklin Gothic*
Publisher / *The Monacelli Press*
Paper / *Monadnock Dulcet 80# Text*

Slow Space

PROJECT STATEMENT

For the cover design of *Slow Space,* through the use of
fluorescent colors against metallic inks, thin typographic
outlines, and corroded images to form the title of the book,
I attempt to convey a sense of instability, addressing the
primary idea of the book's content: matter as a delay.

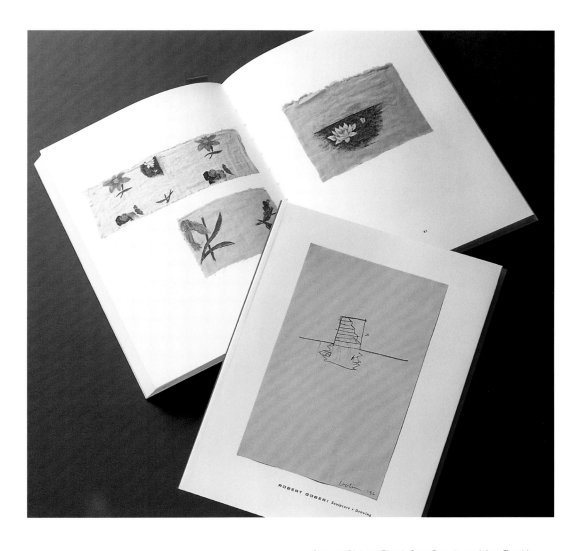

Authors / Richard Flood, Gary Garrels, and Ann Temkin
Publisher / Walker Art Center
Design Firm / Walker Art Center, Minneapolis, MN
Designer / Aaron King
Typefaces / Cooper Black, Eurostile, Jansen
Printer / Friesens
Paper / Mohawk Superfine

Robert Gober: Sculpture and Drawing

PROJECT STATEMENT

The exhibition catalogue *Robert Gober: Sculpture and Drawing* was intended to chronicle primarily the drawings of this contemporary artist and includes three critical essays, an extensive interview with the artist, and comprehensive illustrations of the work. The concept and aesthetic evolved out of collaborative discussions between the designer, the curator, and the artist. The book uses a toothy, off-white uncoated paper to highlight the subtle textures and hues of the artist's drawings, from coffee-stained pen-and-ink drawings on crinkled paper to floral patterns painted on fabric. Using the poetry of Walt Whitman and the films of Alfred Hitchcock, the essay by curator Richard Flood is treated visually as a cinematic journey through the American psyche. Meant to be subdued, informal, yet elegant (a red ribbon is used as a bookmark), the catalogue retains a certain amount of the restrained drama found in Robert Gober's work. Like the artist's work, the book expresses an apparent simplicity and classicism that reveal an edgier psychology upon deeper reflection.

Author / *K. Michael Hays*
Publisher / *MIT Press*
Design Firm / *MIT Press, Design Department, Cambridge, MA*
Designer / *Jean Wilcox*
Illustrators / *Stan Allen and Jean Wilcox*
Typeface / *Meta*
Printer / *Phoenix Color, Quebecor Books*
Paper / *Finch Fine*

Hays: Architecture Theory Since 1968

PROJECT STATEMENT

The typographic elements — rules, bars, and dashes —
suggest a timeline for this anthology on architectural theory.
The text is set up linearly: the running heads, author names,
and folios run continuously on one line. "Hot keys" appear
in the margins, linking the reader to other texts in the book.

The linear theme extends to the cover, where a diagram
and embossed typographic terrain merge. The cover best
embodies the book's design concept, which reflects the
author's view that there is not one architectural theory but
many, and they can intersect with one another at random. The
diagram represents architecture, the superimposed embossing conveys the multiplicity of interpretations in the field.

Author / *Eve Blau*
Publisher / *The MIT Press*
Design Firm / *The MIT Press, Design Department, Cambridge, MA*
Designer / *Jean Wilcox*
Typeface / *Geometric*
Printer / *Phoenix Color, Quebecor Books*
Paper / *Utopia #3 Matte*

Architecture of Red Vienna

PROJECT STATEMENT

This book is about the housing and programs initiated in socialist Vienna from 1919 to 1934. The design was inspired by the exhibitions the municipality erected for public dissemination of information. As the book designer, my concerns were no different from those of the city planners — to present and communicate clearly the vast archive of visual and written materials. The twenty-one-figure grid for the chapter openers and cover emphasize the breadth of work that went on at that time.

Author / *Chief Lelooska*
Publisher / *Callaway Editions*
Design Firm / *Callaway Editions, New York, NY*
Art Director / *Nicholas Callaway*
Designer / *Jennifer Wagner*
Illustrator / *Chief Lelooska*
Typeface / *Mrs Eaves*
Printer / *Palace Press International*
Paper / *140 gsm NPI Woodfree*

Spirit of the Cedar People

PROJECT STATEMENT

Spirit of the Cedar People is the second book in a story-
telling series devoted to preserving the spoken word. It was
made for both parent and child and is oversized to give a
sense of enveloping the entire family. I wanted the book to
look and feel magical to complement the unusual tales. Each
book in the series will capture the spirit of a particular region
and present the art with as much pride as possible, giving
the words the power they deserve.

Author / *Mother Goose*
Publisher / *Harry N. Abrams, Inc.*
Design Firm / *Harry N. Abrams, Inc., New York, NY*
Designer / *Darilyn Lowe Carnes*
Illustrator / *Vernon Grant*
Typeface / *Weiss*
Printer / *Canale Printing*
Paper / *135 gsm Perigord Matte, Coated Stock*

Vernon Grant's Mother Goose

PROJECT STATEMENT

The design of this book is simple, yet witty, especially in the handling of the typography. Vernon Grant's whimsical, boldly colored illustrations made him "America's favorite children's artist," according to *Life* magazine. Letters tumbling, lines zig-zagging, and words jumping were a natural outgrowth of his humorous caricatures. To move the eye sprightly from illustrations to rhymes, titles were eliminated in favor of bold type for the first line of the rhyme. The eye finally drops to the folios, which are bracketed by the slanted parallel lines that characteristically adorn Grant's signature in the illustrations.

Author / *Willi Kunz*
Publisher / *Verlag Niggli AG*
Design Firm / *Willi Kunz Associates, Inc., New York, NY*
Designer / *Willi Kunz*
Typeface / *Univers*
Printer / *Heer Druck AG*
Fabricator / *Burkhardt AG*
Paper / *Hanno Art 170 gr.*

Typography: Macro- and Microaesthetics

PROJECT STATEMENT

The design of effective typography — that is, typography
the reader can comprehend and understand — is based
on certain fundamental principles. Without these principles,
typography cannot communicate, as language cannot
communicate without grammar, vocabulary, and syntax. As
long as letters, words, and sentences are used to transmit
information, these principles will remain valid — even in
the dawning age of electronic media. In demonstrating how
these principles are put into practice, *Typography: Macro-
and Microaesthetics* provides artistic and technical instruc-
tion for students, typographic designers, architects, and
professionals in allied creative fields.

Author / *Randall Rothenberg*
Publisher / *The Monacelli Press*
Design Firm / *Pentagram Design, New York, NY*
Art Director / *Lowell Williams*
Designer / *Julie Hoyt*
Photographer / *David Grimes*
Typefaces / *Century Expended, Helvetica*
Printer / *CS Graphics*
Paper / *Condat Matte*

Pentagram Book Five

PROJECT STATEMENT

Pentagram Book Five is intended to be a valuable resource
for designers, illustrators, artists, photographers, and image-
makers as well as anyone inspired by a Pentagram design.
It presents a body of work produced in the last five years in
the firm of fifty case histories, each with an overview stating
the project's objective, an analysis of the design process,
the rationale for the design recommendations, and the
"moral of the story" — anecdotal narratives told from the
point of view of the designers and clients.

Publishers / *Art Center College of Design/Archetype Press*
Design Firm / *Archetype Press, Pasadena, CA*
Art Director / *Vance Studley*
Designers / *Students of the Art Center College of Design*
Typefaces / *53 fonts of foundry, wood, and*
digital polymer plates
Printer / *Archetype Press*
Paper / *Neenah Classic Crest 80# Text*

Pressing Issues

PROJECT STATEMENT

The intent of *Pressing Issues*, a completely hand-produced book, was to reveal through foundry type and digital plastic plates the subtle nuances of language in letterforms. The text describes personal observations about social dilemmas we are experiencing as we approach the new millennium. Printing these "headlines" of today by methods of fine presswork lifts the text from the level of newspapers and periodicals and places it at the level of high literature.

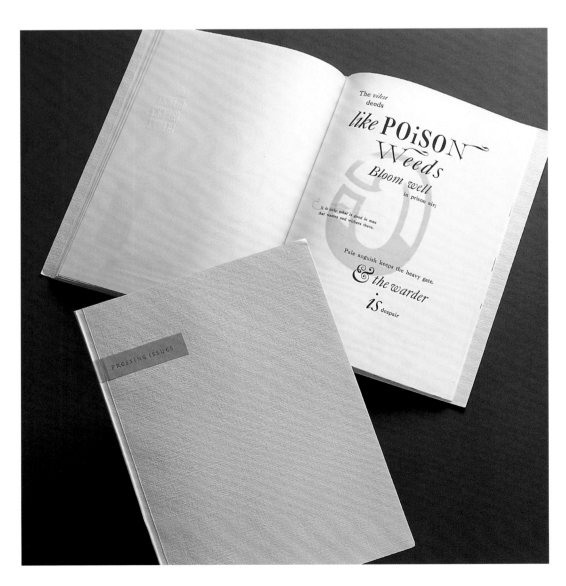

Author / Dan Wakefield

Publisher / The Herron Press

Design Firm / Paul Brown, Bloomington, IN

Art Director / Paul Brown

Illustrator / Paul Brown

Typeface / Bulmer

Printers / Aaron Alvis, Sarah Nevin

Fabricators / Debra Ikeda, Mary Hamilton Shaw

Paper / Frankfort White, French Marbled

Autumn Full of Apples

PROJECT STATEMENT

This edition of *Autumn Full of Apples* continues the imagery created by the author through the illustrations, the use of materials, and the packaging.

Author / *Ben Katchor*

Publisher / *Pantheon Books*

Design Firm / *Alfred A. Knopf Publishing Group, New York, NY*

Art Directors / *Chip Kidd and Marjorie Anderson*

Designers / *Chip Kidd and Misha Beletsky*

Illustrator / *Ben Katchor*

Printer / *R. R. Donnelley & Sons*

Paper / *80# French Vanilla Opaque*

The Jew of New York

PROJECT STATEMENT

Ben Katchor's characters roam a waking dream world set in New York circa 1830. The atmosphere is realistic and fantastic, concrete and absurd. Plans to carbonate all of Lake Erie for bottling purposes seem to make perfect sense, as do newspaper ads decrying the evils of onanism and menus that feature "Oarlock Soup" and "Bullock Heart Stuffed with Veal Forcemeat." You don't see the two embossed characters on the front right away — they enter your subconscious first, as does this winsome, enigmatic story.

Author / *Michael Tobias*
Publisher / *Smart Art Press*
Design Firm / *Smart Art Press, Santa Monica, CA*
Designer / *Tracey Shiffman*
Photographer / *Rocky Schenck*
Typefaces / *Centaur, Centaur Expert*
Printer / *Delta Graphics*
Paper / *Starwhite Vicksburg 70# Text, Gilbert Gilclear Vellum*

Jan & Catharina

PROJECT STATEMENT

From the beginning, the author and editor knew that this novella — a contemporary mystery and love story spanning three centuries — should be illustrated. Marrying the contemporary and antique qualities of the story while retaining the air of "mystery" led to the selection of Rocky Schenck's photographs and the use of details from Vermeer's paintings. Tracey Shiffman's choice of vellum for the illustrations, so that the text is revealed through the veil of the Vermeer paintings, brilliantly expressed the multi-layered content of the book, and her refined design sensibility deftly resolved the historical sweep of the novella.

Author / *Umberto Eco*
Publisher / *Columbia University Press*
Design Firm / *Columbia University Press, New York, NY*
Art Director/Designer / *Linda Secondari*
Typefaces / *Trajan, Shelly Andate, Bembo*
Printer / *Maple Vail*

Serendipities: Language and Lunacy

PROJECT STATEMENT

The target audience for this book is the general reader, one familiar with the work of Umberto Eco and interested in a slim volume exploring the benefits resultant of misunderstandings. The designer explored, visually, the nature of surfaces as a vehicle for understanding. By laying the title over itself, she created a surrealist sense of a shadow not relating to the image that is casting it — an idea of beauty through confusion that seems to address Eco's basic argument.

Author / *Patti Seery*

Client / *The E.M. Bakwin Collection of Asmat Art*

Design Firm / *Kerosene Halo, Chicago, IL*

Art Directors/Designers / *Thomas Wolfe and Greg Sylvester*

Photographers / *Patti Seery, Mike Pepper, and Don Hasman*

Typeface / *Hoefler Text*

Printer / *Jet Lithocolor*

Paper / *Gmund Bier Papier 92# Cover and Mokuba (Flysheet);
Georgia-Pacific Proterra 70# Text; Appleton Utopia One Dull
80# Text; Wyndstone Kabok 52# Cover*

Journey to Asmat

PROJECT STATEMENT

This book was created to commemorate the exhibition
of the E.M. Bakwin Collection of Asmat Art. This private
collection features exotic wood carvings from Asmat, a
cultural group located on the western coast of the island of
New Guinea. The book is divided into two sections, the first
of which presents the history of art in the culture of the
Asmat people. The essay for this section details their roots
in head-hunting and cannibalism and its influence on their
wood carvings. The second section showcases artwork
from the Bakwin collection and provides an explanation of
the work, as well as the meaning of the symbols found in
each piece.

Author / *Jock McDonald*
Design Firm / *Seven Design, San Francisco, CA*
Art Director / *Michael Cronan*
Designer / *Lee Hutchinson*
Photographer / *Jock McDonald*
Typeface / *Adobe Bembo*
Printer / *The Stinehour Press*
Paper / *Starwhite Vicksburg Archiva 100# Text*

The China Book

PROJECT STATEMENT

This is a limited-edition book, showcasing the beautiful photography of Jock McDonald taken while traveling in China. The goal of the project was to showcase the collection in a simple, elegant format that would allow the photographs to speak for themselves. Using simple Chinese elements such as a square cover, Chinese fabric, and an accordion fold, this goal became a reality in a very inviting package.

The China Book brings together classic design principles to give the viewer a pleasant journal into the alluring photography of Jock McDonald.

Author / *Joan L. Naess Lewin*
Publisher / *Joan L. Naess Lewin and*
the Marian Chance Foundation
Design Firm / *Greany Design, Baltimore, MD*
Art Director/Designer / *Gerry Greany*
Illustrators / *Joel Holland and Gerry Greany*
Typefaces / *Memphis, New Baskerville*
Printer / *Collins Lithographing*
Paper / *Mohawk Options Cover, Mohawk Opaque Text*

Dance Therapy Notebook

PROJECT STATEMENT

Dance Therapy Notebook is a collection of Joan Lewin's thoughts about her work as a dance therapist. Compiled over several years, these notes have been organized to serve as a resource and inspiration for other therapists. The overall texture of the book picks up on the idea of a journal with thin horizontal background rules that also suggest the "floor" referred to in the text. Joel Holland created the spontaneous folio collages that enhance the personal qualities of the text and provide a surprise at the bottom of each page.

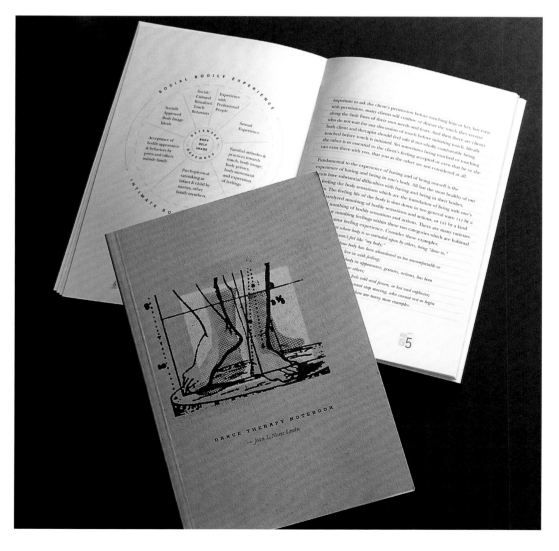

Author / *Naomi Sawelson-Gorse*
Publisher / *The MIT Press*
Design Firm / *The MIT Press Design Department,*
Cambridge, MA
Designer / *Ori Kometani*
Typefaces / *Cheltenham, Monotype Grotesque, Shelley*
Printer / *Quebecor Printing*
Paper / *70# Utopia 3*

Women in Dada

PROJECT STATEMENT

This book makes the case that women's changing role
in European and American society was critical to Dada. The
image of a woman's leg on the cover is also a graphic motif
in the book, used as an alternative to the conventional point-
ing index finger icon.

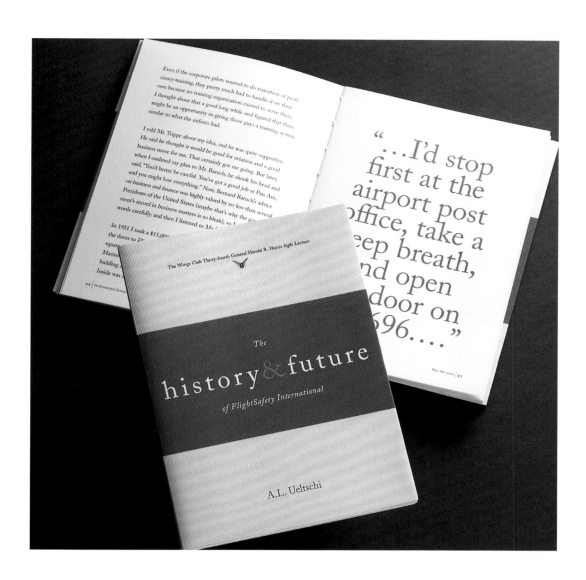

Author / William Garvey

Publisher / FlightSafety International, Inc.

Design Firm / Fuller Dyal & Stamper, Austin, TX

Designer / Christophe Muñiz

Typeface / Adobe Caslon

Printer / The Whitley Company

Paper / Mohawk Superfine Ultrafelt, Smooth, and Eggshell

The History and Future of FlightSafety International

Author / *Logan Ward*

Publishers / *The Field Museum, University of Chicago Press*

Design Firm / *studio blue, Chicago, IL*

Art Director / *Kathy Fredrickson and Cheryl Towler Weese*

Designers / *Cheryl Towler Weese and Gail Wiener*

Illustrator / *studio blue*

Photographer / *Michael Tropea*

Typefaces / *Theserif, Trade Gothic*

Printer / *Mondadori*

An Explorer's Guide to the Field Museum

PROJECT STATEMENT

This guidebook, geared to an audience of kids and grand-
parents, tries to convey the excitement of scientific pursuit
and clearly guide a visitor through a complex natural history
museum. Objects from the collection are removed from
their vitrines and presented as specimens for the reader to
study, or environments for the reader to explore. Maps
on the inside front cover and each spread locate every speci-
men in the museum.

Editors / *Peter Hall, Michael Bierut, and Tibor Kalman*
Publisher / *Princeton Architectural Press*
Design Firm / *Pentagram Design, New York, NY*
Art Directors / *Michael Bierut and Tibor Kalman*
Designers / *Michael Bierut, Tibor Kalman, and Michael English*
Typeface / *News Gothic*
Printer / *Dai Nippon*

Tibor Kalman: Perverse Optimist

PROJECT STATEMENT

Tibor Kalman: Perverse Optimist is the comprehensive monograph of the late designer's work and ideas, with essays and other commentary from clients, collaborators, critics, and friends.

Reducing a lifelong body of work to a single volume was not easy, especially when the subject was the notoriously provocative and contrary but essentially big-hearted Tibor. He worked closely with the designers and editors throughout the process, lovingly questioning every convention of book design, including the need for a title page or table of contents (the book contains neither). On the other hand, the book is generous with information, with many different voices weighing in at various points on Tibor and the history of M&Co. The text-free cover was meant to turn the book into an object.

With Tibor's reputation as a maddening collaborator, I began this project with some trepidation. To my surprise, the experience was a joy from start to finish. I miss him.

Author / *Catherine Puglisi*
Publisher / *Phaidon Press*
Design Firm / *Phaidon Press, New York, NY*
Art Director / *Alan Fletcher*
Designer / *Isambard Thomas*
Typeface / *Univers Condensed*

Caravaggio

PROJECT STATEMENT

Caravaggio is the first monograph to explore the artist's work, making full use of new research and dramatic recent discoveries. The colorful and lucid design breathes new life into works that are centuries old.

Author / T. A. Marder
Publisher / Abbeville Press
Design Firm / Abbeville Press, Inc., New York, NY
Art Director / Patricia Fabricant
Designer / Joel Avirom
Photographer / Joseph S. Martin
Typeface / Stempel Schneidler
Printer / Dai Nippon Printing Co.
Paper / 157 gsm Japanese Matte Coated Stock

Bernini

Author / *Lloyd Jones*
Publisher / *John Ross*
Design Firm / *High Tide Press, New York, NY*
Art Director/Designer/Illustrator / *John Ross*
Typefaces / *Palatino, Wood Type*
Typographer / *Kent LeFebvre/Signs Plus*
Printer / *High Tide Press*
Binding / *Hope Bindery*
Paper / *Arches Cover, Rives BFK, Lenox 100, Stonehenge,
Lana Cover, Coventry, French Speckletone*

Birds of Manhattan

PROJECT STATEMENT

My printshop contains a motorized Brand etching press and
a Vandercook 219 proving press. The type is printed letterpress, either from Linotype slugs or hand set. Display type
is from a collection of wood and metal faces assembled over
the years, including some old fonts from the nineteenth
century. The collagraph (a print pulled from a collage plate
of cardboard, paper, sand, fabric, and found objects) is a particularly favored technique of mine and most of my images
are created by this method.

I do not bind my books, but use several binders whose
work I have come to respect for their craftsmanship and ability. I have clear ideas as to what form these bindings should
take to complement my own work. I am also convinced that
text and image should reinforce and relate to each other:
simple concept, but difficult achievement.

Authors / *Harriet Stratis, Martha Tedeschi,*
Bridd Salvesen, et al.
Publisher / *The Art Institute of Chicago*
Design Firm / *studio blue, Chicago, IL*
Art Director / *Kathy Fredrickson and Cheryl Towler Weese*
Designers / *Joellan Kames, Cheryl Towler Weese,*
and Gail Wiener
Typographer / *Paul Baker Typography*
Typeface / *Monotype Walbaum, Monotype Grotesque,*
Franklin Gothic
Printer / *Meridian Printing*
Paper / *Mohawk Vellum*

The Lithographs of James McNeill Whistler

PROJECT STATEMENT

Whistler was a prolific lithographer, and this *catalogue raisonné* lovingly documents each stage of every lithograph the artist made. It also catalogues much of the ephemera related to Whistler's lithography — the artist's correspondence with his printmaker, his accounting, his personal and publication history, and the watermarks embedded in each of the papers Whistler used.

Throughout this 1,000-page tome, we tried to introduce visual variety and a clear system of organization while remaining true to the fussy, aesthetic, Victorian minimalism that characterizes Whistler's work.

Publisher / University of Nebraska
Design Firm / University of Nebraska, Lincoln, NE
Designer / Richard Eckersley
Illustrator / Edward Hopper
Typeface / Kim Essman
Printer/Binder / Data Reproductions Corporation
Typefaces / Adobe Sabon, Helvetica Condensed
Paper / Glatfelter 55# Natural
Printer / University of Nebraska Printing Department

Bordeaux

Author / John Hopkins
Publisher / Cadmus Editions
Design Firm / Cadmus Editions, Belvedere Tiburon, CA
Creative Director/Designer / Jeffrey Miller
Illustrator / Ahmed Yacoubi
Typeface / Guardi
Printer / Cushing-Malloy
Fabricator / James Tapley, Hand Bookbinder
Paper / Glatfelter 60#

The Tangier Diaries, 1962–1979

PROJECT STATEMENT

The Tangier Diaries, 1962–1979 is intended for an audience
interested in contemporary literary culture. Given that
this work is extracted from seventeen years of diary entries
chronicling literary life in Tangier, Morocco, I wanted the
presentation to appear informal — but within a tight format
that would allow both a compact trade edition in wrappers
and an elegant signed limited edition in boards. Excellence of
design was, I believe, achieved by managing the stretch
between a utilitarian trade edition and an elegant signed limited edition from the same set of printed sheets.

Design Firm / *Chermayeff & Geismar Inc., New York, NY*
Creative Director / *Tom Geismar*
Designers / *Tom Geismar and Emanuela Frigerio*
Photographer / *Dave Hoffman*
Typefaces / *Adobe Monotype Bodoni, Bodoni Book*
Printer / *Grafiche Mariano*
Paper / *Bias gr150*
Authors / *Tom Geismar and Harvey Kahn*
Publisher / *Harry N. Abrams Inc.*

Spiritually Moving

PROJECT STATEMENT

Over sixty years ago, the photographer Walker Evans proposed to photograph various collections of the Metropolitan Museum of Art "in such a way that all atmosphere of scholarship, art history, aesthetic theory and analysis, cultural explanation, and academic tabulation is absent; so that the pictures are presented solely for the excitement and surprise these things carry in themselves." In recording and presenting this extraordinary collection of American folk art sculpture, we have attempted to capture that same spirit, employing specially photographed, highly detailed images, an unusually large format, and the best-quality platemaking, paper, and printing technology to create a virtual museum visit, and to demonstrate convincingly that folk art can indeed be art.

Author / *Albert Watson*
Publisher / *Rizzoli International*
Design Firm / *No. 11, Incorporated, New York, NY*
Art Director / *Giovanni C. Russo*
Designers / *Giovanni C. Russo and Carrie Hunt*
Photographer / *Albert Watson*
Typeface / *Requiem*
Printer / *Sergio Tramontano*
Fabricator / *Fabio Fassolino, Studio F.P.*

Maroc

PROJECT STATEMENT

Albert Watson's *Maroc* was designed to reflect an artist's journal. I kept the typography and layout timeless, yet graphically dynamic, striving to create a modern sense of elegance for an audience of art book lovers. I feel the piece develops a harmony between photography and type that creates rhythm and surprise while one flips through the book.

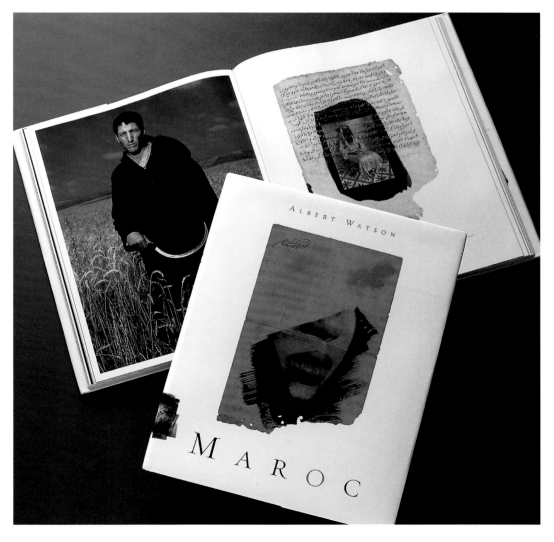

Publisher / *Phaidon Press*
Design Firm / *Phaidon Press, New York, NY*
Art Director / *Alan Fletcher*
Designer / *Julia Hasting*
Typeface / *Din Mittelschrift*

Cream: Contemporary Art in Culture

PROJECT STATEMENT

For *Cream: Contemporary Art in Culture,* the goal was to create a book that serves as both an *objet* of contemporary design and as an exhibition-in-a-book. One hundred emerging artists are featured in its giant, full-color pages. The large size requires the reader to engage with the book physically as well as mentally.

Publisher / *Hammond, Incorporated*
Design Firm / *Pentagram Design, New York, NY*
Art Director / *Michael Gericke*
Designer / *Su Matthews*

Hammond Atlas of the World

PROJECT STATEMENT

The Atlas of the World was the result of an ambitious five-year effort that brought together designers, mathematicians, cartographers, editors, and digital technology. The maps were created using a new projection based on fractal geometry called Optimal Conformal Projection, developed for Hammond by Mitchell Feigenbaum, a noted physicist known for his work in chaos theory. The collaboration led to the creation of the most accurate maps yet published.

The computer-generated maps were placed on three-dimensional digital models of the Earth's topographical features. The results are startlingly clear and textural. Pentagram's designers were consulted to develop a very strict system of type and color usage that would enhance the information, and embrace cartography's rich visual tradition. The atlas included an easily accessible index and introductory sections describing the world's languages, religions, and environmental concerns as well as the theory behind the new projections.

Exhibit.

AIGA Communication Graphics 19

December 9, 1998 – January 14, 1999
The Strathmore Gallery at the AIGA

Exhibition designed by Luke Hayman

Photograph by Jennifer Krogh

An exhibition celebrating the entries selected from the AIGA's prestigious *Communication Graphics 19* competition, the winning entries of which were profiled in last year's annual, *Graphic Design USA: 19.*

ions in the Strathmore Gallery

A Century of Innovative Book Design

January 27–February 26, 1999
The Strathmore Gallery at the AIGA

Commissioned and presented by
the University of Akron

Exhibition curated and designed by
Christopher Hoot

Photograph by Jennifer Krogh

The exhibition explored the influences of art, design theory, and technology on book design. Books were selected based on innovative presentation of text and images, use of materials, historical impact, and application of new technology.

Heavyweight Titles A Selection from the Pacific Titles Archives

March 15–April 16, 1999
The Strathmore Gallery at the AIGA

Photograph by Jennifer Krogh

An exhibition of historic film titles from the Pacific Titles Archives in Los Angeles that was presented in conjunction with the AIGA conference DFTV.001 (Design for Film and Television). The archival film titles, hand-painted on glass, date back to the Silent Era of motion pictures.

AIGA/Minnesota

20th Annual Design Competition Winners

June 23 – July 30, 1999
The Strathmore Gallery at the AIGA

Photograph by Jennifer Krogh

An exhibition of the twentieth annual celebration of design excellence from the Minnesota chapter of the AIGA. The competition was judged by John Fahy of Miramax Films (New York), Bonnie Siegler of Number Seventeen (New York), Jennifer Sterling of Jennifer Sterling Design (San Francisco), and Martin Venezky of Appetite Engineers (San Francisco)

Brand Design 50

May 6 – June 4, 1999
The Strathmore Gallery at the AIGA

Presented by the
Brand Design Association

Photograph by Jennifer Krogh

An exhibition of winners from *Brand Design 50,* the first competition to award excellence specifically in brand design as well as package design. *Brand Design 50* emerged from the tradition of the Package Design Council International's Gold Awards, its purpose redefined to acknowledge new challenges to the design profession, as package design has become part of a broader discipline of branding strategy. Winners were selected in three categories based on their function: consumer branding programs, corporate branding programs, and brand packaging. A complete list of winning entries and participants can be found online at: www.branddesign.org.

During 1999, the AIGA commissioned a series of posters to define functional areas of the new National Design Center and several to define critical issues faced that are germane to the organization, such as its mission statement, the definition of graphic design, or the staff's core values. Each designer working on a poster for a location was told the space where his or her piece would hang and offered total creative freedom except for a consistent motif across the bottom of each poster.

Posters

For the National Design Center

Printing: Noblet Serigraphie Inc., New York
Framing: Mascot Studio, New York

AIGA/Brand Design

Designed by Jack Anderson and Margaret Long
Hornall Anderson Design Works, Seattle

AIGA/NY

Designed by Paula Scher
Pentagram Design, New York

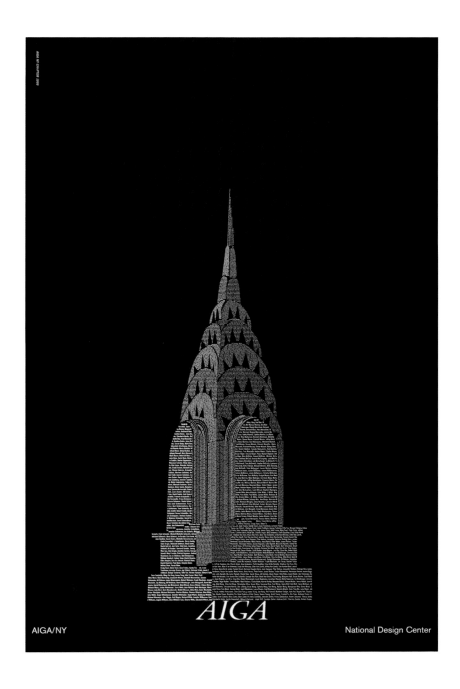

AIGA Mission

Designed by Kit Hinrichs
Pentagram Design, San Francisco

THE PURPOSE OF THE AIGA IS TO ADVANCE EXCELLENCE IN GRAPHIC DESIGN AS A DISCIPLINE, PROFESSION, & CULTURAL FORCE. THE AIGA PROVIDES LEADERSHIP IN THE EXCHANGE OF IDEAS & INFORMATION, THE ENCOURAGEMENT OF CRITICAL ANALYSIS & RESEARCH, AND THE ADVANCEMENT OF EDUCATION & ETHICAL PRACTICE. THE AIGA IS THE OLDEST & LARGEST MEMBERSHIP ASSOCIATION FOR GRAPHIC DESIGN.

AIGA

Chapter Relations

Designed by Luba Lukova
Luba Lukova Studios, New York

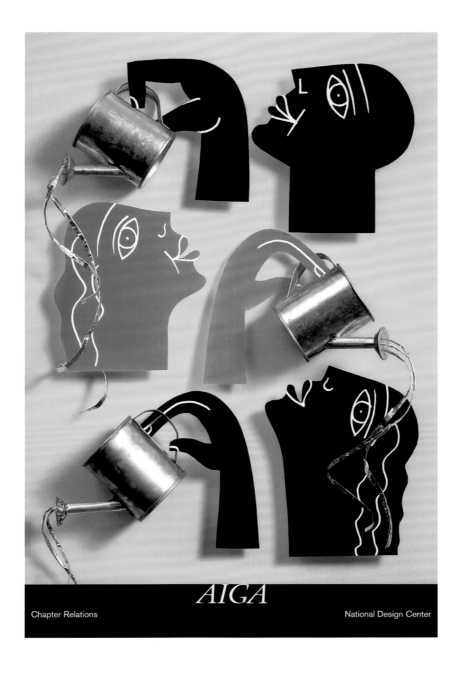

Competitions and Exhibitions

Designed by Steff Geissbuhler
Chermayeff & Geismar Inc., New York

Dance Captain

Designed by Michael Vanderbyl
Vanderbyl Design, San Francisco

Finance and Administration

Designed by Lynda Decker
Decker Design, Inc., New York

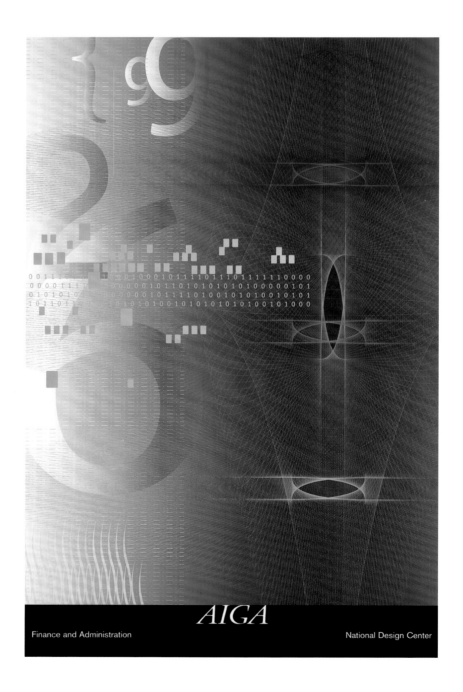

National Membership Center, Third Floor

Designed by Michael Mabry
Pentagram Design, New York, NY

Library

Designed by Lucille Tenazas
Tenazas Design, San Francisco

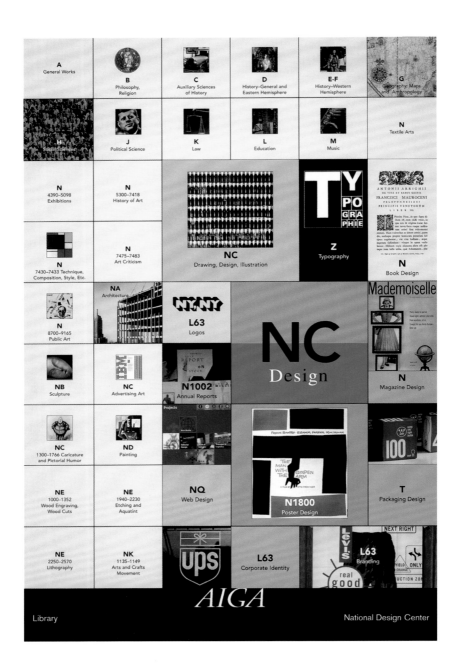

Membership

Designed by Woody Pirtle
Michael Mabry Design, San Francisco

National Presidents

Katie Chester
Context, Bristol, Rhode Island

I knew a man who taught himself

the meaning of words

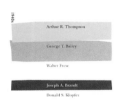

by listening to other people talking.

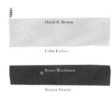

He thought "President" and "Precedent" were the same word.

AIGA

AIGA National Presidents

National Design Center

Publications

Designed by Jilly Simons
Concrete, Chicago

ed. 1. edition; editor. **2.** education.

E.D. election district.

Edam cheese. A mild, yellow Dutch cheese, pressed into balls and usually covered with red paraffin.

E·den (edn) *n.* **1.** In the Bible, the first home of Adam and Eve; Paradise. Also called "Garden of Eden." **2.** Any delightful place or dwelling; paradise. **3.** A state of bliss or ultimate happiness. [Middle English, from Late Latin *Eden*, from Greek *Eden*, from Hebrew *edhen*, "the place of pleasure."]

edge (ej) *n.* **1. a.** The usually thin, sharpened side of the blade of a cutting instrument, weapon, or tool. **b.** The degree of sharpness of a cutting blade. **2.** Keenness, as of desire or enjoyment; zest: *"His simplicity sets off the satire, and gives it a finer edge"* (William Hazlitt). **3.** A rim, brink, or crest, as of a cliff or ridge of hills. **4.** A dividing line or point of transition; a margin; a border: *"an edge of wintery chill"* (John Knowles). **5.** The line of intersection of two surfaces of a solid: *the edge of a brick.* **6.** A margin of superiority; an advantage: *a slight edge over the opposition.* —See Synonyms at **border.** —**on edge. 1.** Highly tense or nervous; irritable. **2.** Eagerly anticipatory; impatient. —**set one's teeth on edge.** *Informal.* **1.** To give one an unpleasant nervous reaction or sensation, as of tingling. **2.** To provoke strong feelings of irritation or annoyance. —**take the edge off.** To soften or dull, as the pleasure, excitement, or force of. —*v.* **edged, edging, edges.** —*tr.* **1.** To give an edge to; sharpen. **2.** To put a border or edge on. **3.** To advance or push gradually. —*intr.* To move gradually or hesitantly: *"She smiled almost slyly as she edged toward the mescal barrel"* (Malcolm Lowry). [Middle English *egge*, Old English *ecg*, edge, point, sword. See **ak-** in Appendix.*]

edg·y (eje) *adj.* **-ier, -iest. 1.** On edge; tense; nervous. **2.** The way one feels after setting an entire dictionary page. **3.** Daring to eliminate the tedious task of implementing phonetic spelling in hopes that no one will notice. **4.** With a sharp edge. **5.** With excessively sharp definition, as in painting or sculpture. —**edginess** *n.*

ed·i·ble (edebel) *adj.* **1. a.** Capable of being eaten. **b.** Fit to eat; nonpoisonous. **2.** Ready to be eaten. —*n.* Something fit to be eaten; food. Usually used in the plural. [Late Latin *edibilis*, from Latin *edere*, to eat. See **ed-** in Appendix.*] —**ed·ibility, edibleness** *n.*

e·dict (edikt) *n.* **1.** A decree or proclamation issued by an authority: *"The edict…extended to all natives… the rights of Roman citizenship"* (James Bryce). **2.** Any formal proclamation, command, or decree. [Latin *editum*, from *edicere*, to speak out, proclaim: *ex-,* out + *dicere,* speak (see **deik-** in Appendix*).]

ed·i·fi·ca·tion (edifekashen) *n.* Intellectual, moral, or spiritual improvement; enlightenment: *"this very day, in which I am now writing this book for the edification of the world"* (Sterne).

ed·i·fy (edefi) *tr.v.* **-fied, fying, -fies.** To instruct or enlighten so as to encourage moral or spiritual improvement. [Middle English *edifien*, from Old French *edifier*, from Latin *aedificare*, to build, instruct. See **edifice.**]. —**edifier** *n.*

ed·it (edit) *tr. v.* **-ited, -iting, -its. 1. a.** To make (written material) suitable for publication or presentation. **b.** To prepare an edition of for publication: *edit a collection of short stories.* **2.** To supervise the publication of (a newspaper or magazine, for example). **3.** To omit or eliminate; delete. Usually used with *out.* **4.** To integrate the component parts of (film, electronic tape, or sound track) by cutting, combining, and splicing. [Back-formation from EDITOR.]

edit. edition; editor.

e·di·tion (idishen) *n. Abbr.* **ed., edit. 1. a.** The entire number of copies of a publication printed from a single typesetting or other form of reproduction. Compare **printing. b.** A single copy from this group. **c.** A facsimile of an earlier publication having substantial changes or additions. **2. a.** Any of the various forms in which something is issued or produced, as publications, music, or stamps. **b.** Any of the forms in which a publication is produced: *a leather-bound edition.* **c.** One closely similar to an original; a version: *The boy was a smaller edition of his father.* **3.** An issue of a work identified by its editor or publisher: *the Oxford edition of Shakespeare.* **4.** All the copies of a single press run of a newspaper: *the morning edition.* [Old French, from Latin *editio,* a bringing forth, publication, from *edere* (past participle *edictus*), to bring forth, publish: *ex-,* out + *dare,* to give (see **do-** in Appendix*).]

e·di·ti·o prin·ceps (idisheo prinseps). *Latin.* First edition.

ed·i·tor (edeter) *n. Abbr.* **ed., edit. 1.** A person who edits a literary, artistic, or musical work for publication or public presentation. **2.** A person who supervises the policies or production of a publication. **3.** A person in charge of a department of a publication: *a sports editor.* **4.** One who writes editorials. **5.** A device for editing film, consisting basically of a splicer and viewer. [Late Latin, publisher, from Latin *edere,* to bring forth, publish. See **edition**]

ed·i·to·ri·al (edetoreel, -toreel) *n.* **1.** An article in a publication expressing the opinion of its editors or publishers. **2.** A commentary on radio or television expressing the opinion of the station or network. —*adj.* **1.** Of, concerning, or prepared by an editor or editors. **2.** Having the nature of an editorial in expressing opinion: *editorial comments.*

¹⁻³designer's notes (see **edg·y***)*

AIGA

Publications   National Design Center

AIGA **Confer**

AIGA **164 FIFTH AVENUE**
NEW YORK NY 10010

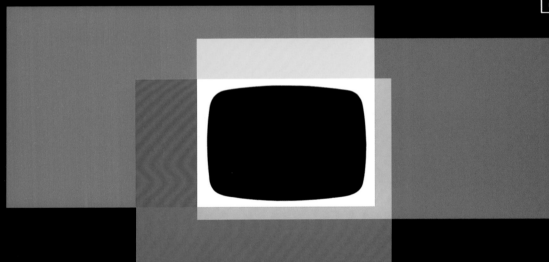

Presenting the first AIGA conference devoted to DESIGN for FILM + TELEVISION

AIGA/DFTV.001* American Institute of Graphic Arts Design for Film and Television Number One

March 12–13, 1999
New York, New York

Sixteen speakers, eight films, and four breaks — that was
the fast-paced, jam-packed format of DFTV, the AIGA's first
conference devoted to design for film and television. The booked-
to-capacity small-scale conference, programmed by guest conference directors Emily Oberman and Bonnie Siegler of Number
Seventeen in New York, was the AIGA's first exploration of
this young, vibrant, constantly mutating discipline. The two-day
conference took both a critical and a loving look at the visual
language being created at the intersection between the film,
television and graphic design disciplines.

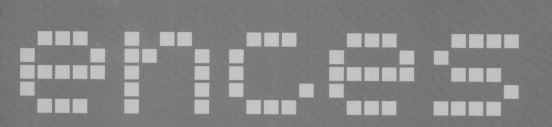

Upcoming Conferences

Collision
An AIGA Digital Design Conference
April 12–14, 2000
The Equitable Center, New York

Risk/Reward
AIGA National Business Design Conference
October 8–10, 2000
Center for the Arts, Yerba Buena Gardens,
San Francisco

America: Cult and Culture   The AIGA's Eighth Biennial National Design Conference

September 29–October 2, 1999
Las Vegas, Nevada

The AIGA's eighth biennial national design conference took place in Las Vegas — a surreal place where no juxtaposition is too absurd, no extravaganza too lurid, no sign is too big. "America: Cult and Culture" examined the production of design, media, and culture in our times at the grassroots, below-the-radar level, and on a mass scale. Organized by guest program director Chee Pearlman of *I.D. Magazine,* New York, with AIGA president Michael Bierut, AIGA executive director Richard Grefé, and an extended committee of design opinion leaders, "America: Cult and Culture" provided a nonstop, 24-hour visual and intellectual design barrage with something for everyone.

The American Institute of Graphic Arts (AIGA) is the oldest and largest professional association serving graphic designers in the United States. It is dedicated to the advancement of excellence and professionalism among designers, educators, and students engaged in type and book design, publications design, communications and corporate design, posters, package and branding strategy, interface and web design, and new-media design. Founded in 1914, the AIGA serves over 14,000 members organized in more than forty local chapters, through professional interest groups and on-campus student groups. AIGA activities offer designers the opportunity to develop relationships within the profession, share information, and advance respect for and understanding of the value of graphic design excellence on the part of business and the public. The AIGA conducts a program of competitions, exhibitions, professional seminars, educational activities, and publications to communicate the value of effective design. Publications include *Graphic Design USA,* the annual of the AIGA, which chronicles the work selected in national competitions each year for exhibition by the AIGA; the *AIGA Journal of Graphic Design;* a yearly membership directory; and occasional topical books. The AIGA regularly produces two biennial conferences in alternate years: the AIGA Design Conference, which celebrates American and international graphic design; and the AIGA Design Business Conference, which focuses on strategic business issues. The AIGA awards the most prestigious award in the graphic design profession — the AIGA Medal — and selects each year's most notable graphic design work in two juried competitions, *AIGA Communications Graphics* and *AIGA 50 Books /50 Covers.*

About the AIGA

AIGA

American Institute of Graphic Arts

The Capital and Capstone Campaign renovation of the AIGA National Design Center at 164 Fifth Avenue started five years ago. In 1998, we concluded the initial phase of the campaign.

We invested $2.5 million in the center by purchasing it and renovating it during that period, supported by a $1.3 million bond we will pay off over thirty years. The balance was raised from those who believe in the profession and its future, giving sums from $25 to $100,000.

Our most generous donors are now memorialized in steel on the mezzanine of the National Design Center. We want to thank everyone who has supported us and encourage others to contribute to the Capstone Campaign, which we hope will raise the final sums needed over the next eighteen months to complete the building's façade renovation and the Fund for the Future, which will continue to support new programming initiatives for the profession.

Supporters of these campaigns will also be memorialized on the mezzanine, next to the names of those generous and accomplished designers listed here.

$50,000+
Benefactors
Champion International Corporation
Digex, Inc.
Pentagram Design, Inc.

$25,000+
Patrons
Apple Computers, Inc.
Crosby Associates, Inc.
The I. Grace Company
Pentagram Design, Inc.

$10,000+
Sponsors
Addison Corporate Annual Reports
Harvey Bernstein Design Associates
Brennan Brothers
Chermayeff & Geismar, Inc.
Designframe, Inc.
Donovan and Green
Doyle Partners
Fine Arts Engraving Company
Frankfurt Balkind Partners
Gr8
Milton Glaser
Jessica Helfand/William Drenttel
Mirko Ilic
Jet Pak
Larsen Design Office, Inc.
Steve Liska
Emanuela Frattini Magnusson
Clement Mok
The Overbrook Foundation
Stan Richards
Anthony Russell
Arnold Saks Associates
Siegel and Gale, Inc.
Jennifer Sterling Design
TeamDesign
Vignelli Associates
Wechsler & Partners, Inc.

$5,000+
Donors
AdamsMorioka, Inc.
Primo Angeli
Appleton Papers
Bass/Yager & Associates
Buddy Berke
Carbone Smolan Associates
James Cross
David Cundy
Richard Danne & Associates
GL Lites On
Diana Graham
Hansen Design Company
Hawthorne/Wolfe
Steven Heller
The Hennegan Company
Hornall Anderson Design Works, Inc.
Alexander Isley
Kinetik Communication Design, Inc.
Judy Kirpich
Monica Little
Eric Madsen
Mary Scott
Beth Singer
Karen Skunta
Robert Star
Sussman/Prejza & Co., Inc.
Typogram, Inc.
Vanderbyl Design, Inc.
Ann Willoughby Design
Weyerhaeuser

$3,000+
Contributors
BlackDog
Doug Byers
Bob Callahan Design
Mark Coleman
Concrete [The Office of Jilly Simons]
Concrete Design Communications, Inc.
Michael Cronan
Joe Duffy
Joseph and Susan Feigenbaum
Martin Fox
Georgia-Pacific Papers
Bill Grant
Kent Hunter
Meyer Design Associates, Inc.
J. Abbott Miller
Milocraft, Inc.
Monadnock Paper Mills, Inc.
Elizabeth O'Keefe
Poulin + Morris
Wendy Richmond
Dugald Stermer

$1,000+
Contributors

Samuel N. Antupit
Dana Arnett
Eric Baker
Merrill Berman
Bernhardt Fudyma Design
Richard Bird
Roger Black
R.O. Blechman
David Boorstin Associates
John Coleman
Cooper Union
Tad Crawford
David Day
Sheila de Bretteville
Hugh Dubberly
John DuFresne
Alvin Eisenman
Miu Eng
Nancy and Joseph Essex
David Franek
Stephen Frykholm
Howard Glener
Roz Goldfarb
Richard Grefe
Carla Hall
Hallmark Cards,
    in honor of Saul Steinberg
Sylvia Harris
Jennifer Howard
Heidi Humphrey
Michael Josefowicz
Fritz Klaetke
Tamera Lawrence
David Leigh
Lippincott & Margulies
Ellen Lupton
Michael Mabry
Judith Majher
Anthony McDowell
Wynn Medinger
Jennifer E. Morla
Mark Murphy
Janou Pakter
Chee Pearlman
Shel Perkins
Grant Pound
Karen Salsgiver
Ellen Shapiro
Paul Shaw
Michael Soha
Lucille Tenazas
Beth Tondreau,
    in honor of Elissa Ichiyasu
George Tscherny
Clair Ultimo
Veronique Vienne
Wiggin Design Inc.
Fo Wilson
Allen Woodard
Bob Zeni

$100-1,000
Friends

Colleen M. Abrams
Dana Ahlfeldt
Justin C. Ahrens
Antonio Alcala
Jim Ales
Jason Anderson
Marty Anderson
Carol A. Ash
Kimberly Baer
Gary R. Baker
Georgette Ballance
Didier Bardon
Dennis Barnett
Andrea Baron
Jennifer Bass
Arthur Beckenstein
Helene R. Benedetti
Dominique Bernard
Timo Andrew Berry
Michael Bierut
Karl Bischoff
Jon Anders Bjornson
Jodi Bloom
Sharon Bodnar
Scott Bowers
Keith Branscombe
Robin Williams Brohm
Janine A. Bruttin
Ronn Campisi
Andrew Cantor
Scott Carroll
George T. Casale
Bernadette Castor
Lisa M. Catalone
Ken Cato
David Robert Cecchi
Mojca Cerjak
Susan T. Chait
Herman Chandra
Howard Clare
Annemarie Clark
Christopher Clark
John Clark
David Cohen
Timothy S. Cook
Thomas Corey
Susan Cotler-Block
Brett M. Critchlow
Edith S. Crocker
Stephen Crooks
Rita Daly
Donna David
Ken Diamond
Joseph A. DiGioia
Roseanne DiSanto
Kenneth Doherty
Melanie Doherty
Dan Donovan
Cynthia Eyring
Marlena Faxon
Martin Fiorillo
Peter Fishel
Gill Fishman

Martin Fitzpatrick
Leslie C. Fleming
Hope Fonte
Polly Franchine
Gretchen Frederick
Laurie Medeiros Freed
David A. Freedman
Kelly Hutchin Frey
Mark Freytag
David Fridberg
Joel Vann Fuller
Tony Gagliardi
Leslie Gans
Arch Garland
Judy Glenzer
Mieke Gondobintoro
Evelyn Goutas
Hester Greene
Edward Grigg
Robert Guthrie
Anissa Gutierrez
Jennifer Haas
Selina Hall
Nathan Hanneman
David Douglas Haring
Jeff Harrington
Kunio Hayashi
Tricia Hayden
Becky Heavner
Walter Herrington
Ken Hiebert
Linda Hinrichs
Susan Hochbaum
Sherrie Holdeman
Nigel Holmes
Samuel Hope
Linda L. Huber
Megan Hug
Rose L. Hunter
Daniel Jennewein
Paul Jensen
Mitchell Jones
Mary H. Junda
Karen Karabasz
Sebastian Kaupert
Nan Keeton
Eileen Kessler
Renee Khatami
Richard A. Klevgard
Jay Koenig
Denise Korn
Thomas Kowalski
Stephen Kraft
Charles Kreloff
Deanna Kuhlmann-Leavitt
Laura Latham
Michael Lauretano
Peggy Lauritsen
Marcia Lausen
David Lecours
Val Lefevre
Bob Leu
Joan D. Libera
Carlene Liscinsky

Theodore Lopez
Barbara J. Loveland
Claire Lukacs
Anthony Ma
Dennis Mabry
Laura MacKay
Nancy Mallett
Dave Malone
Erin Malone
Susan Marcus
Anne Masters
Mitchell Mauk
Marc Alain Meadows
Claudia Mendelsohn
Wendy Meyer
Scott Mires
Ron Miriello
Clement Mok
Hugh Montgomery
Robert Morehouse
Margaret Morton
Alfredo Muccino
Beth Nagy
Tori Napier
Cristiana Neri
Marty Neumeier
Jenny W. Ng
Claudia Nierman
Chris Noel
William O'Connor
Manuel A. Olmo
Andrew Patapis
Bennett Peji
Joyce Pekala
Stephanie Pesakoff
Bryan L. Peterson
Elaine Petschek
Leslie Phinney
Elizabeth J. Placke
Karen Pomeroy
Eduardo Posada del Real
Kashka Pregowska-Czerw
Wendy Pressley-Jacobs
Christopher Pullman
Patrick V. Racelis
Floyd M. Rappy
Kenneth Resen
Forrest Richardson
Valerie Richardson
Kay Ritta
Juliette Robbins
Jana M. Rocheleau
Marcia Romanuck
Lance Rutter
Dan Saal
Mark E. Sackett
Linda Santopietro
Lara Santos
Daniel Scharfman
Cara Schiavone

Ward Schumaker
Fred Seibert
Rochelle Seltzer
Jennifer Serota
Scott Severson
Jessica Shatan
Jonina Skaggs
Carol Sly
Grant Smith
Howard C. Smith
Tim Smith
Elizabeth Somoff
Tony Spaeth
Elliot Strunk
Tom Suzuki
Barbara Taff
Jill Tanenbaum
Kathleen Taylor
Megan A. Taylor
Robert Pat Taylor
Len Temple
Rick Tharp
Liz Throop
Steven J. Tomkiewicz
Annie W. Tong
Cheryl Towler Weese
Andres E. Tremols
Stephen Turgi
Ryo Urano
Edgar Uy
Andrea Van den Brulle
Bill Van Ingen
Petrula Vrontikis
Raymond L. Wandling
David L. Wasson
Cheryl A. Watson
Janine Weitenauer
Ann Werner
Lorraine Wild
Pamela L. Williams
Andrew Wilson
Soung Wiser
Jason Wittwer
Brad Woodworth
Jack Wooster
Marilyn Worseldine
Ann Worthington
Wang Xu
Chin-Chih Yang
Laurie Young
Edward H. Zahra, Jr.
Joanne Zamore

1998–1999
Board of Directors

Michael Bierut, *President*
Richard Grefé, *Executive Director*
Sam Shelton, *Chapter Presidents'
Council Chair*

Directors
Sean Adams, Maxey Andress,
Bart Crosby, Michael Donovan,
Steff Geissbuhler, Eric Madsen,
Clement Mok, Emily Oberman,
Samina Quraeshi, Lana Rigsby,
Mary Scott, Beth Singer, Lucille
Tenazas, Michael Vanderbyl

1999–2000
Board of Directors

Michael Bierut, *President*
Beth Singer, *Treasurer*
Richard Grefé, *Executive Director*
Mark Oldach, *Chapter Presidents'
Council Chair*

Directors
Sean Adams, Maxey Andress,
Bart Crosby, Michael Donovan,
Marc English, Peter Girardi, Eric
Madsen, Clement Mok, Jennifer
Morla, Emily Oberman, Lana
Rigsby, Mary Scott, Beth Singer,
Thomas Suiter

AIGA National Staff

Richard Grefé
Executive Director

Denise Wood
*Director of Information and
Member Services*

Deborah Aldrich
Director of Corporate Partnerships

Carolynn Jennings
*Director of Finance and
Administration*

Gabriela Mirensky
Program Coordinator

Alice Twemlow
Conference Program Coordinator

Rita Grendze
Special Projects

George Fernandez
Membership Coordinator

Marc Vassall
*Finance and Administration
Associate*

Jennifer Rittner
Project Coordinator

Megan Hackett
Information Assistant

Liv Vogel
Chapter Liaison

Christine Fischer
Customer Service Associate

Michelle Piano
Customer Service Associate

Johnny Ventura
Facilities Assistant

Joel Holland
Project Assistant

AIGA Chapters and Chapter Presidents 1998–1999

Arizona • David Rengifo
Atlanta • Bill Grant
Austin • Marc English
Baltimore • Kristin Seeberger
Birmingham • MaryAnn Charles
Boston • Jan Moscowitz
Chicago • Mark Oldach
Cincinnati • Tim Smith
Cleveland • Sheila Hart
Colorado • Rick Griffith
Dallas • John J. Conley
Detroit • Michael Besch
Honolulu • Michael Horton
Houston • Shawn Collier
Indianapolis • Stacy Kagiwada
Iowa • Steve Pattee
Jacksonville • Florence Haridan
Kansas City • Deb Lilla
Knoxville • Leland Hume
Las Vegas • Andrew Hershberger
Los Angeles • Moira Cullen
Miami • Maggy Cuesta
Minnesota • Douglas Powell
Nebraska • Trish Farrar
New Orleans • John Barousse
New York • Paula Scher
Upstate New York • Marj Crum
Oklahoma • Sarah Sears
Orange County •
  Anthony Columbini
Philadelphia • Caren Lipkin
  and Steve Williams
Pittsburgh • Bernard Uy
Portland • Susan Agre-Kippenhan
Raleigh • Jim Briggs
Richmond • Donand McCants
Salt Lake City • Dave Malone
San Diego • Maelin Levine
San Francisco • Shel Perkins
Seattle • David Betz
  and Richard Smith
St. Louis • Karen Handelman
Washington, DC •
  Tamera Lawrence
Wichita • Sherrie Holdeman

AIGA Chapters and Chapter Presidents 1999–2000

Arizona • David Rengifo
Atlanta • Peter Borowski
Austin • Sean Carnegie
Baltimore • Carl Cox
Birmingham • Jennifer Tatham
Boston • Amy Strauch
Chicago • Lance Rutter
Cincinnati • Tim Smith
Cleveland • Sheila Hart
Colorado • Clare Kelly
Dallas • John J. Conley
Detroit • Michael Besch
Honolulu • Michael Horton
Houston • Shawn Collier
Indianapolis • Stacy Kagiwada
Iowa • Karen Beach
Jacksonville • Florence Haridan
Kansas City • Michael Lamonica
Knoxville • Kenneth White
Las Vegas • Andrew Hershberger
Los Angeles • Moira Cullen
Miami • Maggy Cuesta
Minnesota • Douglas Powell
Nebraska • Brenda Lyman
New Orleans • Christy Bracken
New York • Paula Scher
Upstate New York • Marj Crum
Oklahoma • Casey Twenter
Orange County •
  Anthony Columbini
Philadelphia • Caren Lipkin
  and Rosemary Murphy
Pittsburgh • Bernard Uy
Portland • Susan Agre-Kippenhan
Raleigh • Christy White
Richmond • Donand McCants
Salt Lake City • Linda Sullivan
San Diego • Maelin Levine
San Francisco • Diane Carr
Seattle • David Betz
  and Richard Smith
St. Louis • Steve Hartman
Washington, DC •
  Tamera Lawrence
Wichita • Jeff Pulaski

Past Presidents
of the AIGA

1914–1915 William B. Howland
1915–1916 John Clyde Oswald
1917–1919 Arthur S. Allen
1920–1921 Walter Gilliss
1921–1922 Frederic W. Goudy
1922–1923 J. Thompson Willing
1924–1925 Burton Emmett
1926–1927 W. Arthur Cole
1927–1928 Frederic G. Melcher
1928–1929 Frank Altschul
1930–1931 Henry A. Groesbeck, Jr.
1932–1934 Harry L. Gage
1935–1936 Charles Chester Lane
1936–1938 Henry Watson Kent
1939–1940 Melbert B. Carey, Jr.
1941–1942 Arthur R. Thompson
1943–1944 George T. Bailey
1945–1946 Walter Frese
1947–1948 Joseph A. Brandt
1948–1950 Donald S. Klopfer
1951–1952 Merle Armitage
1952–1953 Walter Dorwin Teague
1953–1955 Dr. M. F. Agha
1955–1957 Leo Lionni
1957–1958 Sidney R. Jacobs
1958–1960 Edna Beilenson
1960–1963 Alvin Eisenman
1963–1966 Ivan Chermayeff
1966–1968 George Tscherny
1968–1970 Allen Hurlburt
1970–1972 Henry Wolf
1972–1974 Robert O. Bach
1974–1976 Karl Fink
1976–1977 Massimo Vignelli
1977–1979 Richard Danne
1979–1981 James Fogleman
1981–1984 David R. Brown
1984–1986 Colin Forbes
1986–1988 Bruce Blackburn
1988–1991 Nancye Green
1992–1994 Anthony Russell
1994–1996 William Drenttel
1996–1998 Lucille Tenazas

Past Recipients
of the AIGA Medal

Norman T.A. Munder, 1920
Daniel Berkeley Updike, 1922
John C. Agar, 1924
Stephen H. Horgan, 1924
Bruce Rogers, 1925
Burton Emmett, 1926
Timothy Cole, 1927
Frederic W. Goudy, 1927
William A. Dwiggins, 1929
Henry Watson Kent, 1930
Dard Hunter, 1931
Porter Garnett, 1932
Henry Lewis Bullen, 1934
Rudolph Ruzicka, 1935
J. Thompson Willing, 1935
William A. Kittredge, 1939
Thomas M. Cleland, 1940
Carl Purington Rollins, 1941
Edwin and Robert Grabhorn, 1942
Edward Epstean, 1944
Frederic G. Melcher, 1945
Stanley Morison, 1946
Elmer Adler, 1947
Lawrence C. Wroth, 1948
Earnest Elmo Calkins, 1950
Alfred A. Knopf, 1950
Harry L. Gage, 1951
Joseph Blumenthal, 1952
George Macy, 1953
Will Bradley, 1954
Jan Tschichold, 1954
P. J. Conkwright, 1955
Ray Nash, 1956
Dr. M. F. Agha, 1957
Ben Shahn, 1958
May Massee, 1959
Walter Paepcke, 1960
Paul A. Bennett, 1961
Wilhelm Sandberg, 1962
Saul Steinberg, 1963
Josef Albers, 1964
Leonard Baskin, 1965
Paul Rand, 1966
Romana Javitz, 1967
Dr. Giovanni Mardersteig, 1968
Dr. Robert R. Leslie, 1969
Herbert Bayer, 1970
Will Burtin, 1971

Milton Glaser, 1972

Richard Avedon, 1973

Allen Hurlburt, 1973

Philip Johnson, 1973

Robert Rauschenberg, 1974

Bradbury Thompson, 1975

Henry Wolf, 1976

Jerome Snyder, 1976

Charles and Ray Eames, 1977

Lou Dorfsman, 1978

Ivan Chermayeff and
  Thomas Geismar, 1979

Herb Lubalin, 1980

Saul Bass, 1981

Massimo and Lella Vignelli, 1982

Herbert Matter, 1983

Leo Lionni, 1984

Seymour Chwast, 1985

Walter Herdeg, 1986

Alexey Brodovitch, 1987

Gene Federico, 1987

William Golden, 1988

George Tscherny, 1988

Paul Davis, 1989

Bea Feitler, 1989

Alvin Eisenman, 1990

Frank Zachary, 1990

Colin Forbes, 1991

E. McKnight Kauffer, 1991

Rudolph de Harak, 1992

George Nelson, 1992

Lester Beall, 1992

Alvin Lustig, 1993

Tomoko Miho, 1993

Muriel Cooper, 1994

John Massey, 1994

Matthew Carter, 1995

Stan Richards, 1995

Ladislav Sutnar, 1995

Cipe Pineles, 1996

George Lois, 1996

Lucian Bernhard, 1997

Zuzana Licko and
  Rudy VanderLans, 1997

Louis Danziger, 1998

April Greiman, 1998

**Past Recipients of the
Design Leadership Award**

IBM Corporation, 1980

Massachusetts Institute of
  Technology, 1981

Container Corporation of America,
  1982

Cummins Engine Company, Inc.,
  1982

Herman Miller, Inc., 1984

WGBH Educational Foundation,
  1985

Esprit, 1986

Walker Art Center, 1987

The New York Times, 1988

Apple and Adobe Systems, 1989

The National Park Service, 1990

MTV, 1991

Olivetti, 1991

Sesame Street, Children's
  Television Workshop, 1992

Nike, Inc., 1993

Champion International
  Corporation, 1998

AQUENT

the official *AIGA* talent agency

For over a decade, Aquent has been placing and supporting graphic design professionals using their extensive portfolio of career planning and placement services to serve over 30,000 clients worldwide. As a global company dedicated to helping independent professionals succeed, Aquent has joined with the AIGA this year as the AIGA's Official Talent Agency to support AIGA activities related to digital design, communicating the value of design to business, information design, and research on the design economy, starting with a comprehensive salary survey that will be published annually and be made available free to members. The AIGA and Aquent announced this partnership at the 1999 National Design Conference in Las Vegas, where Aquent was presenting sponsor of the opening night reception.

As the partnership progresses, Aquent will work with the AIGA to develop national programs to educate AIGA members about professional advancement and career planning issues and will collaborate with the AIGA to create financial service offerings, including insurance, retirement, and cash-flow management benefits for AIGA members who practice as independent professionals or in small studios. Also, AIGA members who are independent professionals will have direct access to freelance opportunities through Aquent's talent agency and international network of clients.

*Crane's 100% Cotton Papers
is the Official Sponsor of
AIGA Educational Activities*

This year, a generous, long-time supporter of the AIGA, Crane & Co. Inc., joined the AIGA as a national sponsor by focusing its corporate, financial, and staff resources toward educational programming for the AIGA's 4,000 student members and more than 80 student groups. In addition, working with the AIGA and members of the AIGA's board, Crane developed and distributed reference materials to help students and young professionals in creating effective letterhead, business card, and résumé systems to help them in their career searches. The AIGA benefited from Crane's national support and the involvement of its regional staff, who worked with individual chapters on activities.

As the Official Sponsor of AIGA Educational Activities, Crane's was the Presenting Sponsor of VegasOasis, the Student Symposium that preceded the AIGA's biennial National Design Conference in Las Vegas. More than 400 students attended the symposium, which featured presentations and seminars by AIGA board members on such topics as designing for print, branding, and landing a dream job. Crane's commitment to students at the national conference extended beyond the symposium as they presented a student portfolio review, the presentation of the AIGA student medallion winners from 1998 and 1999, a session on the interface of technology and aesthetics, and the VegasOasis student reception, complete with costumed sheik and a desert décor designed by students from the Portfolio Center in Atlanta.

In addition to supporting student conference activities, Crane's goal is to share information about the "real world" of paper and printing and work with the AIGA to educate students about the value, tradition, and techniques of communicating their thoughts, designs, and business presentations on paper. To that end, they have worked with the AIGA to develop the Student Online Services section on the AIGA's website. As the AIGA's website evolves, this section will remain an important focus for the organization and become a central location for students and young professionals.

an official *AIGA* corporate sponsor

Sapient, a leading systems integration firm that acquired StudioArchetype to add experience design to its competitive strengths, has joined the AIGA as a national partner for a new journal that the AIGA will publish highlighting case studies of how business has benefited from interdisciplinary design. The journal will be published in print and on the web twice each year. It will focus on examples of the role of design in business solutions for the network economy.

This partnership will allow the AIGA to pursue an important priority of the membership — to communicate the value of design to business, with a particular emphasis on systems integration projects and solutions requiring design as the comparative advantage in customer experiences. This journal will reinforce the AIGA's increasing support to professionals operating in experience design.

Index

A—DATE DUE SLIP INSIDE FRONT